THE INSTITUTE OF
TAXATION
IN IRELAND

The Institute of Taxation in Ireland was founded in 1967. It has been admitted by the Confederation Fiscale Europeenne (CFE) as a member representing the Republic of Ireland. Under the provisions of the Finance Act 1990, any person who has been admitted a member of the Institute of Taxation in Ireland has the right to be heard by the Appeal Commissioners and at a rehearing before a Circuit Court Judge (Finance Act 1995). The Institute and its AITI qualification are officially recognised in the State for purposes of the EC Directive of 21 December 1988 regarding Standards for Higher Education Qualifications Awarded on Completion of Professional Education and Training of at least Three Year's Duration.

The objects of the Institute include the promotion of the study of tax law and practice, the making of regular submissions on fiscal matters to the Government and through CFE, to the EU Commission, and the establishment of a high standard of professional ethics for persons engaged in the practice of tax consultancy.

To become an Associate, it is necessary to pass examinations set by the Institute. Designatory letters are AITI and FITI. Fellows, Associates, Members, Student and Subscriber Members of the Institute now number over 4,400, and are drawn mainly from the legal, accounting and banking professions and from the revenue service.

It is possible, outside of the examination system to participate in many of the benefits of Institute membership by becoming a Subscriber.

Full details are available from:
Institute of Taxation in Ireland,
19 Sandymount Avenue, Dublin 4.
Telephone (01) 66 88 222, Fax (01) 66 88 088.

iii

FOREWORD

The property market in Ireland tends to be very active and in recent years has received a major boost through the targeted tax incentives introduced under various Finance Acts. It is impossible to evaluate any property deal without taking into account the value added tax aspects. Although the actual legislation is quite concise, the potential permutations and combinations that can emerge from it have given rise to numerous problems. Some time ago the Institute recognised this and commissioned Fergus Gannon to produce a publication dedicated to the topic. He produced an excellent work which dissects and analyses in a logical manner the VAT position, in each case providing detailed examples to clarify the implications. I congratulate Fergus on this fourth edition of *VAT On Property* which brings the position up to date with the latest developments.

RORY MEEHAN
President,
Institute of Taxation in Ireland.

VAT ON PROPERTY
CONTENTS

PART A

A THREE STEP APPROACH TO VAT ON THE MOST COMMON PROPERTY TRANSACTIONS

1.   A three step approach - introduction

In dealing with a problem of VAT on property, I suggest a three step approach. Similar to Caesar's Gaul - it can be divided into three parts.

1.1   Step 1 - Type of transaction

Write down the category of transaction.

Into which of the following categories does the transaction fall?

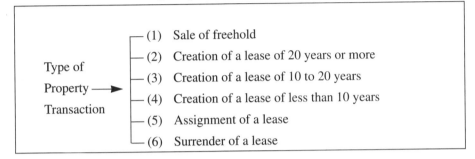

Type of Property Transaction

- (1)   Sale of freehold
- (2)   Creation of a lease of 20 years or more
- (3)   Creation of a lease of 10 to 20 years
- (4)   Creation of a lease of less than 10 years
- (5)   Assignment of a lease
- (6)   Surrender of a lease

1.2   Step 2 - Is the transaction chargeable to VAT

Apply the following check list to find out whether or not the transaction is chargeable to VAT:

1.   Was the property developed or redeveloped in whole or in part since 31.10.1972?

2.   Has the person disposing of the interest or creating the lease got an interest of 10 years or more?

3.   Is the person disposing of the interest or creating the lease doing so in the course or furtherance of any business carried on by him. This is as distinct from doing so in a private capacity. For example, selling one's residence is not a sale in the course or furtherance of business.

4.   Was the person who is disposing of the interest or creating the lease entitled to an input credit?

Note: 'The criterion is **entitlement** irrespective of whether or not input was actually claimed. A person cannot keep a property out of the VAT net by not claiming input credit to which he is entitled.

A person who acquires a vatable property VAT free on transfer of a business is treated as having been entitled to input credit.

(I do not include a further check which is in the Revenue Guide which is that the person making the supply must dispose of a freehold interest or create an interest of 10 years or more. This treats leases of less than 10 years separately. I include leases of less than 10 years as they are also supplies under the Value-Added Tax Act, 1972, Section 3(1)(f) i.e. self-supplies.)

If all four conditions above are not met, you need go no further. The transaction is not chargeable to VAT. For example, the sale of a property now, which has not been developed since 31.10.1972, is not chargeable to VAT.

1.3 Step 3 - Amount on which VAT is chargeable

Ascertain on what amount VAT is chargeable. There are different rules for deciding the amount on which VAT is chargeable for different types of transactions.

For example, there are special rules for valuing the creation of a lease of more than 20 years. I will deal with the methods of valuation as we go through the examples of different types of transactions.

1.4 Summary of 3 Step approach

> **Step 1:** Write down the type of transaction e.g. creation of a lease of 35 years.
>
> **Step 2:** Apply the check list to see if VAT is chargeable.
>
> **Step 3:** Calculate the amount on which VAT is chargeable.

2. Sale of a freehold

2.1 Sale of a freehold - Example 1

Let us start with a simple example. A builder bought land in Waterford in 1990 (i.e. purchased a freehold interest in land), built an office block on it and sold the freehold for £3m. to a firm of accountants. Was the transaction chargeable to V.A.T.?

Step 1 - *Type of transaction*

This transaction was the sale of a freehold.

Step 2 - *Check list used to decide if VAT was chargeable*

The check list used to decide whether or not VAT was chargeable was as follows:

1. Was the property developed after 31.10.1972? Yes.

2. Had the builder got an interest of 10 years or more in the property? Yes, he owned the freehold.

3. Was the supply in the course or furtherance of any business carried on by the builder? Yes, it was not done in a private non commercial capacity.

4. Was the builder entitled to input credit on the property? Yes. The builder was entitled to deduct the VAT charged to him on developing the property.

Therefore, the transaction was chargeable to VAT.

Step 3 - *On what amount was VAT chargeable?*

In the case of the sale of a freehold, VAT is chargeable on the sale price, in this case £3m.

2.2 Sale of a freehold - Example 2

Draper Ennis Ltd owned a freehold property in O'Connell Street, Ennis. The property was acquired in 1954 and rebuilt in 1968. No development has taken place since. The company sold the property in 1989 for £1m. Was VAT chargeable on the sale?

Step 1 - *Type of transaction*

This transaction was the sale of a freehold.

Step 2 - *Check list used to decide if VAT was chargeable*

1. Was the property developed after 31.10.72?

   No.

   Therefore, we need go no further. VAT was not chargeable on the sale of the freehold in 1989.

2.3 Sale of a freehold - Example 3

Jane Ryan, an antique dealer, who is registered for VAT, purchased a new holiday home in 1985 (i.e. she acquired a freehold interest). In 1990 she sold the holiday home (i.e. the disposal of her freehold interest) for £60,000. Was VAT chargeable on the sale?

Step 1 - *Type of transaction*

This transaction was the sale of a freehold.

Step 2 - *Check list used to decide if VAT was chargeable*

1. Was the property developed after 31.10.1972? Yes.

2. Had Jane Ryan got an interest of 10 years or more in the property? Yes, she owned the freehold.

3. Was the supply in the course or furtherance of any business carried on by her?

    No. She did not purchase the house for business purposes, she purchased it as a holiday home.

Therefore, we need go no further. The four conditions of Step 2 are not met and therefore VAT is not chargeable.

2.4   Sale of a freehold - Example 4

Conor Murphy is a solicitor registered for VAT. He decided in 1987 to build a house for the purpose of selling it rather than using it personally. He acquired a freehold interest in land and engaged a contractor to build a house on it. He sold the house (disposal of his freehold interest) for £100,000. Was VAT chargeable on the sale?

Step 1 - *Type of transaction*

This transaction was the sale of a freehold

Step 2 - *Check list used to decide if VAT was chargeable*

1. Was the property developed after 31.10.72? Yes.

2. Had Mr Murphy got an interest of 10 years or more in the property? Yes, he owned the freehold.

3. Was the supply in the course or furtherance of any business carried on by him? Yes.

    The interpretation of the phrase "in the course or furtherance of any business carried on by him" is very wide. All dealings in property are taken as being in the course or furtherance of business except private transactions such as the sale of one's private dwelling. The Revenue Commissioners state: -

    > *Any person who engages in the exploitation of developed property whether by way of the creation or disposal of taxable or other interests is regarded as carrying on a business activity which subject to the other conditions governing liability, is within the scope of VAT.*

In short the Revenue view is that usually any person involved in any property transaction is doing so in the course or furtherance of business except the sale of a private dwelling. The fact that the person carried out only one transaction in property does not make it any the less in the course or furtherance of business.

The word business is defined in VATA 1972 Section 1(1) as follows:

"**business** includes farming, the promotion of dances and any trade, commerce, manufacture, or any venture or concern in the nature of trade, commerce or manufacture, and any profession or vocation, whether for profit or otherwise;"

You will note that the term business <u>includes</u> farming etc. meaning it is not limited to farming etc.

In practice therefore 99 times out of a 100 you will not have to dwell too long on this point in the check list.

Those dealing with Income Tax and/or Corporation Tax should not confuse this requirement with the "badges of trade" as recommended by the 1954 Royal Commission in deciding whether a trade is being carried on. The term business is wider than the term trade.

If you have a case in which you think an argument could be made for a transaction being outside the scope of VAT because it is not in the course or furtherance of any business I recommend you read the following U.K. cases: National Water Council -v- C & E 1978 1 BVC 200 : C & E -v- Royal Exchange Theatre Trust 1979 1 BVC 308.

In the case of Rolls -v- Miller (1884) 27 Ch. D 71 at page 88 Lindley L J stated -

> *"Almost anything which is an occupation as distinguished from a pleasure - anything which is an occupation or duty which requires attention is business".*

However, the Revenue view is that the phrase "in the course or furtherance of any business" can be a useful part of their arsenal in combating VAT planning arrangements which have some non-commercial aspect to them. Their view is that the non-commercial aspect is not" in the course or furtherance of any business" and on that basis will refuse registration.

In the case of W.L.D. Worldwide Leather Diffusion Limited (1993/320 J.R.) the Revenue Commissioners refused to register W.L.D. on the grounds that it was not a bona fide application for many reasons including the view that the purchase and sale by it were not in the course or furtherance of any business. On judicial review the High Court held that W.L.D. was entitled to registration.

Getting back to the example of Conor Murphy, therefore, the transaction is in the course or furtherance of business.

4. Was Conor Murphy entitled to input credit on the property? Yes. Because the transaction was a business one, the VAT on the builder's costs was allowable. The supply by the builder was used by Mr Murphy for the purposes of taxable supplies.

Therefore, since the four points in the check list are answered "Yes", VAT was chargeable.

Step 3 - *On what amount was VAT chargeable?*

VAT was chargeable on the sale price, i.e. on £100,000.

2.5   Sale of a freehold - Example 5

An insurance broker acquired freehold land in Cork in 1990 on which an office block had recently been built. It was unlet when he bought it. He bought it not for his own use but to sell it, which he did for £1m. in December 1990. Was VAT chargeable on the sale in December 1990?

Step 1 - *Type of transaction*

This transaction was the sale of a freehold.

Step 2 - *Check list used to decide if VAT was chargeable*

1.   Was the property developed after 31.10.72? Yes.

2.   Had the broker got an interest of 10 years or more in the property? Yes, he owned the freehold.

3.   Was the supply in the course or furtherance of any business carried on by him? Yes.

4.   Was he entitled to input credit on the property? Yes. (Contrast this with the next example).

     Therefore, since the four points in the check list are answered "Yes", VAT was chargeable.

Step 3 - *On what amount was VAT chargeable?*

VAT was chargeable on the sale price i.e. on £1m.

The point this example seeks to illustrate is that the transaction was not an exempt one because it was carried out by an insurance broker. His insurance broking activities are exempt but his dealing in property is taxable.

It is sometimes mistakenly thought that insurance brokers, insurance companies, pension funds, banks, religious orders and charities are exempt from VAT. They are not. It is the activities usually carried on by these people or organisations that are exempt. For example, if St Vincent de Paul sold property which met the criteria, it would be obliged to register for VAT in respect of that sale. In VAT it's not who you are that is relevant, it's what you do.

In the same way, if any of the above mentioned (insurance brokers, etc) carry out a property transaction which meets the criteria, VAT is chargeable on that transaction.

2.6   Sale of a freehold - Example 6

An insurance broker acquired freehold land in Galway in 1990 on which an office block had recently been built for her exempt insurance broking business. Shortly after moving in, she accepted an offer of £1.5m. for it. Was the sale for £1.5m. chargeable to VAT.?

Step 1 - *Type of transaction*

This transaction was the sale of a freehold.

Step 2 - *Check list used to decide if VAT was chargeable*

1. Was the property developed after 31.10.1972? Yes, developed in 1990.

2. Had the broker got an interest of 10 years or more in the property? Yes, she owned the freehold.

3. Was the supply in the course or furtherance of any business carried on by her? Yes, it was not sold in a private non-commercial capacity.

4. Was she entitled to an input credit? No. She acquired it for the purposes of exempt supplies (i.e. insurance broking services).

   Therefore, VAT was not chargeable on the sale of £1.5m.

2.7   Sale of a freehold - Example 7

In 1990, Pat O'Reilly, a civil servant, purchased a freehold site. He built a house on it for the purpose of selling it. His total costs were £100,000. He sold it for £75,000. He was advised that he was not chargeable to VAT for three reasons:

(1) He was not a builder, he was a civil servant.

(2) He lost money on the transaction.

(3) He was not entitled to input credits because he had not registered and therefore he was not chargeable to VAT on the sale.

Was the advice correct?

Step 1 - *Type of transaction*

The transaction was the sale of a freehold

Step 2 - *Check list used to decide if VAT was chargeable*

1. Was the property developed since 31.10.72? Yes

2. Had Pat O'Reilly an interest of 10 years or more in the property? Yes, he owned the freehold.

3 Was the supply in the course or furtherance of business? Yes.

4. Was he entitled to input credit? Yes.

Therefore VAT was chargeable.

As regards whether the supply was in the course or furtherance of business see example **2.4**.

The fact that he sustained a loss was irrelevant.

He was entitled to input credit because he made a taxable supply (Section 12 VATA 1972). The fact that he did not register does not mean he was not entitled to input credit. He was entitled to a refund as the VAT on his costs was greater than the VAT due on the sale.

The advice he got was not correct.

2.8   Sale of a freehold out of which a long lease has been created

When a landlord grants a long lease (one of 10 years or more) he is treated for VAT purposes on disposing of his interest in the property. When he later sells the freehold with the benefit of the lease he should not charge VAT because for VAT purposes he no longer has an interest in the property.

2.9   Sale of a freehold after a long lease has been surrendered back to the landlord

Up to 26 March 1997 if a landlord granted a long lease to a tenant and the tenant surrendered the lease back to him a subsequent sale of the property by the landlord was not chargeable to VAT provided the property was not redeveloped. The reason for this was that the landlord had for VAT purposes disposed of his interest in the property when he created the long lease and the surrender back was ignored for VAT purposes.

Since 26 March 1997 the surrender back of the lease is no longer ignored if the tenant has recovered any input VAT in respect of the property. The landlord is still treated as disposing of his interest when he grants the first lease but since 26 March 1997, on surrender he is treated as acquiring the vatable interest which the tenant surrendered back to him. A subsequent sale of the freehold from 26 March onwards is treated as a sale by the landlord of the vatable interest remaining in the lease which he acquired from the tenant. For example, a landlord granted a 35 year lease to a tenant who recovered the VAT and 10 years later surrendered the lease back to the landlord. The landlord sold the property immediately afterwards. If the sale was before 26 March 1997 in the absence of redevelopment of the property VAT was not chargeable. Since 26 March VAT is chargeable on the sale of the freehold as if it were the creation of the 25 year vatable interest acquired from the tenant. If the landlord sold the property a year after he took the surrender from the tenant the sale would have been treated as the creation of a 24 year vatable interest. The amount of VAT is based on a market rent for the property which is capitalised using the multiplier, the formula or a valuation (See later creation of a lease of more than 20 years)

3.   Creation of a lease of 20 years or more

3.1   Introduction

The creation after development of a first lease of 20 years or more is a supply (i.e. sale) of property for the purposes of VAT.

For example: A owns a freehold property and grants B a lease for 999 years. Granting the 999 year lease is a supply by A for VAT purposes. VAT will be chargeable on the creation of the lease if it meets the criteria applied to sales of property.

If B, who has a 999 year lease of the property, grants a sub-lease to C for 500 years, granting the sub-lease is a supply by B for VAT purposes, which will be chargeable to VAT if it meets the criteria for VAT on sales of property.

If C, who has a 500 year lease of the property, grants a sub-lease to D for 35 years, that in turn is a supply of property by C which will be chargeable to VAT if it meets the criteria applied to sales of property.

Two questions have to be answered when dealing with VAT on the creation of a lease:

1)   Is the transaction chargeable to VAT?

2)   If so, on what amount is VAT charged?

3.2   Creation of first lease of 20 years or more

Example 1

An accountant purchased freehold land in Thurles. He had the existing buildings demolished and had new offices built on the land. He used half the office for his own practice. On 1.1.1990 he leased the other half on a 35 year lease to an insurance broker at a rent of £18,000 per annum, with the first rent increase on 1.1.1995. What were the VAT implications?

The accountant was allowed an input for all the VAT charged to him by the builder while the property was being built. He was also allowed an input for VAT on the solicitor's fees and VAT on any other costs in relation to the building.

Was VAT chargeable on the creation of the lease?

Step 1 - *Type of transaction*

The creation of a lease of 20 years or more.

Step 2 - *Check list used to decide if VAT was chargeable*

1.   Was the property developed after 31.10.72? Yes.

2.   Had the accountant got an interest of 10 years or more in the property? Yes, he owned the freehold.

3.   Was the creation of the lease in the course or furtherance of any business carried on by him? Yes, it was not in a private non commercial capacity.

4. Was the accountant entitled to an input credit? Yes.

Therefore, VAT was chargeable on the creation of the lease.

Step 3 - *On what amount was VAT chargeable*

What the Thurles accountant found was that the lease that he was granting was valued and VAT was charged on that value. What was valued was the capital value of the rent he will receive.

He found that because there was not a rent increase within 5 years, he had a choice of three methods of valuation. Had he a right to a rent increase within 5 years, he would not have had any choice of valuation - the only method of valuing would have been to get a valuation from a competent valuer (i.e. an auctioneer).

However, the accountant had a choice of three methods of valuing the lease:

1) a valuation by a competent valuer; or

2) a formula; or

3) a multiplier of the rent.

He looked at each as follows:

1) The valuer valued the lease at £220,000.

2) The formula used was - the rent x 3/4ths x the number of years in the lease: £472,500

3) A multiplier of the rent. On 1 January 1990 the multiplier was 11.41. Therefore, the capital value on the basis of the multiplier was £205,380

The multiplier can be obtained from the VAT Office. The multiplier is 14.43 at time of writing (July 1997).

In the example the Thurles accountant chose the multiplier value of £205,380 and VAT was charged on this amount.

The insurance broker who leased the property was not entitled to recover the VAT.

TAX TIP: If a client is creating a lease of 20 years or more and the tenant cannot recover all the VAT make sure that the first rent increase is not earlier than the end of the 5th year after the lease is created. By doing this you give your client the choice of the three methods of valuation.

3.3 Creation of a first lease of 20 years or more

Example 2

A pension fund purchased freehold land in Kilkenny in 1990 on which an office block had recently been built. The pension fund leased the property to an insurance company on a 35 year lease with the first rent increase after 3 years. Was VAT chargeable on the creation of the lease?

Step 1 - *Type of transaction*

Creation of a lease of 20 years or more.

Step 2 - *Check list used to decide if VAT was chargeable*

1. Was the property developed after 31.10.1972? Yes.

2. Had the pension fund got an interest of 10 years or more in the property? Yes, it owned the freehold.

3. Was the creation of the lease in the course or furtherance of any business carried on by the pension fund? Yes. (see example 4 on sale of freehold for further details).

4. Was the pension fund entitled to an input credit? Yes, because the subsequent creation of the lease was subject to VAT. (If the pension fund had purchased it for its own administration then it would not have been entitled to the input credit).

Therefore, the pension fund was chargeable to VAT on the creation of the lease.

Step 3 - *On what amount was VAT chargeable*

VAT was chargeable on the value of the lease as valued by a competent valuer.

The pension fund did not have the choice of the other two methods of valuation because the first rent increase was earlier than 5 years after the creation of the interest.

TAX TIP: Sometimes clients will ask for an immediate rough estimate of the VAT that will arise on the creation of a long lease. To facilitate him/her you can advise that on the current multiplier (14.43) the amount of VAT will be equal to about 1^3/$_4$ year's rent.

3.4   The reversion

Where a person disposes of an interest in property which is a lesser interest than his own, the undisposed interest is known as "the reversion".

For example, where a person who holds a freehold grants a 35 year lease to a tenant, the right the freeholder has to his property after the lease expires is known as his reversion.

For VAT purposes, a person who creates a lesser interest and retains a reversion is carrying out two transactions:

1. the creation of the interest; and

2. the retention of the reversion.

The creation of the interest is chargeable to VAT if it meets the criteria set out in earlier examples.

The retention of the reversion is also a disposal for VAT purposes and is charged to VAT at the time of creation of the lease. Where the interest created is more than 20 years, the value of the reversion is disregarded for VAT.

3.5 Creation of a first lease of 20 years or more

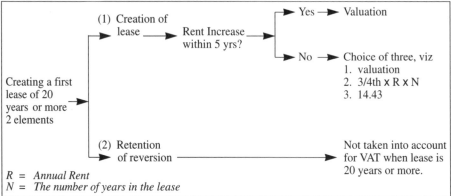

Creating a first lease of 20 years or more 2 elements

(1) Creation of lease → Rent Increase within 5 yrs? → Yes → Valuation

No → Choice of three, viz
1. valuation
2. 3/4th x R x N
3. 14.43

(2) Retention of reversion → Not taken into account for VAT when lease is 20 years or more.

R = *Annual Rent*
N = *The number of years in the lease*

3.6 Creation of a second lease of 20 years or more

Up to 26 March 1997 if a landlord granted a long lease to a tenant and the tenant surrendered the lease back to him a second lease created by the landlord was not chargeable to VAT provided the property was not re-developed. The reason for this was that the landlord had for VAT purposes, disposed of his interest in the property when he created the long lease and the surrender back was ignored for VAT purposes.

Since 26 March 1997 the surrender back of the lease is no longer ignored if the tenant was entitled to recover any of the VAT on the first lease. The landlord is still treated as disposing of his interest when he grants the first lease but since 26 March 1997 on surrender he is treated as acquiring the vatable interest which the tenant surrenders back to him. A second lease by the landlord is treated as the creation of a lease of the vatable interest remaining in the lease acquired from the tenant.

If the vatable interest that the landlord is disposing of is less than 10 years the supply is an exempt supply of goods with the option to the landlord to charge VAT on the supply (at 12½%). For example, a landlord granted a 21 year lease on which the tenant was entitled to input deduction. After 13 years, the tenant surrendered the lease back to the landlord. The landlord then created a new 21 year lease. The landlord was treated as making an exempt supply of an eight year vatable interest in the property with the right to opt to charge VAT available to him. The amount of VAT is based on the rent under the new lease using the multiplier, the formula or a valuation. Where appropriate 4A can be used.

If the vatable interest is 10 years or more (and the second lease is 20 years or more) VAT is chargable on the second lease based on the length of the vatable interest using the rent under the new lease and applying the multiplier, the formula or a valuation. Where appropriate 4A can be used.

4.   Creation of a lease of 10 years to 20 years

4.1   Lease and reversion

> **TAX TIP: Beware when creating a lease of 10 to 20 years. It gives rise to irrecoverable VAT. The option to overcome this by electing to be taxed on the rents does not arise. That option is only available for lettings of less than 10 years.**

Where a person creates a lease of 10 to 20 years, he is disposing of his interest for the period of the lease but retaining his right of reversion at the end of the period of the lease.

This gives two elements to the transaction:

1.   the creation of the lease - any VAT on which will be chargeable to the tenant; and

2.   the retention of the reversion - any VAT on which is a self-supply to the landlord and is irrecoverable.

4.2   Creation of a first lease of 10 years to 20 years - Example 1

An insurance company purchased i.e. acquired a freehold interest in a newly built unlet shopping centre in May 1993 for £5m. plus £625,000 VAT. It intended to let the units. It let all the units on 15 year leases at a total rent of £250,000 per annum. The first rent increase was 6 years after the creation of the leases.

Was VAT chargeable on the transaction and, if it was, on how much?

Step 1 - *Type of transaction*

The transactions were the creation of leases of 10 to 20 years.

Step 2 - *Check list used to decide if VAT was chargeable*

1.   Was the property developed after 31.10.1972? Yes.

2.   Had the insurance company got an interest of 10 years or more in the property? Yes, it owned the freehold.

3.   Was the creation of the leases in the course or furtherance of any business carried on by it? Yes.

4.   Was the insurance company entitled to an input credit? Yes, for it was making taxable supplies.

Therefore, VAT was chargeable on the creation of the leases.

Step 3 *On what amount was VAT chargeable?*

There are two supplies to be valued

1.   The value of the lease; and

2.   the value of the reversion.

The lease is valued first. It is valued in the same way as a lease of more than 20 years (see paragraph **3.2**). Since the rent increase is not earlier than 5 years after the creation of the lease there was the choice of 3 methods of valuation. The three methods were:

1.   Valuation by a competent valuer at, say, £3m.

2.   The value of the lease using the formula was:-

     Rent (R) x no. of years (N) x 3/4ths

     £250,000 x 15 x 3/4ths = £2,812,500

3.   The value of the lease using the multiplier was:

     £250,000 x 10.98 = £2,745,000

The multiplier at the time of the transaction (May 1993) was 10.98.

Value of reversion

The value of the reversion is the difference between the total value of the property at the time of creating the lease and the value of the lease as ascertained above.

Since the reversion gives rise to an irrecoverable VAT cost, the person creating the lease will choose the highest value for the lease to give the lowest value for the reversion.

The value of the reversion in this case was:

Total value	£ 5 m.
Value of lease created	£(3 m.)
Value of reversion	£ 2 m.

The insurance company charged the tenants:

£3m. @ 12$\frac{1}{2}$%   =   £375,000

And it included a notional sale in its VAT return for the reversion:

£2m. @ 12$\frac{1}{2}$%   =   £250,000

The £250,000 was an irrecoverable VAT cost to the Insurance Company.

> **TAX TIP: Make sure the first rent increase is not within 5 years for maximum choice and choose the highest value for the supply, giving the lowest value for the self supply.**

4.3 Creation of a first lease of 10 to 20 years - Example 2

Galway Hardware Ltd. acquired a freehold premises in 1968 and redeveloped it in 1970. It moved to a new premises in 1990 and let the old premises on a 17 year lease. Was VAT chargeable on the creation of the 17 year lease?

Step 1 *Type of transaction*

The transaction was the creation of a lease of 10 to 20 years.

Step 2 *Check list used to decide if VAT was chargeable*

1. Was the property developed after 31.10.1972? No.

There is no need to go any further. The transaction was not chargeable to VAT because the property was not developed since 31.10.1972.

4.4 Creation of a first lease of 10 to 20 years

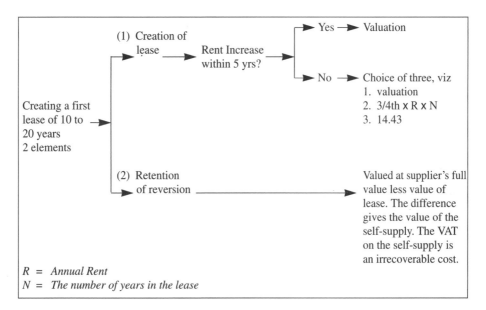

R = *Annual Rent*
N = *The number of years in the lease*

4.5   Creation of a second lease of 10 to 20 years

Up to 26 March 1997 if a landlord granted a long lease to a tenant who surrendered the lease back to him a second lease created by the landlord was not chargeable to VAT provided the property was not redeveloped. The reason for this was that the landlord had for VAT purposes disposed on his interest in the property when he created the long lease and the surrender back to him was ignored for VAT purposes.

Since 26 March 1997 the surrender back of the lease is no longer ignored if the tenant was entitled to recover any VAT in respect of the first lease. The landlord is still treated as disposing of his interest when he grants the first lease but since 26 March 1997 on surrender he is treated as acquiring the vatable interest which the tenant surrenders back to him. A second lease by the landlord is treated as the creation of a lease of the vatable interest remaining in the lease acquired from the tenant.

If the vatable interest that the landlord is disposing of is less than 10 years the supply is an exempt supply of goods with the option to the landlord to charge VAT on the supply (at 12½%).

If the landlords vatable interest is longer than the length of the second lease the landlord has an irrecoverable VAT cost on the reversion retained.

For example, a landlord created a 21 year lease on which the tenant was entitled to input credit. After 2 years the tenant surrendered the lease back to the landlord and he granted a second lease for 12 years. The second lease was chargeable to VAT but in addition the landlord had an irrecoverable VAT cost on the reversion of 7 years. The amount on which VAT was chargeable using the formula was as follows:

19 year interest £10,000 x 19 x ¾	£132,500
12 year interest £10,000 x 12 x ¾	£ 90,000
	£42,500

VAT on the lease was £11,250	(£90,000 @ 12½%)
VAT on the reversion was £5,312	(£42,500 @ 12½%)

5.   The shift mechanism

A landlord may (subject to the Inspector's approval) agree with his tenant that responsibility for the VAT arising on the creation of a lease of 10 years or more shifts from him to the tenant provided the tenant is entitled to full input recovery.

The way this works in practice is as follows:

(i)   the landlord and the tenant complete a form known as a VAT 4A and send it to the landlord's Inspector,

(ii) the inspector sends a form VAT 4B to both the landlord and the tenant telling them that the shift mechanism applies, and

(iii) the landlord's invoice must have the following words on it instead of the amount of VAT:

> *"In accordance with Section 4A of the Value Added Tax Act 1972 the lessee is liable for Value Added Tax of £*   ."*

> * being the amount of VAT arising on the creation of the lease.

(iv) The tenant enters the amount of VAT arising on the creation of the lease in both the sales part (Box T1) and the deduction part (Box T2) of his return. The entries are self-cancelling.

There is no obligation on the landlord or the tenant to agree to transfer responsibility for the VAT arising on the creation of the lease. However it is in both their interests to do so.

It is in the landlord's interest because if he retains responsibility for the VAT and the tenant fails to pay it to him the landlord must still pay the VAT to the Revenue Commissioners and is not entitled to VAT bad debt relief despite the tenants failure to pay him.

It is in the tenants interest to take responsibility for the VAT arising on the creation of the lease for by doing so he will overcome the cash flow disadvantage of paying VAT to the landlord and then reclaiming it from the Revenue Commissioners.

The question has been raised whether or not opting for the shift mechanism puts the landlord's entitlement to input credit in doubt. The thinking being that since he does not make a taxable supply of the property he is not entitled to input credit. In my opinion, a supply by a landlord to which Section 4A applies is a taxable supply by the landlord which gives entitlement to input credit. What the shift mechanism does is transfer the liability to pay the tax from the landlord to the ternant. The Revenue Commissioners have confirmed that they agree with my interpretation.

In the case of leases of 10 to 20 years, the shift mechanism will apply only in respect of the supply to the tenant. VAT on the reversion, if any, will remain the liability of the landlord.

Form VAT 4A

Value Added Tax - Section 4A, VAT Act 1972

To: Inspector of Taxes,

Application by a Lessor and a Lessee to have the provisions of Section 4A VAT Act 1972 applied to a letting of property deemed to be a supply of goods under Section 4, VAT Act 1972. (Note 1)

[BEFORE COMPLETING THIS FORM PLEASE READ THE ATTACHED NOTES]

SECTION A - (To be completed by the Lessor)

1. Name of Lessor _____

2. Address of Lessor _____

_____

_____

3. Trading Name _____

4. Telephone Number _____

5. VAT Number   *IE* ⬜⬜⬜⬜⬜⬜⬜⬜

6. Address of Premises to be Leased _____

_____

_____

7. Is the letting of the property a taxable supply of property under Section 4, VAT Act 1972   Yes ⬜   No ⬜   (Note 2)

8. Period of Proposed Lease _____ (Note 3)

9. Capitalised Value of the Lease _____ (Note 4)

10. VAT Due _____ (Note 5)

SECTION B - (To be completed by the Lessee)

11. Name of Lessee   _____

12. Address of Lessee   _____

                                           _____

                                           _____

13. Trading Name   _____

14. Telephone Number   _____

15. VAT Number   *IE* ☐☐☐☐☐☐☐☐

16. Describe the purpose for which the premises
     at No. 6 overleaf is being leased   _____   (Note 6).

17. Are you entitled to full deductibility in respect of   Yes ☐   No ☐   (Note 7)
     the VAT chargeable on the lease of the premises

DECLARATIONS   (Note 8)

To be Completed by the Lessor

I/We declare that the information provided in **Section A** of this form is correct and I/we undertake to supply any further information which may be requested.

Signed: _____   Date: _____

Status: _____

To be Completed by the Lessee

I/We declare that the information provided in **Section B** of this form is correct and I/we undertake to supply any further information which may be requested. I further declare that I am entitled to full deductibility in respect of the amount of VAT shown at No. 10 overleaf and that I will account for that VAT on my VAT return.

Signed: _____   Date: _____

Status: _____

NOTES ON FORM VAT 4A

NOTE 1

Section 4A VAT Act 1972 provides that a lessor, who is letting property which is deemed to be a supply of goods to a lessee who is entitled to take a full deduction in respect of VAT charged on the supply of the property does not have to charge VAT on the supply of the property. The lessee will be obliged to account for the VAT due on his Return but may also take a credit for the VAT on the same Return. Both the lessor and the lessee must agree to the application of the provisions before they can be applied.

NOTE 2

A number of conditions apply before the supply of a property becomes liable to VAT. If you are in doubt as to whether VAT should be charged on the supply you should consult your local Tax Office.

NOTE 3

A lease of property must be for a period of at least ten years before it constitutes a taxable supply.

NOTE 4

There are various methods of capitalising a taxable lease of property. These are contained in Regulation 19 of the VAT Regulations 1979 and if you require assistance in this matter you should consult your local Tax Office.

NOTE 5

The invoice issued by the lessor in accordance with Section 17, VAT Act 1972 should show the following endorsement in lieu of the amount of VAT chargeable. "In accordance with Section 4A of the Value Added Tax Act 1972 the lessee is liable for the Value Added Tax of £XXX".

NOTE 6

A full description should be given as to what the premises will be used for. If it is intended to use any part of it for purposes other than in connection with taxable supplies of goods and services by the lessee e.g. short term letting of part of the premises, full details should be given on a separate sheet if necessary.

NOTE 7

A trader will normally be entitled to full deductibility in respect of the VAT charged as a taxable supply of property where it is exclusively used for the purposes of the traders taxable supplies of goods or services.

NOTE 8

This form, when completed and signed by both the lessor and the lessee should be **returned to the lessor's local Tax Office.**

6. Creation of lease of less than 10 years – surrender of possession

6.1   Introduction

> **TAX TIP: Be wary of creating leases of less than 10 years and of the surrender of possession of a property if it is chargeable to VAT. The creation of a lease of less than 10 years gives rise to an irrecoverable VAT cost. This can be overcome by electing to be accountable for VAT on all short-term rents. They are taxable at 21%. Late elections to be taxable on rents are only allowed by the Revenue in certain circumstances and they have legislative authority for refusal. The election must be made in writing during the VAT period in which the lease is created.**

6.2   Creation of a lease of less than 10 years before 26.3.1997 – Example 1

In 1977 Vladimir & Estragon, a firm of architects, purchased the freehold on which a newly constructed office block had been built. It was for their use as architects that they purchased it. The building cost £3m plus £90,000 VAT (£3m @ 3%: The rate of VAT on property in 1977 was 3%). They reclaimed the VAT and, on inspection, the Inspector agreed to their entitlement.

In May 1993, the firm cut back and let half the space on a lease of 9 years.

Step 1 - *Type of transaction*

Lease of less than 10 years.

Step 2 - *Check list used to decide if VAT was chargeable*

1.   Was the property developed after 31.10.1972? Yes.

2.   Had the landlord got an interest of 10 years or more in the property? Yes.

3.   Was the creation of the lease in the course or furtherance of any business carried on by the landlord? Yes.

4.   Were Vladimir & Estragon entitled to input credit? Yes.

Therefore, the transaction was chargeable to VAT.

Step 3 *On what amount was VAT chargeable*

The view of the Revenue Commissioners is that strictly as it is a supply of property (albeit a self-supply) it is chargeable to VAT on the market value (VATA 1972 10(9)(b)). An alternative view is that is chargeable to VAT on the cost which is the basis of assessment for self supplies (VATA 1972 10(4)).

Assuming the market value of the building in May 1993 was £4m Vladimir & Estragon faced an irrecoverable VAT cost on half of £4m. But the rate in May 1993 was $12\frac{1}{2}\%$. Therefore, the irrecoverable VAT cost based on market value was £250,000 (£4m x $\frac{1}{2}$ x $12\frac{1}{2}\%$). On the basis a self-supply at cost they faced an irrecoverable VAT cost of £187,500 (£3m x $\frac{1}{2}$ x $12\frac{1}{2}\%$). These figures are in contrast with total VAT recovered of £90,000.

However in practice its not as grim as that. The current practice of the Revenue Commissioners is to deal with a self-supply by clawing back the input VAT already recovered rather than treating it as a notional sale at market value at cost.

In practice the disallowable VAT for Vladimir & Estragon was £45,000.

Had Vladimir & Estragon sent a letter to the Inspector of Taxes (known as a waiver of exemption) within the VAT period in which the short term letting commenced telling him that they would charge VAT on all short term rents the self-supply would not have arisen.

6.3   Short term letting from 26 March 1997

If the same happened to Vladimir & Estragon on 26 March 1997 or afterwards they could take remedial action. Under new regulations effective from 26 March 1997 in the circumstances outlined for Vladimir & Estragon they could apply for a back dated waiver. To get a back dated waiver, the landlord must apply in writing to the Inspector stating:

(i)   his name

(ii)   his address

(iii)   his VAT registration number

(iv)   the tenant's name

(v)   the tenant's address

(vi)   the tenant's VAT registration number

(vii)   details of the letting agreement

(viii) the date from which the waiver should have effect (this cannot be earlier than 26 March 1997)

The landlord should attach a letter from the tenant stating:

(i)   that (s)he (the tenant) is entitled to full recovery of VAT on the rents.

(ii)   that (s)he (the tenant) agrees to the back dating

The effect of the back dated waiver is as follows:

(i)   No adjustments are required for the past. The landlord is deemed to have paid the VAT and the tenant is deemed to have deducted it. All obligations such as invoicing are deemed to have been complied with. Any other short term rents are unaffected as regards the past.

(ii)   the application for back-dating is treated from the date of application (or agreed later time) as a waiver of exemption in respect of all short term lettings from then on.

A back dating is only allowed where a person was in the first instance entitled to input credit and subsequently short term let the property. It is not allowed where a property has been let short term from the beginning and the waiver is not sent in on time.

6.4   Short term letting pre and post 26.3.1997 – Example 2

Peter Ryan owns all the shares in Peter Ryan Ltd. He decided to buy a new premises in his own name for use by the company. He purchased a newly developed property at a cost of £1m. plus £125,000 VAT. The company reclaimed the £125,000 VAT. What is the correct VAT position?

Step 1 *Type of transaction*

Letting of less than 10 years by Peter Ryan to Peter Ryan Ltd.

Step 2 *Check list used to decide if VAT was chargeable*

1.   Was the property developed after 31.10.1972? Yes.

2.   Had Mr. Ryan got an interest of 10 years or more in the property? Yes.

3.   Was the surrender in the course or furtherance of any business carried on by him? Yes.

4.   Was Mr. Ryan entitled to input credit? No.

Mr Ryan is not entitled to input credit because he never used the property for vatable supplies. He has allowed a tenancy at will to his company. The company is not entitled to the input because it did not purchase the property. On inspection the VAT Inspector will disallow the £125,000 VAT claimed by the company.

6.5   Taxable self supplies on lettings of less than 10 years

There is some confusion as regards the technical position on lettings of less than 10 years. In my opinion the correct interpretation is as follows:

1. If the purchaser of the property lets it short-term he/she is not entitled to input credit because the short term letting is an exempt supply. Input credit is not allowed where property is put to an exempt use. There is not a self supply in these circumstances there is a blockage of input credit. (See Peter Ryan example above).

2. Where the property is first used for a vatable purpose there is entitlement to input credit. A subsequent short-term letting gives rise to a self-supply.

The amount of irrecoverable VAT under a blockage of input credit may be different from the amount under a self-supply (See Vladimir & Estragon example above).

6.6   Tax Tip - Advantageous use of lease of less than 10 years – Example 3

In June 1975 a company purchased a freehold interest in a new office block for £250,000 plus VAT of £7,500, which it reclaimed.

In May 1993 the company was offered £1m. for its freehold interest. The purchaser was not registered and said he would not bear the VAT.

Step 1 - *Type of transaction*

Sale of freehold.

Step 2 - *Check list to decide if VAT was chargeable*

1. Was the property developed since 31.10.1972? Yes.

2. Had the person making the disposal an interest of 10 years or more in the property? Yes.

3. Was the supply in the course or furtherance of any business carried on by him? Yes.

4. Was the firm entitled to input credit? Yes, for it was making taxable supplies.

Therefore, VAT was chargeable on the sale.

Step 3 - *Amount on which VAT was charged*

The amount of VAT was £111,111 (£1m x 12.5/112.5) as the sale price was a VAT inclusive £1m.

Alternative

The firm first sub-lets the property for 6 months to the purchaser. This results in a self-supply. Self-supplies are valued at cost. VAT arises on the original cost, £250,000 @ $12^{1}/_{2}\%$ (i.e. £31,250 irrecoverable).

This results in a saving of £79,861. (Ref. Sections 3(1)(f) and 10(4), VAT Act, 1972).

As this involves tax planning it is to be expected that Revenue would challenge it and argue that the self-supply was chargeable to VAT at market value in accordance with VATA 1972 Section 10(9) (b). The normal Revenue practice in the case of self-supplies is to block inputs or claw-back the input VAT recovered.

The subsequent disposal of the freehold is not chargeable to VAT.

7.   Assignment of a lease

The assignment of a lease means the transfer of a lease by the existing tenant to a new tenant. Up to 26 March 1997 VAT was charged on the assignment of a lease if the assignor was entitled to input credit on being granted the lease. It was charged on the money passing for the assignment. Often as not, no money passed and there was no VAT charge.

Since 26 March 1997 the assignment of a lease is chargeable to VAT not by reference to the money passing but by reference to the capitalised value of the interest passing.

For example, a landlord granted a tenant a 35 year lease the VAT on which the tenant was entitled to recover. The tenant assigned the lease after 5 years to tenant number 2. VAT arose on the capitalised value of the 30 year vatable interest which was assigned.

The value of the interest for VAT purposes is arrived at using the formula, the multiplier or a valuation by a competent valuer. For example, if the rent was £10,000 per annum the VAT using the multiplier would be £18,054 calculated as follows:

$$£10,000 \times 14.43 \times 12\tfrac{1}{2}\% = \qquad\qquad £18,054$$

8.   Surrender of a lease

The surrender of a lease in property law means giving back the lease to the landlord before it has expired. In VAT law its meaning is extended to take in abandonments, ejectments, forfeitures and failure to exercise an option.

The surrender of a lease is similar for VAT purposes to the assignment of a lease. A tenant, for example, who has a 35 year lease and who surrenders it after 10 years is disposing of a 25 year vatable interest. Assuming he was entitled to input VAT, the surrender is chargeable as the disposal of a 25 year vatable interest. VAT arises on the capitalised value arrived at by using the multiplier, the formula or a valuation by a competent valuer. For example, if the rent was £10,000 per annum the VAT using the multiplier would be £18,054.

$$£10,000 \times 14.43 \times 12\tfrac{1}{2}\% = \qquad\qquad \underline{\underline{£18,054}}$$

9. Reverse charge

Normally the person who sells the goods or services is the one who has to collect VAT from the customer and pass on that VAT to the Revenue. Under the reverse charge mechanism the reverse happens. The seller does not charge VAT but rather the purchaser is responsible to the Revenue for the VAT arising. This happens every day when registered persons import goods from other EU countries. The purchaser accounts for VAT to the Revenue by including the amount of VAT in the sales box (T1) of his VAT return. To the extent that he is entitled to recovery he claims back VAT by including the appropriate amount in box T2 of the return.

The reverse charge applies to the majority of assignments and surrenders from 26 March 1997. That means in the case of assignments or surrenders it is usually the assignee or landlord who accounts for the VAT and the assignor or tenant does not.

The reverse charge applies to the assignments and surrenders if the assignee or landlord is one of the following:

1. a vatable person

2. a Department of State or a local authority

3. a person supplying exempt property

4. a person supplying financial services

5. a person letting property short term

6. a travel agent

7. an insurance company

8. an insurance broker

9. An Post

10. RTE

11. transporter of people e.g. a taxi, airliner.

I have tried to keep the above list readable and in doing so have lost some of the legal precision. You should refer to the legislation (VATA 1972 Section 4(8)).

The tenant who is disposing of an interest either by surrender or assignment should get confirmation from the landlord or assignee that he (the landlord or assignee) is a person within VATA 1972 Section 4(8) and that he (the landlord or assignee) will account for the VAT.

The landlord or assignee should get confirmation from the tenant that the interest in question is a vatable one and should get details of the vatable interest.

10. Summary Chart

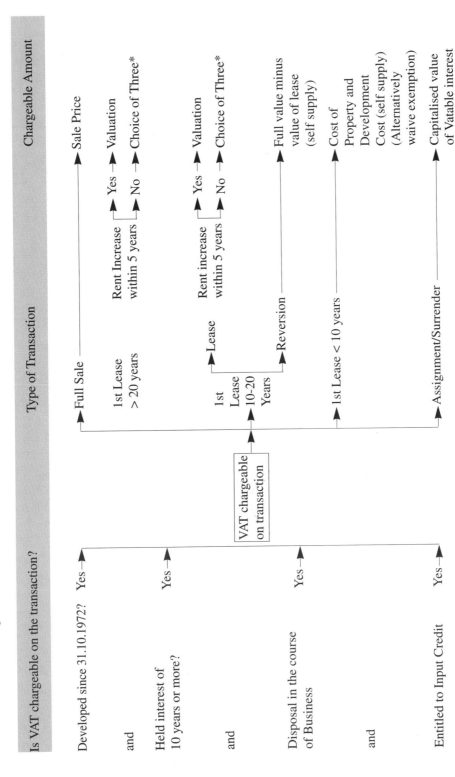

Is VAT chargeable on the transaction?

| Type of Transaction | Chargeable Amount |

*Choice of (i) valuation or (ii) ³/₄ths of R x N or (iii) Multiplier 14.43

11. Second Leases from 26 March 1997 – Summary Chart

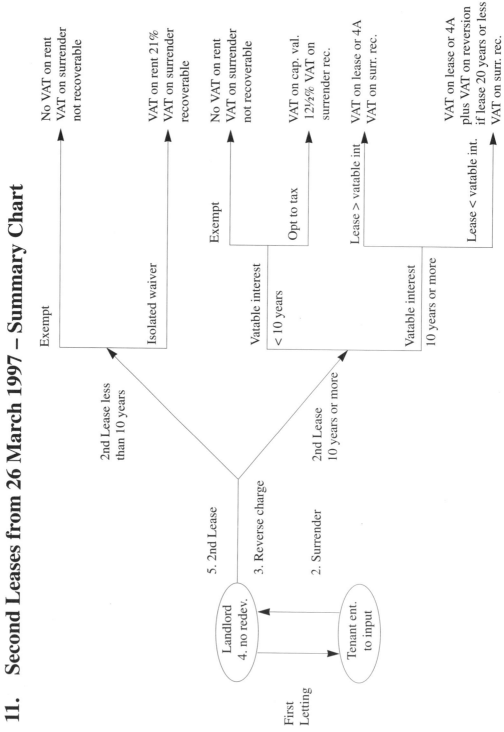

12. Check List

A property transaction requires that much more than VAT is considered. The following check list may help to ensure that all taxes are considered:

1. Income Tax.

2. Corporation Tax.

3. Balancing allowances.

4. Balancing charges.

5. Capital Gains Tax

6. Capital Gains Tax Clearance Certificate.

7. Development Land Tax.

8. Capital Acquisitions Tax.

9. Capital Acquisations Tax Clearance Certificate.

10. Sub-contractors Tax.

11. Stamp Duty.

12. Residential Property Tax.

13. Residential Property Tax Clearance Certificate.

14. Value Added Tax.

15. Rates.

16. Foreign Taxes.

PART B

THE DETAILED ASPECTS OF FREEHOLDS

1.   The development of a freehold

1.1   Introduction

As you know from Part A a freehold must be developed since 31.10.1972 before its sale is chargeable to VAT. Therefore, it was necessary for the legislators to define development.

Development in relation to land for VAT is defined in VATA 1972 Section 1(1). The definition is the same as the definition in Finance (Miscellaneous Provisions) Act 1968 Section 16(1). The interpretation of the meaning of the term development is more art than science. The view taken is often coloured by the result desired.

The definition falls into two main parts, each setting out the circumstances in which land will be developed land for VAT. Part (a) sets down that land shall be developed for VAT purposes if certain things are done to a building on the land. Part (b) sets down that land shall be developed for VAT purposes if certain work is done to the land itself "to adapt it for materially altered use".

1.2   WORK ON A BUILDING ON THE LAND

1.2.1   Types of work on a building

Under part (a) of the legislative definition of development and developed, if any of five types of work are done to a building on the land then the land shall be treated as developed land for VAT. The five things which, if done to a building on the land, result in the land being developed land for VAT are:

(1) the construction of any building on the land;

(2) the demolition of any building on the land;

(3) the extension of any building on the land;

(4) the alteration of any building; and

(5) the reconstruction of any building on the land.

What comes within part (a) is the construction of new buildings and the alteration, reconstruction, extension and demolition of existing buildings. For example, if a person bought an old run-down building and knocked it down, the very act of knocking it down is a development of the land on which it stands for VAT.

1.2.2   Materially altered use of building

The legislation does not require that the work on the building is to adapt it for materially altered use. The actual work of constructing, demolishing etc. is sufficient in itself to result in development irrespective of whether the work is for an existing use or for an altered use. For example, alteration to a building which will continue to be used as an office will result in the land being developed for VAT purposes. The materially altered use requirement is only in part (b) of the definition.

However, in practice, the concept of "materially altered use" has spilled over into the application of what is known as the 10% rule as that rule is applied to part (a) of the definition.

1.2.3 10% Rule

In strict law, any additions or alterations to a building will result in the property being developed for VAT purposes. In practice, the property may be treated as not having been developed if:

(1) there is no essential change in the use of the property; and

(2) if the work has not cost more than 10% of the amount on which tax would be payable on the next disposal of the property.

This is not to say that in all cases where the expenditure is in excess of 10% that the property is developed for VAT purposes. The expenditure must be in one of the five categories — construction, demolition, extension, alteration or reconstruction. For example, repair work even though more than 10% does not result in the property being developed.

Example: A Trader Ltd. bought a premises in 1969. In 1974 it extended the premises at a cost of £120,000, on which it claimed the VAT inputs. It sold the property in 1990 for £1.5m. VAT was not charged because the cost of the addition was less than 10% of the sale price. No adjustment to the 1974 costs is made for inflation. It is a straight comparison of cost against 10% of the selling price.

1.2.4 Demolition

Demolition work does not come within the 10% rule. Any amount of demolition work constitutes development. It is only additions or alterations that are covered by the 10% rule. The VAT practice in the UK is that to demolish a building is to reduce it to no more than the foundations and a single wall.

1.2.5 Repairs & Maintenance

Neither repairs nor maintenance of a building give rise to development for VAT. "Repairs" and "maintenance" are defined as "work which leaves the property essentially as it was" (VAT Property Transactions, Revenue Commissioners VAT Leaflet No 2).

1.2.6 UK Cases

(1) Conversion of Cinema into Bingo Hall: In the case of C&E Comms. -v-Morrison Dunbar Ltd. and Mecca Ltd. (1978) 1 BVC 165, the QB found that the word "alterations" means structural alterations to a building.

(2) Underpinning Defective Foundations: The House of Lords held that "alteration" meant structural alteration - something which affects the fabric of the building. They held that the construction of an additional foundation to a building in danger of subsidence was not repair or maintenance but an alteration. (ACT Construction -v- C&E Commrs. 1981 1BVC 451).

(3) Building Damaged by Fire: The QB held that when a building is extensively badly damaged by fire, it is more correct to say that it is "rebuilt" or "reconstructed" than to say it is repaired. (Parish Council of St. Luke -v- C&E, 1982 1BVC 521). In the case of Thomas Briggs (London) Limited (1977) the VAT Tribunal held that the replacement of a large factory wing which was gutted by fire was a repair (VATTR 212 London August 1977)

(4) Re-roofing - repair or alteration: The Court of Appeal held that the replacement of old clay tiles with modern concrete roof tiles was properly described as work of "repair" or "maintenance" and was not an alteration. (Sutton Housing Trust -v- C&E Commrs., 1984 2 BVC 200036).

(5) Installation of gas fires: The House of Lords held that the installation of gas fires in houses which had not previously had such fires was an alteration (C&E Commrs. -v- Viva Gas Appliances Ltd., 1983 1BVC 588). It should be noted that the installation required an amount of alteration work to the building.

There is a good summary of the U.K. cases on the meaning of the word alteration in Tolleys VAT Cases 1997 at 49.12 to 49.42.

The wording in the UK legislation under which these cases arose is not the same as ours. The legislation allowed zero rating on the supply of services "in the course of alteration or demolition of any building..." The relevant U.K. legislation is now contained in VATA 1994, 8 Schedule Group 6, Item 2.

1.2.7   Aide-Memoire

An aide-memoire for the five types of work on a building which result in the land on which it stands being developed is

C A R E D –
— Construction
— Alteration
— Reconstruction
— Extension
— Development.

1.3   WORK ON THE LAND

1.3.1   Types of Work: Under part (b) of the definition, the land is developed for VAT purposes if any engineering or other operation is carried out in, on, over or under the land to adapt it for materially altered use. There are four element to this:

1. An engineering or other operation must be carried out.
2. The engineering or other operation must be "in, on, over or under the land".
3. The engineering or other operation must be to adapt the land for altered use.
4. The altered use must be material.

This covers work such as levelling, construction of roads, laying of sewers, water or gas mains all of which adapt the land for materially altered use.

1.3.2 Planning Permission: Obtaining planning permission does not constitute a development of the land.

1.3.3 Area Developed: This is a matter of fact. Carrying out a development on land does not mean that the entire holding is treated as developed. For example, a farmer who builds a house on his land would only have developed the portion on which the house stands plus a reasonable plot surrounding it.

On the question of the area developed the Revenue state:

> *"The exact area which has been developed can be determined only by considering all the material circumstances. Thus, if a site is prepared for building work by having road and sewers laid, the entire area which would be reasonably regarded as served by the roads and sewers would be regarded as developed."*

I don't agree with this. If roads and sewers are laid in my opinion land untouched by the roads and sewers remains undeveloped even if it will be served by the roads and sewers. The definition of development in VATA 1972 Section 1 sets down that the work must be:

> *in the land*
> *on the land*
> *over the land or*
> *under the land.*

Work carried out "beside" the land does not give rise to development. I do not agree with the Revenue Commissioners interpretation that the preparation of a site for building work by having roads and sewers laid results in development of the entire area. That land which has not had work done in, on, over or under it remains undeveloped land despite the fact that roads and sewers run beside it. However the land which has no work done to it may be chargeable to VAT in accordance with VATA 1972 Section 4(5) – see 10.4 below

1.3.4 Materially Altered Use of Land: Work on land which is not designed to make a material alteration to which the land is put is not a development. Thus no account is taken of fencing, land drainage, laying of roads for agricultural purposes.

1.4   RELEVANCE OF WHETHER PROPERTY IS DEVELOPED OR NOT

The relevance from the seller's point of view of whether or not a property is developed is that if it is, VAT is chargeable on the sale and VAT inputs on its development and costs of sale are allowed.

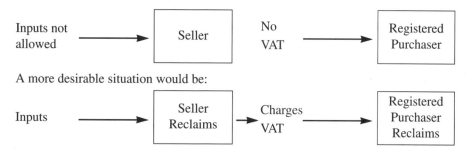

A more desirable situation would be:

From the purchaser's point of view a VAT charge is not desireable. It results in a cash flow disadvantage and usually a VAT inspection. In addition if the purchaser is in arrears with his/her tax payments the VAT repayment will be offset against the outstanding tax.

1.5   Building

In practice, this word does not normally cause a problem except in the case of a pre-fab type of structure the existence of which may result in the land on which it stands being developed. The definition in our legislation VATA 1972 (Section 1(1)) is extensive and detailed and contrasts with the brief definition in Article 4(3)(b) of the Sixth Directive. It states:

> *"A building shall be taken to mean any structure fixed to or in the ground."*

A taxpayer has the right to invoke EU law where the domestic law is inconsistent with Community law   [Amministrazione della Finanze dello Stato V Simmenthal SpA {1978} ECR 629].

Therefore, a taxpayer can choose the EU definition of building over that in the domestic legislation.

1.6   The Emmen Case

The question of whether or not land was developed and thus vatable was considered by the European Court of Justice in the case of Gemeente Emmen and Belastingdienst Grote Ondernemingen (Case C-468/93).

The municipality of Emmen supplied eight sites which had not been built on and were earmarked for housing. The land was equipped with roads and sewers and the sites were connected up to the water, gas, electricity, telecommunications and cable television networks.

The Netherlands Regional Court referred the question of whether the sites were chargeable to VAT in accordance with the EU 6th Directive to the European Court of Justice.

The E.C.J. held

It is for the Member States to define the concept of 'building land' within the meaning of the combined provisions of Article 13B(h) and Article 4(3)(b) of the Sixth Directive. In the view of the Court it was not for the Court to specify what degree of improvement land which has not been built on must exhibit in order to be categorized as building land within the meaning of the directive.

2.   The amount on which VAT is charged on the sale of a freehold

2.1   The majority of sales

In the majority of cases VAT is charged on the sale price. If the contract is for £1m VAT is charged on £1m. VAT is charged on the total consideration the supplier is entitled to receive including all taxes, commissions, costs and charges excluding VAT on the supply. (VATA 1972 Section 10(1)).

2.2   Stamp Duty

The stamp duty payable is not part of the consideration the supplier "becomes entitled to receive" and so stamp duty is not included in the figure on which VAT is charged.

On the other side of the stamp duty/VAT coin, stamp duty is not chargeable on the VAT payable on the sale. For a short while, in 1993 and early 1994 there was doubt about this and a change of practice by the stamp duty office. It is now set down clearly in the Finance Act 1994 S.108 that stamp duty is not chargeable on VAT.

2.3   Market Price

The general rule in VAT law is that market price only applies where there is a non business reason for the selling at below market price. This allows below market pricing for commercial reasons (e.g. January sales) to be the basis for the VAT charge. However, the sale of product at below market price for non-commercial reasons is caught by the market price rules. For example, if a computer distributor sells a computer to his brother for 10% of the market price VAT should be accounted for on the full market price (VATA 1972 Section 10(3)(a)).

In the case of property sales, VATA 1972 Section 10(9) applies. It is a very difficult sub-section to understand and I have asked a number of specialists what in their view it means. None were clear what exactly it means.

The Revenue however, have no bothersome scruples or doubts about what it means. In their view, Section 10(9) simply imposes market value on all property transactions.

If you have a case where an Inspector is contending that market value should apply I suggest you:

1. Consider Article 11 of the EU 6th Directive on VAT and Ireland's derogations, if any, from that Article. Article II sets out the rules for determining the amount on which VAT is charged. Market value is only allowed in very limited circumstances under the Directive.

2. Read the European Court's decision in the case of EC Commission v France (Ref. 50\87). In that case, French law restricted input credit where the related outputs were below market price. The Court held that French law controvened the EU 6th Directive.

3. Read the European Courts decision in the Skripalle case (Ref. C-063/96). In that case, German law imposed a notional price above market value. The Court held against the German authorities.

I think you will find a study of the foregoing will lead you to the conclusion that it is not quite as clear as Revenue would have you believe.

3. The rate at which VAT is charged on the sale of a freehold

3.1 The majority of sales

The present rate at which VAT is charged on the sale of a freehold is $12^1/_2\%$ (VATA 1972 Sixth Schedule (xxviii))

The rates of VAT in the past on the sale of a freehold were:

From	To	Rate
1.11.1972	28.2.1983	3%
1.3.1983	28.2.1985	5%
1.3.1985	28.2.1993	10%
1.3.1993		$12^1/_2\%$

The Government's intention, in line with EU requirements, is to increase the rate on commercial property to 21%. It has not yet been decided when this will be done. The Minister in his 1993 Budget Speech said

> *"EC law requires a fundamental change to the VAT treatment of building services. A division has ultimately to be made between house building, which may continue at a reduced rate, and other building, which must become subject to the standard rate. I do not, however, propose to introduce this distinction at this point."*

3.2   Package Supply

Where a number of goods and/or services are sold for an all inclusive price, the highest rate of VAT that applies to any of the goods or services applies to the total consideration. The package rule is VAT's version of what the nuns used to tell children long ago about one bad apple in a barrell making all the apples rotten. If a vatable item is included with one or more non-vatable ones and the whole lot is sold for one price VAT is chargeable on the entire consideration at the highest rate of VAT in the package.

Therefore the sale of a house with a cooker, a fridge and a washing machine for an all inclusive price is liable to VAT at the rate of 21% rather than $12\frac{1}{2}$%. (VATA 1972 11(3)). However, on request the Inspector may allow a builder to account for VAT @ 21% on the open market value of such fittings and at $12\frac{1}{2}$% on the balance of the sale proceeds.

To avoid any risk it is prudent to separately charge for the fittings.

3.2.1   Example of a package supply

Developer Limited acquired 5 adjoining undeveloped sites with a view to building an office block. He had done extensive work on the first site when he ran short of money. He sold all 5 sites together for £2m. As the first site was developed the package rule applied i.e. VAT was chargeable on the total consideration. The question of inputs would also have to be considered.

4.   The VAT clause in a contract for the sale of a freehold

4.1   Special Condition 3

The Law Society's standard contract for sale has a clause for VAT known as Special Condition 3. It reads as follows:

3.   *"In addition to the purchase price, the Purchaser shall pay to the Vendor an amount equivalent to such Value-Added Tax as shall be exigible in relation to the sale or (as the case may be) the Assurance same to be calculated in accordance with the provisions of the Value-Added Tax Act, 1972, and to be paid on completion of the sale or forthwith upon receipt by the Purchaser of an appropriate invoice (whichever shall be the later)."*

(Delete if inappropriate)

This clause makes it clear that the consideration is net of VAT and prevents doubt which could otherwise arise whether the price was VAT inclusive or VAT exclusive. The clause protects the vendor even against his own miscalculations. The clause does not protect the vendor against interest charges.

If the clause is deleted the vendor does not have the right to collect VAT from the purchaser.

4.2.1   *Example:* — Special Condition 3 deleted

A seller sold a property for £1m. Special condition 3 was deleted. On inspection 3 years later it transpired that the seller should have charged VAT.

The seller sent a VAT invoice to the buyer for VAT of £100,000 (the 10% rate applied at the time). The buyer returned the invoice demanding an invoice for £909,090 plus VAT of £90,910.

The seller had to pay the Revenue Commissioners £90,910 plus interest of £40,910 (15% p.a. for 3 years).

The buyer submitted a supplementary VAT return and got a repayment of £90,910.

4.2.2   *Example:* — Special Condition 3 not deleted

Although the seller thought VAT was not chargeable on the sale of her property she insisted that special condition 3 was left in the contract. On inspection 3 years later it transpired that she should have charged VAT. She sent an invoice to the purchaser for VAT.

The purchaser paid her the VAT and recovered it from the Revenue Commissioners.

The Revenue agreed not to charge her interest as there was no loss to the Exchequer. At time of writing (July 1997) the Revenue have indicated that in future they will not accept the no loss to the Exchequer argument. In all but very exceptional circumstances, interest will be charged on late payment of VAT. The rate of interest charged on late payment of VAT is 1.25% per month. This interest is not an allowable deduction for Income Tax or Corporation Tax. Thus making it equivalent to a rate of interest of 24% per annum when compared with bank interest that is allowable for corporation tax. The Institute's Indirect Taxes Committee are in consultation with the Revenue on this at time of writing.

5.   The country in which the sale of a freehold is charged to VAT – the place of supply rule.

The place of supply rule is quite simple. The sale of a freehold is charged to VAT in the country in which the property is situated. (VATA 1972 Section 3(6)(c).)

5.1   *Example:* — Place of Supply Rule

A German GmbH sold a freehold office block in Cork to a U.S. Corporation. The sale is treated as taking place in Ireland where the property is situated.

5.2   *Example:* — Place of Supply Rule

Mr. Maxwell Smart owned a property in Ireland which he had recently developed. He sold it to Mr. Bright. They signed the contract for sale in the Isle of Man. In what country is the sale charged to VAT? The answer is Ireland i.e. where the property is situated.

6.   The time when the charge to VAT on the sale of a freehold arises -the triggering event.

6.1   On completion

The supply of a freehold interest takes place when a person disposes of his freehold interest (VATA 1972 s.4(2)). The VAT Act does not state when a disposal takes place.

In practice the supply is treated as taking place on completion. This practice is supported by the wording in the Law Society's standard contract for sale. Special condition 3, in the standard contract, which deals with VAT, states:

> *"....... to be paid on completion of the sale or forthwith upon receipt by the Purchaser of an appropriate invoice (whichever shall be the later)".*

The practice is also in accord with the Supreme Court Judgement in the case of Tempany v Hynes (1976 IR 101) which held that the equitable interest passed on payment – equity follows the money. The deposit is held by the stakeholder until completion and it is handed over on completion as is the balance of the purchase money, plus VAT if appropriate. It follows from this that the legal and equitable interest both pass on completion. From this it follows that the supply for VAT purposes takes place on completion. There is sometimes confusion about this arising from the fact that prior to the 1976 decision the interpretation of our law was in line with interpretation under U.K. law which is that equity passes on contract.

There are counter arguments that the supply takes place when the contract is signed. It is unlikely that many will argue this as it brings forward the date of payment of VAT.

6.2   Payment received in advance:

Where payment is received in advance by the vendor a VAT charge arises at the time of receipt (VATA 1972 Section 19(2)). Therefore where the vendor receives a deposit the receipt of the deposit by him is the triggering event (the supply) for VAT. However, in most sales of freeholds the vendor does not receive the deposit but rather his solicitor receives it as his stakeholder. In those circumstances a VAT charge does not arise on the deposit.

When the deposit is received by the vendor's agent (e.g. an auctioneer) the receipt is a supply for VAT.

6.2.1   *Example:* — Deposit received by stakeholder

Sir Charles Clore signed a contract for the sale of an office block in Limerick on 1 July for £2m. His solicitor received a deposit of £200,000 as stakeholder when the contract was signed. Conveyance and completion took place on 12 August.

Sir Charles received £2.25m on 12 August made up as follows:

Balance of purchase price	£1.80m
Deposit from Stakeholder	.20m
	2.00m
Value Added Tax @ $12^1/_2\%$	.25m
Total	2.25m

The supply for VAT purposes took place on 12 August.

6.2.2 *Example: — * **Deposit received by agent**

On 1 June, a housebuilder's auctioneer received a £5,000 deposit for a new house. The sale was completed on 12 August. The sale price was £70,000. The housebuilder made two supplies for VAT as follows:

Date of Supply	*Amount*
1 June	£ 5,000
12 August	£65,000

7. The VAT Invoicing requirements on the sale of a freehold

7.1 Governing Legislation

The invoicing requirements on the sale of a freehold are governed by:

1. VATA 1972 Section 17 and

2. Value Added Tax (Invoices and Other Documents) Regulations 1992.

7.2 Requirement to issue an invoice

The vendor is obliged to give a VAT invoice to the purchaser if

1. The sale of the freehold is chargeable to VAT and

2. The purchaser of the freehold is a taxable person.

7.3 What should be on a VAT Invoice

There are eleven items that should be on the VAT Invoice on the sale of a freehold:

1. The name of the vendor

2. The address of the vendor

3. The VAT number of the vendor

4. The name of the purchaser

5. The address of the purchaser

6. The date of issue of the invoice

7. The date of supply of the freehold

8. A description of the freehold

9. The consideration net of VAT

10. The rate of VAT

11. The amount of VAT

7.4   Example:

THE PROPERTY DEVELOPER PLC
125 MERRION SQUARE
DUBLIN 2.

VAT NO. I.E. 1357911 P
DATE: 22 JULY 1994

Shoe Importers Limited
140 Lower Leeson Street,
Dublin 2.

Freehold interest in Unit 12

Sandyford Industrial Estate,

Dublin 16.

Supplied on completion on 22 July 1994	600,000
Value Added Tax @ $12^1/_2\%$	75,000
	£675,000

7.5   Time Limit for issuing the Invoice

Under S.I. 276 of 1992 the invoice should be issued by the 15th day of the month following the month of supply. For example a sale completed in July should be invoiced by the 15th August.

In practice the vendor will produce the VAT invoice on completion to ensure he gets paid the VAT on completion.

8   The appropriate return for VAT on the sale of a freehold

8.1   The General Rule

The general rule is that VAT arising in the VAT period should be included in the return for that period. For example VAT on a sale completed in September should be included in the September\October VAT return.

8.2   Exceptions to the general rule

There are two exceptions to the general rule:

1.   VAT on an advance payment is accounted for when received. A deposit received by the vendors agent (eg. an auctioneer) is treated as received by the vendor and VAT is chargeable on it on receipt. A deposit received by the vendor's solicitor as stakeholder is not treated as received by the vendor and does not trigger a VAT charge.

2.   VAT on an invoice to a taxable person is accounted for when the invoice is issued. If the invoice is not issued on time it is treated as issued on the 15th of the month following sale.

8.3   The majority of cases

In practice in the majority of cases the VAT invoice is issued on the day of completion and payment of the VAT is received on that day with the result that the VAT charge arises in the VAT period in which completion takes place.

8.4   Example

Mr. Donald Trump signed a contract for the sale of a vatable freehold in Galway on 3rd May. On signing his solicitor as stakeholder received a deposit of £250,000. The sale was completed on 12 July and the VAT invoice was issued on that date. The VAT charge arose in July-August.

9.   The date on which VAT on the sale of a freehold is payable

VAT is payable to the Revenue Commissioners by the 19th of the month following the VAT period in which the supply takes place. This means that in the majority of cases VAT on the sale of a freehold is payable to the Revenue Commissioners on the 19th of the month following the VAT period in which completion takes place. The VAT periods are 2 monthly ending in the even numbered months. In the majority of cases the VAT on the sale of a freehold will be payable as follows:

VAT period in which the sale is completed	Date by which VAT is payable
January – February	19 March
March – April	19 May
May – June	19 July
July – August	19 September
September – October	19 November
November – December	19 January

VAT paid late is subject to an interest charge of 1.25% per month.

10. Special instances when a VAT charge arises on a freehold

10.1 The self-supply of a freehold

Certain actions give rise to a notional sale of a freehold for VAT purposes even though in fact there has been no sale. This means that VAT has to be paid as if there had been a sale. Being a notional sale there is no debtor from whom the VAT can be collected and therefore it is an irrecoverable cost to the owner of the freehold. Notional sales are known as self-supplies.

The actions which trigger the notional sale of a freehold are:

1. Transfer to private use of a freehold on which input tax was claimed (VATA 1972 S.3(1)(f)).

2. The application of a freehold to exempt or partly exempt activities (VATA 1972 S3(1)(e)).

3. The surrender of possession of freehold by way of letting of less than ten years (VATA 1972 S4(2))

10.1.1 Transfer to private use

A simple example of the transfer to private use of a freehold is where a builder takes a house on which he has claimed input credit for his private use. This triggers a notional sale and the builder must account for VAT on this notional sale. Under VATA 1972

10(4) the amount on which self-supplies are chargeable to VAT is cost that is total cost, not just the costs on which VAT inputs were claimed.

Example

Jack Ryan a builder incurred the following costs in building a house:

	Cost	Input VAT
	£	£
Site	30,000	Nil
Development	20,000	2,500
Building	50,000	6,250
	100,000	8,750

When he incurred the costs he (correctly) claimed the input VAT of £8,750. He decided after the house was built to move into it himself i.e. he self-supplied the house. In his VAT return he included £12,500 (£100,000 @ $12^1/_2\%$) as additional VAT on goods and services thus increasing his liability by £12,500 (Box T1 on the return). He complied with the requirements of VATA 1972 Sections 3(1)(f) and 10(4).

However under Article 5 (6) of the EU 6th Directive the amount of the site should not have been included and since the EU Directive is superior in law to the domestic legislation Jack Ryan should have accounted for VAT on £70,000 i.e. £8,750 not on £100,000 (Ref: de Jong – v – Staatssecretaris Van Financien Case C 20/91).

10.1.2 The application of a freehold to exempt or partly exempt activities

I will illustrate this self-supply by the following example:

Megabucks Limited purchased a freehold office block for its leasing activity. It reclaimed the VAT on the purchase of the office block. Later the leasing staff moved to another premises and staff dealing with lending moved in. The lending activity is VAT exempt. There was transfer of use of the premises from a vatable activity (leasing) to an exempt activity (lending). The transfer of use triggers a self-supply at cost (VATA 1972 S3(1)(e) and 10(4). In practice such a self-supply is dealt with by clawing back VAT on inputs.

10.1.3 The surrender of possession of a freehold

I will deal with surrender of possession by way of lease of less than ten years later in the part dealing with short term lettings.

10.2   Gifts

Gifts are often categorised as self-supplies because in most cases they give rise to an irrecoverable VAT cost. A gift is not a self-supply. It is a supply to the person to whom the gift is given.

10.2.1 Example

A builder gave a house to his daughter free of charge triggering a charge to VAT (VATA 1972 S 3(1) (f)) which is an irrecoverable cost to the builder.

10.2.2 Example

A business woman gave a freehold office to her son free of charge for her son's accountancy business. The business woman charged her son VAT and her son recovered VAT. There was no irrecoverable VAT.

10.3   The "sale" of a freehold by compulsory purchase or by seizure

It is specifically provided in VATA 1972 S.3(1)(d) that the compulsory acquisition by the state or a local authority is a sale for the purposes of VAT. It also provides that seizure by a person acting under statutory authority is a sale for the purposes of VAT.

10.4   The sale of a freehold interest in undeveloped building sites

The sale of undeveloped land is not chargeable to VAT. There is a special provision in the VAT Act (Section 4(5)) which makes the sale of undeveloped land chargeable to VAT in certain circumstances. I will illustrate the provisions by the following:

10.4.1 Example

In January 1994 a farmer who was not registered for VAT agreed with a builder to sell him 1 acre of land. In an effort to avoid VAT they gave effect to the sale as follows:

1.   The farmer retained title to the land but granted the builder license to build a house on the land.

2.   The builder built a house for the customer.

3.   The farmer transferred his freehold interest in the land to the customer after the house was built.

The farmer was selling land which had not been developed by him or on his behalf. Under "normal" rules he would not have to charge VAT. Under the special provisions of VATA 1972 Section 4(5) the farmer is obliged to register and account for VAT on the sale of the land.

10.4.2 Example

A builder sold an undeveloped site to a customer in January 1996. Under a separate contract with the builder's company the customer engaged the company to build a house on the site. The sale of the undeveloped site by the builder is chargeable to VAT in accordance with VATA 1972 Section 4(5).

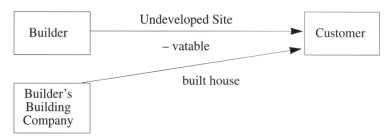

Section 4(5) was amended by Section 122(a) of the Finance Act 1995 because it was considered that as originally drafted it was defective in achieving its objective. The revised Section 4(5) is very widely drawn.

If you are advising on the sale of undeveloped land it would be prudent to confirm with the Inspector that Section 4(5) does not apply.

10.5 The sale of a freehold within a VAT Group

Transactions between companies within the same VAT group are ignored for VAT purposes. The sale of a vatable freehold from one company within a VAT group to another company within the same VAT group is excluded from the VAT group relieving provisions (VATA 1972 8(8)(a)(ii)(I). This means that VAT must be charged on the inter group sale of a vatable freehold. An invoice must be raised and a deduction claimed.

10.5.1 Example:

A Limited and B Limited were group registered for VAT. A Limited was the remitter for the group. B Limited sold its freehold interest in a recently developed property to A Limited for £100,000. B Limited issued a VAT invoice to A Limited. In the group return A Limited included an additional £12,500 (£100,000 @ $12^{1}/_{2}\%$) in Box T1 of the return thus increasing the VAT payable by the group. In the return A Limited also included a claim for £12,500 input credit (Box T2 of the return) in respect of the purchase by A Limited. A Limited was entitled to full recovery. The transaction was self-cancelling. If A Limited was entitled to say 20% input the cost of the transaction would have been £10,000 made up as follows:

Additional liability in group return (Box T1)	£12,500
Input deduction in group return (Box T2)	£2,500
Increase in VAT payable	£ 10,000

The VAT implications of moving a property within a VAT group are the same as if the property was purchased from outside the group.

11.   Special instances where a VAT charge does not arise on the sale of a freehold

11.1   The sale of a freehold in connection with the transfer of a business

Even if the disposal of a freehold is chargeable, VAT should not be charged if the disposal is "in connection with the transfer of a business or part thereof to another taxable person". (VAT Act 1972 Section 3(5)(b)(iii)).

The practice is that the seller gets and retains independent evidence that the buyer is registered for VAT – e.g. a letter from the VAT Inspector to the seller confirming that the buyer is a taxable person.

It is not an optional relieving sub-section but is mandatory where there is such a disposal VAT should not be charged.

The Revenue once took a broad view of the scope of the sub-section even to the extent of treating the sale of an asset of a business as being the transfer of "part thereof" of the business but are less inclined to take such a broad view now.

A broad interpretation is in line with the EU 6th Directive. Article 5.8 allows Member States to enact legislation providing for no VAT

> "*In the event of a transfer........... of a totality of assets or part thereof*"

Some refer to the relief as the transfer of a going concern. The words "going concern" are neither in the VAT Act 1972 nor in EU 6th Directive. The words going concern are imported from the parallel U.K. legislation (Value Added Tax (Special Provisions) Order 1992 – SI 1992/3129). In the U.K. the provision is known by the acronym TOGC (i.e. Transfer of Going Concern). Despite the fact that the words "going concern" are not in the VAT Act nor the EU legislation I understand they have been taken into account in some appeal cases.

The main problem that has arisen with Section 3(5)(b)(iii) is where the seller has charged VAT and failed to pass it on to the Revenue Commissioners. In such circumstances Inspectors have refused entitlement to input credit to the purchaser.

There is a risk to a purchaser who accepts a VAT charge on the transfer of a business or on the purchase of assets which have been used in a business.

11.1.1 Example

Mr. Dodgy sold his business and the freehold premises from which it was operated to Mr. Innocent for £300,000 plus VAT @ $12^1/_2\%$. Mr. Dodgy did not account for VAT on the sale to the Revenue Commissioners. The Inspector refused to repay Mr. Innocent the VAT charged to him because VAT should not have been charged since it was in connection with the transfer of a business. Had Mr. Dodgy paid the VAT it is likely that the Inspector would have allowed the refund to Mr. Innocent.

> **Tax Tip: Be careful in advising your client to accept a VAT charge on the purchase of a freehold used by the seller for his business.**

The relief is available even where the purchase is not entitled to full input credit. The requirement is that the purchaser is a taxable person. However, a freehold acquired VAT free under 3(5)(b)(iii) by a person not entitled to full input recovery should be considered in the light of VATA 1972 3(1)(e).

The VAT costs incurred by the seller of a freehold within 3(5)(b)(iii) are allowable [(VATA 1972 S.12 (1)(a)(iic)].

11.2   Sale of a Freehold out of which a long lease has been created

In 1989, Thomas Ryan purchased a freehold interest in land. He had an office block built on the land and granted a lease of 35 years.

He registered for VAT, claimed the inputs on the development and charged VAT on the lease.

In 1990, he sold his freehold interest to a pension fund for £1m. Was VAT chargeable on the sale?

The answer is "No".

The reason the answer is no is that when he granted the lease he sold his interest in the property for years 1 to 35 and transferred the reversion to non-business. The subsequent sale of the reversion was not in the course or furtherance of business. VAT costs in connection with the sale were not recoverable.

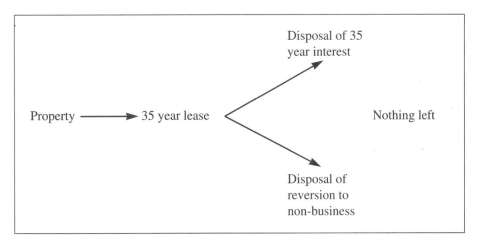

12   Miscellaneous points on freeholds

12.1   The forfeiture of the deposit on failure to complete.

In my opinion there are two types of forfeited deposits:

1. A deposit which is received by the vendor or agent at the time of the agreement for sale

2. A deposit which is not received by the vendor or his agent but is initially held by the vendors solicitor as stakeholder and is only released to the vendor after the sale has collapsed.

The deposit which is received by the vendor at the time of the agreement for sale of the vatable freehold (the first type) is chargeable to VAT at that time (VATA 1972 S.19 (2) at the rate appropriate to the intended sale i.e. $12^{1}/_{2}\%$.

Where the deposit is received from the stakeholder after the sale collapses there is in my view no supply and therefore no charge to VAT. If you have an instance of a forfeited deposit I advise that you get the Inspector's agreement to your conclusions as to the correct VAT treatment.

12.2   The mortgage and repossession of a freehold

The most common type of mortgage is a legal mortgage. In a legal mortgage the mortgagor (the borrower) conveys his interest in the property to the mortgagee (the lender). The lender has a legal interest in the property and the borrower has the right to get it back (the equity of redemption) when the borrowing is cleared.

It is provided that the transfer of ownership of goods as security for a debt is not a supply for the purposes of VAT Act 1972 Section 3(5)(b)(i). Neither is the transfer of the property back to the owner when the debt is cleared a supply for VAT purposes. (VATA 1972 3(5)(b)(ii)).

If a borrower defaults on his repayments and a vatable freehold formed part of the assets of the borrowers vatable business the disposal by the lender is treated as being made by the borrower (VATA 1972 Section 3(7) but it is the duty of the lender to account to the Collector General for the VAT (VATA 1972 Section 19(3)(b)). A liquidator or receiver is also responsible to account to the Collector General on the sale of a vatable freehold which formed part of the assets of the borrowers vatable business.

12.3   Options on a freehold

12.3.1 There are two types of options

1. Call options and

2. Put options

12.3.2 Call options

A call option on a freehold is the right to buy a freehold at a fixed price within a given time. For example on 1 January 1994 Farmer Browne granted an option to Mr. Builder to buy 100 acres of land for £2m at any time up to 31 December 1996. Mr. Builder paid Farmer Browne £75,000 for this option. For the £75,000 Mr. Builder got the option to call on Farmer Browne to sell the 100 acres to him for the agreed price of £2m. Mr. Builder can exercise his option at any time between 1 January 1994 and 31 December 1996.

In my opinion the option money is a separate supply chargeable to VAT at 21% (VATA 1972 Section 5). However, if the option money is treated as part payment for the land, I think the option should follow the land for VAT. If the land is exempt then the option is exempt while if the land is developed the option is chargeable at the same rate as the land i.e $12^1/_2$%. In summary the VAT treatment of options on freeholds in my opinion is as follows:

1. Option not exercised   — VAT on option at 21%

2. Option exercised but option money
    not offset against price of land   — VAT on option at 21%

3. Option exercised and option money
    offset against price of land   — VAT at rate appropriate to the land

There are arguments for an alternative VAT treatment for call options in particular circumstances.

There will be a practical difficulty in some cases because the time of supply will be at the time of granting the option at which time it will not be known if the option will be exercised. For example on 1 January 1996 a farmer granted a call option to a builder to buy 100 acres of land for £2m at any time up to 31 December 1998. The builder paid the farmer £75,000 which will be offset against the purchase price if the option is exercised. The difficulty that arises is that the time of supply is 1 January 1996 at which time it is not known if the transaction is chargeable at 21% or is exempt. It will be exempt if the option is exercised and the option money is offset against the sale of the undeveloped (exempt) land. In the practical administration of VAT it should be possible to come to an arrangement with the Inspector.

12.3.3 Put options

A put option on a freehold is a right of the vendor to sell a property at a fixed price within a given time. For example on 1 January 1996, Developer Limited granted a put option to Speculator Limited giving Speculator Limited the right to sell 50 acres of land to Developer Limited for £1m at any time up to 31 December 1998. Speculator paid Developer £45,000 for the put option.

Put Option

Developer ————————————————————————————————————> Speculator

Limited   <———————————————————————————————————— Limited

£45,000

A put option on a freehold is most unusual. Revenue have not had to consider the issue. Prima facie they consider it would be chargeable to VAT at 21% in accordance with VATA Section 5(1).

PART C

THE DETAILED ASPECTS OF LONG LEASES

1.   What is a long lease

A long lease for VAT purposes is a lease of 10 years or more. (A short lease is a lease of less than 10 years.)

1.2   Option to extend (Finance Act 1997)

A lease which gives the tenant an option to extend it to 10 years or more is treated for VAT purposes as one which runs to the latest date possible. For example, a 7 year lease with an option to the tenant to extend it to 35 years is a 35 year lease for VAT purposes. Likewise a 15 year lease with an option to extend it to 25 years is a 25 year lease for VAT purposes.

A lease which contains an option to extend it to less than 10 years is unaffected. For example, a 3 year lease which contains an option to the tenant to extend it to 9 years is a 3 year lease for VAT purposes.

It is interesting to note that the legislation is quite clear that the option to extend must be contained in the lease itself. This means that a 7 year lease which contains an option of extension to 35 years is a 35 year lease for VAT purposes. In contrast if there was a separate option agreement the lease would not be affected. It would remain a 7 year lease for VAT purposes. A lease which contains an option to extend it to less than 10 years in unaffected. For example, a 3 year lease which contains an option to the tenant to extend it to 9 years is a 3 year lease for VAT purposes.

The second interesting point to note about options is that the extending effect only arises where the tenant has the option to extend. If a 7 year lease contained a clause whereby the landlord could extend the lease to 35 years the lease for VAT purposes would remain a 7 year lease.

2.   Development of a property by the tenant

The meaning of development has been fully considered in Part B Paragraph 1.

A tenant who develops a property is entitled to input credit subject to the normal rules. If all his supplies are taxable he is entitled to full recovery on the development of the property in which he has a leasehold interest.

I will deal later with subsequent supplies by the landlord where the property has been developed by the tenant.

3. The amount on which VAT is charged on the creation of a first long lease

3.1 Introduction

You will remember from part A that the act of creating a long lease (one of 10 years or more) is a sale for VAT purposes. The problem with such a sale is there is no sale proceeds. This problem is overcome by arriving at a value for the lease. There is choice of three ways of valuing a long lease provided there is no provision for a rent increase within 5 years. The three ways of valuing a long lease for VAT purposes are:

1. Valuation by a competent valuer or

2. The formula: 3/4 x annual rent (R) x no. of years in the lease (N) or

3. The multiplier

Where there is provision for a rent increase within 5 years, valuation by a competent valuer is the only method of valuation allowed.

The term "competent valuer" is not used in the legislation but comes from the Revenue's Booklet on Property. What is required under the relevant Regulation (No. 19 of the VAT Regulations 1979) is evidence of the open market price of the lease. In my opinion the term competent valuer is used to mean a professional valuer indicating that the Revenue will accept a valuation by a professional valuer but will not accept a "DIY" valuation by the landlord.

3.2 The multipliers used in valuing a long lease

The multipliers used in valuing a long lease are derived from the yield on Government Stocks with the result that the multipliers change from time to time. As interest rates decrease the multiplier increases. The multipliers since 14 August 1987 have been:

From	14.08.87 to 19.07.89	8.89
"	20.07.89 to 20.05.91	11.41
"	21.05.91 to 23.01.92	10.75
"	24.01.92 to 13.06.93	10.98
"	14.06.93 to 14.10.93	13.57
"	15.10.93 to 16.08.94	14.56
"	17.08.94 to 14.05.95	11.68
"	15.05.95 to 25.3.97	11.74
"	26.03.97 to 16.09.97	14.43
"	17.09.97 to	15.97

You can find out what the multiplier is by contacting your local tax office.

3.3 Rent free periods in valuing a long lease

Sometimes as an inducement to lease the property the landlord allows the tenant a rent free period or a period at a reduced rent.

3.3.1 Example — Rent free period

Landlord Limited has a draft 35 year lease with Reluctant Tenant Limited. The rent is £30,000 p.a. with the first rent increase after 5 years. As an inducement to the tenant the landlord changes the lease to nil rent for the first year and £30,000 p.a. thereafter. The change results in the first rent increase (Nil to £30,000) being within 5 years. This means that the only permissible valuation is that of a competent valuer. Obviously, the valuer will take the rent free period into account in valuing the lease.

3.3.2 Example — Rent free period

The lease is drawn up between the landlord and tenant for a 35 year lease with the first rent increase after 5 years. By separate agreement the landlord waives his entitlement to rent for the first year. The landlord has the choice of three methods of valuing the lease and the rent free period is ignored for VAT purposes. The Income Tax/Corporation Tax implications of such a waiver would also have to be considered.

3.4 Premium in valuing a long lease

A premium on a lease is an amount payable up-front by the tenant in addition to the rent under the lease. Where there is a premium on a lease it is added on to the value of the lease, based on the capital value of the rents, to arrive at the amount for VAT.

3.5 Reverse premium in valuing a long lease

A reverse premium is an amount paid by a landlord to a tenant as an inducement to the tenant to take up the lease.

The current practice of the Revenue is to treat the transaction as not being a supply for VAT purposes and the reverse premium is therefore ignored irrespective of whether the reverse premium clause is contained in the lease or not. They do however caution that one could interpret the reverse premium as the supply of a service by the tenant and they might very well choose to do so if the practice of ignoring the reverse premium was used in a contrived way to avoid VAT.

3.5.1 Example — Reverse premium

Dr. Johnson owned a developed property in Sligo. In negotiating to let the property to Art and Design Consultants it transpired that their fitting out costs would be £75,000. Dr. Johnson agreed to pay them a reverse premium of £50,000. This can be illustrated by a diagram as follows:

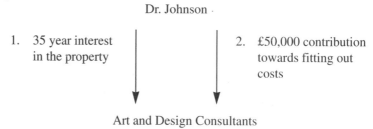

Dr. Johnson

1. 35 year interest in the property	2. £50,000 contribution towards fitting out costs

Art and Design Consultants

The £50,000 contribution towards fitting out costs was ignored for VAT purposes.

Art and Design Consultants recovered all VAT on the fitting out cost as they were entitled to full recovery.

3.6   Stamp duty in valuing a long lease

Stamp Duty is not chargeable on the VAT that arises on the creation of a long lease. See my comments earlier as regards stamp duty on the sale of a freehold (Part B paragraph 2.2). They apply equally to stamp duty on the creation of a long lease.

3.7   Long leases at less than open market price

As a long lease is as much a supply of immoveable goods for VAT as a freehold, my comments on freehold sales at less than open market price apply equally to long leases at less than open market price.

3.8   Unencumbered Rent

Sometimes connected landlords and tenants put restrictive conditions in a lease to support a low rent and thus reduced the leases value for VAT.

To stop this type of VAT planning the new rules, effective from 26 March 1997, require the valuer to ignore restrictive conditions when arriving at a market rent for a property. The valuer must arrive at the market rent that the property would fetch if let without restrictive conditions. Restrictive conditions are not defined in the legislation. I suspect the draftsman purposely avoided defining a restrictive condition on the basis that like the elephant, it is hard to define, but you will know one when you see one! The reality is that most, if not all leases, have conditions that it could be argued are restrictive.

If you have a case where the Inspector is attempting to impose an unencumbered rent as the basis for arriving at a VAT charge you might find it useful to consider whether or not the domestic legislation in this regard is in line with the Directive. Article 11 of the EU 6th Directive sets down the rules for determining the amount on which VAT is charged. Unencumbered rent seems to go beyond Article 11. In addition the derogation sought by Ireland did not include a request for permission to use unencumbered rent. It merely sought permission to use the reverse charge.

In a recent decision, the E.C.J. considered the question of taxable amount of rent under Article 11 (Finanzampt Bergisch Gladbach v Skripalle (Case C - 63\96)). In that case, Werner Skripalle charged a market rent on letting a property to a connected company. The German tax authorities attempted to impose a higher charge based on a notional amount in accordance with German VAT legislation. The Court found against the German authorities.

If you are considering the vires of the Irish legislation (Finance Act 1997) in the light of the Directive you might also find it useful to read the E.C.J. decision in the case of EC Commission v France (1989) 1 CMLR 505, ECJ 50\87. In that case, French law attempted to deal with below market rents for social housing by restricting the entitlement to inputs. The E.C.J. held that the French domestic legislation contravened the provisions of the EU 6th Directive and that input entitlement could not be restricted in the circumstances.

However, it is unlikely you will have a problem with unencumbered rent in the majority of cases. The Revenue Commissioners have stated in their "Guide to the Finance Act 1997 Changes" that there will be no change in the methods of valuing a leasehold interest for VAT where a market rent is charged in a commercial arms-length transaction. The Revenue Guide goes on to say:

> *"In practice,the unencumbered rent will be substituted for the actual rent charged for the purpose of valuing on interest for VAT purposes where:*
>
> *(i)   an exempt (or partially exempt) company or a non- taxable entity develops a property through a development company,*
>
> *(ii)   the conditions contained in a lease restrict the use of the property to a situation where there is effectively no open market for the interest and the exempt company or non-taxable entity or a related party to it is the only possible tenant and*
>
> *(iii) the cost of the development significantly exceeds the value of the interest, based on the actual rent charged, effectively confirming that a non- commercial rent is involved.*

3.9   A break clause in valuing a long lease

A break clause in a lease is a clause which allows the tenant to terminate the lease at a given time or times. For example: A landlord granted a 35 year lease to a tenant with a clause in the lease allowing the tenant to terminate the lease at the end of year five or at the end of year ten. Such a clause is known as a break clause. A break clause in a 35 year lease is attractive to a tenant in that he or she is not locked in for 35 years.

In practice break clauses are ignored in determining the length of a lease. For example, a 35 year lease with a 5 year break clause is a 35 year lease for VAT purposes.

4. The rate at which VAT is charged on the creation of a long lease

The rate at which VAT is charged on the creation of a long lease is $12^1/_2\%$ (VATA 1972 Section 11(1)(d) and the Sixth Schedule paragraph (xxviii)).

4.1 The package rule

The package rule which has been dealt with earlier when dealing with the rate of VAT on the sale of a freehold can also apply in the case of a long lease.

4.1.1 Example of the package rule

Office Properties Limited granted a 35 year lease of a fully furnished office to Insurance Brokers Limited for an all inclusive rent of £100,000 p.a.. VAT was accounted for by Office Properties Limited at $12^1/_2\%$.

This was a package supply with the result that the rate of VAT on the supply was 21%. This could have been avoided if separate rents were specified for the property and the furniture. Inspectors generally are not strict on the application of the package rule, but would in the circumstances such as Office Properties seek the additional VAT due at 21% on the letting of the furniture.

A further complication arises in such circumstances in that the lease of the property is subject to a once-off charge to VAT, while letting the furniture is chargeable to VAT on an on-going basis.

Where the value of the furniture being let is not significant, I am of the view that it would be ignored on de minimis grounds and in line with the substance and reality test (See British Airways Plc v C & E Commrs (1990) STC 643).

> **Tax Tip: When reviewing a lease check what exactly is being leased – is there more involved than just a premises.**

5.   The VAT clause in a long lease

An example of the wording used in a long lease to cover VAT is as follows:

> *"and the lessee hereby covenants with the lessor in the manner following that is to say ....*

> *to pay and discharge all value added tax payable in respect of this lease and to keep the lessor indemnified against payment thereof"*

This was in respect of a 35 year lease. This wording would only be suitable in the case of a 10 to 20 year lease if the tenant was undertaking to pay the landlord the two strands of VAT i.e. the VAT on the supply and the VAT on the reversion. The tenant would not be entitled to input credit on the VAT payable on the reversion.

My comments earlier and the examples on the VAT clause in a contract for sale of a freehold apply equally to the VAT clause in a long lease (Part B paragraph 4).

6.   The country in which a long lease is charged to VAT – place of supply rule.

As the creation of a long lease is a supply of goods, the place of supply rules for goods apply with the result that a long lease is charged to VAT in the country in which the property being let is situated (VATA 1972 S4(2) and Section 3(6)(c)).

7.   The time when the charge to VAT arises on the creation of a long lease – the triggering event

The time when the VAT charge arises (the time of supply) is the earlier of

1.   The date the tenant takes occupancy or

2.   The date the lease is signed.

7.1   An agreement for lease

In some instances, the landlord and tenant sign an agreement for lease in advance of the actual lease. The question arises: Is the agreement for lease without occupation an event that gives rise to a VAT charge? In my opinion, an agreement for lease is not a triggering event for VAT. My thinking runs as follows: An agreement for lease is said to be as good as a lease and on that basis an agreement for lease is a triggering event for VAT. However, an agreement for lease is as good as a lease on the assumption that the Courts would grant a decree of specific performance, based on the agreement for lease. But specific performance, being an equitable remedy, is at the discretion of the Courts, so one cannot assume that a decree for specific performance would be granted in any particular case. Therefore, it follows that an agreement for lease is not a triggering event for VAT.

7.2   Moving in before the lease is signed

Sometimes, concern is expressed where the tenant moves in at a date earlier than the date the lease is signed because it is feared that in the period between moving in and signing the landlord has allowed a short term letting. In practice, there is no difficulty provided it can be shown that the agreement from the start was for a long lease. Copies of correspondence between the solicitors should be able to support this. However, where the long lease is between connected persons it can be more difficult to supply objective evidence.

8.   The VAT invoicing requirements

The VAT invoicing requirements on the grant of a long lease are the same as the invoicing requirements on the sale of a freehold with the exception that the description will be on the lines of the following:

"35 year lease granted on 8 May 1996 on Unit 12
Sandyford Industrial Estate Dublin 16.

Annual Rent £100,000 x 11.74 (multiplier)	£1,174,000
VAT @ $12^1/_2\%$	£ 146,750

However, see under Reverse Charges later which explains the circumstances where a landlord or assignee can be responsible for the VAT arising on a surrender or assignment..

9.   The appropriate return for VAT on the creation of a long lease and payment of VAT

The general rule is that VAT arising in the VAT period should be included in that return. For example VAT on a lease created in January-February should be included in the January-February VAT return.

The rules as regards the appropriate return are the same as set out for the sale of a freehold.

In the majority of cases VAT will be payable on the 19th day of the month following the VAT period in which the invoice is raised.

The triggering event for VAT purposes is the earlier of the date the tenant takes occupancy or the date of the lease. In practice Inspectors allow the VAT to be accounted for when the lease is drawn up even though the tenant has taken up occupancy earlier i.e. the supply has taken place earlier. The amount of VAT is however always calculated according to rules applicable at the date of supply. For example the multiplier used is always the one appropriate at the date of supply.

9.1   Example

Property Owners Limited granted a 35 year lease to Tenant Limited (which is registered for VAT) on 15 February. Property Owners Limited, issued the appropriate VAT invoice on 8 March. The appropriate return for the VAT on the creation of the lease was March-April. The VAT was payable on the following 19th May.

10.   Valuing self-supplies of leasehold interests

Where a tenant first uses a leasehold premises for the purposes of his vatable supplies he is entitled to recover the VAT charged on the lease. If he later uses it for exempt rather than vatable supplies he is obliged under the new rules to repay the VAT initially recovered. The legislative mechanics for this are that the taxpayer treats the application of the leasehold interest to exempt use as a notional vatable sale. The consideration for this notional sale will be the amount on which VAT was charged when he entered into the lease. This is known in VAT parlance as a self-supply.

Previous to the 26 March, VAT on such a self-supply was chargeable on the cost to the tenant. The question arose; what is the cost of a lease to a tenant? Presumably nil!

11.   Sale and lease back

The Revenue Commissioners allow a concession whereby a sale and lease back are both ignored for VAT purposes provided:-

1. The value of the lease corresponds approximately to the value of the interest sold and

2. The lease back is for at least 10 years.

11.1   Example

Car Manufacturers Limited sold it's freehold interest in Unit 20 Shannon Industrial Estate to Property Finance Limited for £1,500,000. Property Finance Limited leased back the unit to Car Manufacturers Limited on a 35 year lease at a rent of £100,000 per annum.

Car Manufacturers Limited	Sale £1,000,000 ⟶	Property Finance Limited
Car Manufacturers Limited	Lease £1,174,000* ⟵	Property Finance Limited

*£100,000 x 11.74 (multiplier)

The concession applied because the conditions were met as follows:

1. The value of the sale and the value of the lease back were approximately the same.

2. The lease back was for more than 10 years.

The advantage of the concession is limited because the VAT arising without the concession is self cancelled by the entitlement to input.

12.   Service charges

Frequently, landlords of shopping centres, apartment blocks, office blocks etc. not only collect rent but also supply services to their tenants such as cleaning, security, insurance, heating and maintenance.

There are two categories of service charges for VAT. The VAT treatment for each is different.

Category 1 – own staff

Category 1 is the category where the landlord supplies the services (e.g. security, maintenance, repairs etc.) using his own staff.

In such circumstances the landlord is carrying on an activity chargeable to VAT at 21% (i.e. property management) and is obliged to remain registered and account for VAT if his vatable turnover is in excess of £20,000 p.a.

Where one charge is made by the landlord for a composite supply of security, maintenance etc. the rate of VAT on the charge is 21%.

The landlord can reduce the VAT by making a separate charge for each service and he can do so on the one invoice.

Example

Cleaning	VAT rate	12.5%
Electricity	VAT rate	12.5%
Heating Oil	VAT rate	12.5%
Security	VAT rate	21%

Category 2 – Cost collection by landlord

In this category, the landlord gathers the costs and shares them between the tenants. All services are bought in and none are supplied by the staff of the landlord.

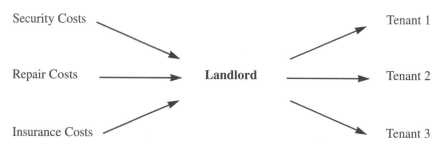

This arrangement caused VAT problems in the past. The Revenue view is that sharing the costs is not a supply for VAT with the result that VAT on the costs is blocked with the landlord. If the landlord was allowed onward charge VAT on the costs the fully vatable tenant could recover it.

The Revenue Commissioners since 1985 allow landlords to pass on the input VAT to the tenant.

The landlord issues one invoice each year covering his accounting year to the vatable tenant. A VAT deduction may not be taken by the tenant for payments on account but is only available on the annual invoice.

A sample invoice is as follows:

Landlord Limited
123 High Street,
Kilkenny,

Date 30.9.1994

VAT No. IE 2468104 B

A Tenant
Unit 1,
Alpha Industrial Estate
Kilkenny.

Service charge year ended 30.9.1994 made up as follows:

	Net of VAT	VAT	Total	Comment
Insurance	£1,000	£Nil	£1,000	Exempt
Electricity	£2,000	£250	£2,250	$12^{1}/_{2}\%$
Heating Oil	£3,000	£375	£3,375	$12^{1}/_{2}\%$
Security	£4,000	£420	£2,420	21%
			£9,045	
Paid on Account			£8,500	
Balance Due			£ 545	

For the Revenue statement on this see H.3.

13.   The termination of a long lease

VAT law on the termination of a long lease was amended with effect from 26 March 1997. In the following paragraphs, I will first of all consider the VAT treatment of terminations before 26 March and then I will set out the VAT treatment from then on.

13.1   Terminations before 26 March 1997

There are five ways a tenant's long term interest in a property can be terminated:

1. The long lease comes to an end e.g. a 21 year lease granted on 1 January 1970 came to an end on 31.12.1991.

2. The tenant is ejected for breach of a term of the long lease (e.g. non-payment of rent).

3. The tenant surrenders the residue of the long lease and returns the premises to the landlord.

4. The tenant assigns his interest in the long lease to someone else who then becomes the tenant.

5. The tenant abandons the long lease.

13.2   Lease came to an end before 26 March 1997

When a long lease came to an end before 26 March 1997 there was no supply by the tenant and therefore no charge to VAT.

A subsequent supply (say another 35 year lease) by the landlord was not chargeable to VAT provided the property was not developed before the second supply. The Revenue Commissioners have confirmed that this was their practice.

13.2.1 Example

Landlord Limited developed a property in 1973 and let it on a 21 year lease from 1 March 1973. It charged the tenant VAT on the creation of the lease. The lease expired 28 February 1994. Landlord Limited re-let the property without further development to Bank Limited for 21 years from 1 March 1994. VAT was not chargeable on the 21 year lease to Bank Limited.

This reflects the view that as a general principle a person could only supply a vatable interest once and once only. As you will see later when dealing with transactions from 26 March onwards a person can re-acquire a vatable interest in a property and dispose of it. If Landlord Limited re-developed the property before the second letting, for VAT purposes it would be a new property and therefore the second long lease would be chargeable to VAT.

13.3   The tenant was ejected before 26 March 1997

Where the tenant was ejected for breach of a term of a long lease (eg. non-payment) before 26 March 1997 there was no supply by the tenant and therefore no charge to VAT.

A subsequent supply of the property was not chargeable provided the property was not re-developed.

The Revenue Commissioners have confirmed that this was their practice.

13.4   Surrender of long lease by the tenant before 26 March 1997

There were three categories for surrenders of long leases before 26 March 1997

1. Surrender of a long lease for which the landlord paid the tenant.

2. Surrender of a long lease for which the tenant paid the landlord.

3. Surrender of a long lease without payment by either.

13.4.1 Surrender of a long lease before 26 March 1997 for which the landlord paid the tenant

The practice of the Revenue Commissioners was to treat this transaction as consisting of two supplies viz.

1. A supply by the tenant of his interest in the property to the landlord. This was a supply of immovable goods which in their view is chargeable to VAT at market value in accordance with VATA 1972 Section 10(9)(b) (assuming the tenant met the requirements for property supplies – entitled to input etc.)

2. The supply of a service by the tenant to the landlord. The service of allowing the landlord terminate the lease (VATA 1972 Section 5 (1)).

This can be illustrated:

(1) Property

(2) Service
    to landlord

Landlord

Cash £100,000
to tenant

Tenant

The total value of the two supplies was £100,000. The Revenue practice was to treat the supply by the tenant of his interest in the property as chargeable to VAT at $12^1/_2\%$ on the market value of his interest. The balance of the £100,000 was in practice treated as a service chargeable to VAT at 21%.

A subsequent supply in the absence of re-development was not chargeable to VAT. This meant that the VAT chargeable by the tenant was not an allowable input to the landlord.

The practice of the Revenue was to treat the surrender of the property by the tenant to the landlord as not being chargeable to VAT if the original lease was not chargeable to VAT. This treatment was in line with the ruling of the European Court of Justice in the case of Lubbock, Fine & Company (Case 63/92). It still left the service chargeable at 21%.

There was an alternative interpretation to the one favoured by the Revenue. The alternative interpretation was that in substance and reality there was only one single supply by the tenant and that was the surrender of his interest in the premises to the landlord. I favour this alternative interpretation. The question at issue goes to the very root of VAT. When is there one single supply made up of its constituent parts and when are there two or more separate supplies. This question has been the subject of many U.K. cases. The courts there initially leaned towards viewing transactions as single composite supplies but in more recent judgements the shift has been towards viewing transactions as separate multiple supplies (See C.& E. v Scott (1977) IBVC 139 and Card Protection Plan v C.&.E. (1992) (BVC 157).

13.4.2 Surrender of a long lease before 26 March 1997 for which the tenant paid the landlord

The practice of the Revenue was that like the previous instance there were two supplies which can be illustrated as follows:

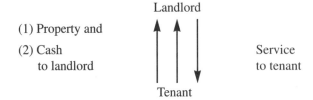

1. Their practice was to treat the tenant as supplying his interest in the long lease to the landlord which was chargeable to VAT at market value in accordance with VATA 1972 Section 10(9)(b). However, if the tenant was paying to surrender, Revenue accepted that in the majority of cases his interest had a negative market value and so no VAT arose.

2. The second leg of the transaction was the supply by the landlord to the tenant of the service of allowing the tenant break the lease. It was chargeable at 21%.

The alternative interpretation is on the lines set out above in respect of surrenders for payment by the landlord to the tenant i.e. there was only one supply.

The practice of the Revenue was to treat a subsequent supply of the property by the landlord as not chargeable provided it was not re-developed.

13.4.3 Surrender of a long lease before 26 March 1997 with no payment by either landlord or tenant

The practice of the Revenue was to treat such a transaction as a supply by the tenant to the landlord at market value which in the majority of cases was nil, so no VAT arose.

The argument has been put that such a supply was a disposal free of charge by the tenant of goods within VATA 1972 Section 3(1)(f) and was chargeable to VAT on the cost to the tenant in accordance with VATA 1972 Section 10(4). This was not the view of the Revenue. Their view was that it was a disposal at market value which in the majority of cases was nil and no VAT arose. In any event the argument that VATA

1972 Sections 3(1)(f) and 10(4) apply gave rise to some doubt as to what the cost was to the tenant on acquiring his leasehold interest. The Finance Act 1997 introduced a proviso to VATA 1972 Section 10(4) which eliminated this doubt.

13.5   An assignment of a long lease by the tenant before 26 March 1997

There were three categories for an assignment before 26 March 1997:

1.   An assignment of a long lease for which the new tenant paid the existing tenant.

2.   An assignment of a long lease with payment by the existing tenant to the new tenant for taking it.

3.   An assignment of a long lease without payment by either.

13.5.1 An assignment of a long lease before 26 March 1997 for which the new tenant paid the existing tenant

The practice of the Revenue was to treat the supply as chargeable to VAT at $12^1/_2\%$ on the consideration. While this could result in a lesser VAT charge than if a sub-lease was created it was accepted by Revenue where it was a bona fide commercial transaction.

The argument was put that assignments should have been valued on the same basis as the creation of a lease (e.g. rent by the multiplier). There was no basis in law for this argument, nor was it the view of the Revenue.

A subsequent assignment or sub-letting by the new tenant was chargeable to VAT, subject to the normal rules (entitlement to input credit etc.).

The transaction can be illustrated as follows:

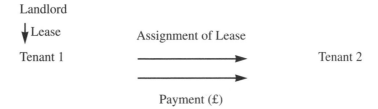

13.5.2 An assignment of a long lease before 26 March 1997 with payment by the existing tenant to the new tenant for taking it

The practice of the Revenue was to treat the assignment of a long lease with payment by the existing tenant to the new tenant as a supply for no consideration so there is no VAT charge. A subsequent assignment or sub-letting by tenant 2 was chargeable to VAT in their view if the new tenant would have been entitled to input credit had there been a charge to VAT.

This transaction can be illustrated as follows:

13.5.3 An assignment of a long lease before 26 March 1997 without payment by either the existing tenant or the new tenant

The practice of the Revenue was, that provided it was a bona fide commercial transaction, no VAT charge arose and a subsequent transaction by the new tenant was chargeable to VAT for the same reason as set out in the previous instance i.e. Tenant 2 would have been entitled to input credit had a VAT charge arisen.

If the transaction was structured to avoid VAT, the Revenue are of the view that it was open to them to treat the assignment as a supply of goods free of charge, under VATA 1972 3(1)(f) at market value under VATA 1972 10(9)(b).

13.6   The abandonment of a long lease before 26 March 1997

The view of the Revenue was that the abandonment of a long lease was a chargeable supply by the tenant to the landlord at market value, in accordance with VATA 1972 Sections 3(1)(f) and 10(9)(b). In practice, when that happened they were of the view that it was usually impractical to pursue collection of the charge. Their view was that in the absence of re-development, a subsequent supply by the landlord was not chargeable to VAT.

13.7   Subsequent supplies before 26 March 1997 – generally

The booklet "VAT on Property Transactions" published by the Revenue Commissioners states that subsequent supplies (e.g. second lettings) were not chargeable to VAT where the property is not re-developed. The current practice of the Revenue Commissioners was to hold with that interpretation, although it must be appreciated that anomalies arose in particular cases because of that. There was an exception to the non-vatability of a second letting before 26 March 1997. The Revenue view was that where the property was re-developed by the tenant, a subsequent supply by the landlord was chargeable to VAT. I do not agree with them.

13.7.1 Example of development by tenant

Mr. Achilles took a 21 year lease on an old premises in 1973. He carried out extensive renovations in 1993 as he knew he would be signing a new lease in 1994. He was entitled to recover the VAT on the cost because the costs were for the purpose of his taxable supplies (i.e. selling shoes).

The Revenue view was that the work by the tenant was by or on behalf of the landlord, thus making the subsequent supply by the landlord chargeable to VAT.

13.8 Schedule of Dilapidations

Normally the lease will provide that the tenant maintains the property as he received it. The lease will provide that the tenant maintains the property in good order. An example of the type of wording used is:

> *"........ to repair and keep in good order repair and condition the demised premises and every part thereof....."*

Where the repair work is carried out by the tenant while in occupation, VAT on the expenditure incurred is normally recoverable under Section 12 as the expenditure comprises of goods and services used by him for the purposes of his taxable supplies.

When the tenant is vacating the premises and under the terms of the lease is obliged to pay the landlord in respect of a schedule of dilapidations – repair work which the landlord may or may not carry out – no supply takes place for VAT purposes. The landlord is not supplying any service to the tenant. No VAT charge arises from the payment by the tenant to the landlord.

13.9 Termination of Leases from 26 March 1997 onwards

Up to 26 March 1997 there was no definition in VAT law for the term surrender. Up to then it had its ordinary property law meaning of a tenant surrendering the residue of a lease back to the landlord and returning the premises to him.

The Finance Act 1997 introduced a special meaning in VAT law for the term surrender, which is now in VATA 1972 Section 1. As well as covering a surrender in the property law meaning of the term, its VAT meaning includes:

1. an abandonment,

2. recovery by ejectment or forfeiture, or

3. failure by the tenant to exercise an option to extend the lease.

The surrender of an interest in a property is chargeable to VAT if the tenant recovered any of the VAT charged on the creation of the lease.

When looking at the pre-26 March 1997 position, I considered five ways in which a tenant's long term interest in a property can be terminated:

1. The long lease comes to an end.

2. The tenant is ejected.

3. The tenant surrenders the lease.

4. The tenant assigns the lease

5. The tenant abandons the long lease.

Under the new definition in the Finance Act 1997, abandonments and ejectments come under the umbrella of surrenders. Therefore, for lease terminations from 26 March 1997 abandonments and ejectments need not be categorised separately. The VAT categories for terminations from 26 March 1997 are as follows:

1.   The long lease comes to an end.

2.   The tenant surrenders his interest. A surrender includes an ejectment, forfeiture, failure to exercise an option and an abandonment.

3.   The assignment of a lease.

13.9.1   Leases ending on or after 26 March 1997

When a long lease comes to an end, there is no supply and therore no charge to VAT. The VAT treatment up to 26 March 1997 and since then is the same.

13.9.2   Surrenders on or after 26 March 1997

As mentioned above, from 26 March 1997 surrenders include abandonments, ejectments, forfeitrues and failure to exercise an otion. From 26 march 1997 a surrender is chargeable to VAT as if it were the creation of a new interest for the period left in the lease, provided the tenant was entititled to an input on the creation of the lease.

13.9.3   Example

A landlord granted a 35 year lease to a tenant. He charged VAT on the creation of the lease and the tenant recovered it. Ten years later on 1 May 1997 the tenant surrendered his interest back to the landlord. No money changed hands. This surrender was treated for VAT purposes as the acquisition by the landlord of a 25 year interest . The landlord accounted for VAT on the reverse charge basis (see Part A). The amount on which VAT was charged was the same amount as would have arisen if the tenant had created a 25 year sub-lease. That is, the capitalised value of the rent in the lease based on the multiplier, the formula or valuation by a competent valuer. Whether the landlord was entitled to recovery of the VAT arising on the reverse charge depends on what he subsequently does with the 25 year interest he has acquired (see below under the heading second leases).

Payment by the landlord to the tenant for the surrender is taken into account in valuing the lease but payment by the tenant (a reverse premium) is ignored.

Break Clauses

A break clause in a lease is a clause which allows a landlord or a tenant or both to terminate the lease before it has run its full length. The question has been asked whether the exercise of a break clause is a surrender within the definition in the legislation (VATA 1972 Section 1).

This question was addressed by Michael O'Connor in his article "Changes in the VAT Regime for Property" published in the July 1997 edition of the Irish Tax Review. He states as follows:

"In the writer's view, a lessee does not make a surrender when his lease expires. The lease automatically comes to an end. The same situation applies where a break clause is exercised. Accordingly, because the definition of surrender in the VAT Act does not specifically include the exercise of a break clause, the exercise of such a clause which enables a lessee or a lessor to terminate a lease is not a supply for VAT purposes if the mechanism used is to terminate the lease rather than to effect a surrender. This assertion is likely to be contradicted by the Revenue in a statement of practice which will be issued shortly."

The Revenue, as Michael predicted, do not agree but do not give any argument to support their view. They rather baldly state:

"If the break clause is exercised .... this is the surrender of an interest for VAT purposes" (Revenue Guide para. 8)"

The Revenue's view reminds me of Humpty Dumpty's words to Alice:

When I use a word", Humpty Dumpty said, in a rather scornful tone, "it means just what I choose it to mean - neither more nor less."

In my opinion, the exercise of a break clause is not a surrender for VAT purposes for the reasons set out in the article in the Irish Tax Review.

13.9.4 Assignment of a lease from 26 March 1997

The assignment of a lease means the transfer of a lease by a tenant (the assignor) to another person who becomes the new tenant (the assignee). For example, a landlord granted a 35 year lease to A and after 5 years A transferred the lease to B. The transfer by A to B is known as an assignment.

For VAT purposes, if the tenant was entitled to recover any input VAT on the creation of the lease the subsequent assignment from 26 March 1997 is chargeable to VAT

13.9.5 Example

A landlord granted a 35 year lease to a tenant at a rent of £100,000 p.a. The VAT amounted to £180,375 calculated as follows:

£100,000 x 14.43 x 12.5% = £180,375

The tenant recovered this VAT.

If in ten years time the tenant assigns the lease, the same amount of VAT will arise on the assignment (£180,375) assuming the same multiplier and the same rent.

14   Second Leases on or after 26 March 1997

A second lease is a new lease which is created after the first one has been surrendered back to the landlord provided the property has not been re-developed since the creation of the first. For second leases after 26 march 1997 there are four categories for VAT purposes:

1.   A second lease for less than 10 years.

2.1 A second lease for 10 years or more and

2.2 the landlord has a vatable interest of less than 10 years.

3.1 A second lease for 10 years or more and

3.2 the landlord has a vatable interest of 10 years or more

and

3.3 the lease is for longer than the vatable interest.

4.1 A second lease for 10 years or more and

4.2 the landlord has a vatable interest of 10 years or more and

4.3 the lease is for a shorter time than the vatable interest.

14.1   A second lease on or after 26 March 1997 for less than 10 years

A second letting by a landlord for less than 10 years is exempt from VAT. The VAT arising on the surrender of the first lease is not recoverable by the landlord. However, the landlord may waive his entitlement to exemption (i.e. charge VAT at 21% on the rents) and recover the VAT on the surrender. A waiver in the case of a second lease is on a property-by-property basis. This contrasts with a waiver on a first letting which is on a "one in all in" basis. A waiver in the case of a second lease does not affect other short term lettings.

14.2   Example

A landlord granted a 35 year lease to a tenant. The tenant was entitled to a full recovery of the VAT charged on the lease. After ten years the tenant surrendered his interest back to the landlord thus giving the landlord a 25 year vatable interest. The landlord let the property on a 4 year 9 month lease. In order to protect his right to recovery of VAT on the surrender, the landlord waived his entitlement to exemption on the rents. The waiver only applied to the second letting in question. The rate of VAT on the rents was 21%. (Reference VATA 1972 Section 4(2c)).

14.3   A second lease on or after 26 March 1997 for 10 years or more; vatable interest less than 10 years

When a landlord creates a lease of 10 years or more but his vatable interest is less than 10 years, he is treated for VAT purposes as making an exempt supply of goods. This means that VAT on the surrendered interest and on any incidental costs is not recoverable. However, he may opt to charge VAT on the vatable interest and thus get entitlement to entitlement recovery of VAT on the surrender and on the incidental expenses. The landlord exercises the option by deducting VAT on the surrender.

14.4 Example

A landlord granted a 21 year lease to a tenant who recovered the VAT charged on the lease. After 13 years the tenant surrendered the lease back to the landlord. The landlord then created a new 21 year lease. The landlord was treated as making an exempt supply of an eight year interest in the property i.e. an exempt supply of his vatable interest. VAT on the surrendered interest was not recoverable. The landlord had the choice of opting to charge VAT on the supply of the eight year interest and thus gaining entitlement to recovery of the VAT on the surrender.

14.5 A second lease on or after 26 March 1997 for 10 years or more; vatable interest 10 years or more; second lease is longer than the vatable interest

Where a landlord grants a second lease for 10 years or more and he has a vatable interest of 10 years or more and the second lease is longer than his vatable interest, VAT arises on the second lease. The second lease is valued based on the rent using the multiplier, the formula or a valuation. Where appropriate, 4A can be used.

14.6 Example

A landlord granted a tenant a 25 year lease which was subject to the 4A procedure. The tenant surrendered the lease back to the landlord after two years and the landlord created a new 25 year lease in favour of tenant 2. VAT was chargeable on the second lease as if it were the creation of a 23 year lease. The amount of VAT being determined by the multiplier, the formula or a valuation. Section 4A applied to the second lease. As the landlord disposed of more than his vatable interest, the question of a reversion did not arise.

14.7 Second lease on or after 26 March 1997 for 10 years or more; vatable interest of 10 years or more; second lease is shorter than the vatable interest.

This category covers a second lease of 10 years or more and vatable interest of 10 years or more and the lease is shorter than the vatable interest. In such circumstances the landlord has to account for a self-supply on the reversion which is based on the difference in years between the vatable interest and the second lease. If the second lease is for more than 20 years, then the reversion is ignored.

14.8   Example

A landlord granted a tenant a 21 year lease which he surrendered back to him after two years. VAT was chargeable on the surrender. The landlord granted a twelve year lease to a new tenant. VAT was chargeable on the second lease and was payable by the landlord on the reversionary interest of 7 years. This gave rise to an irrecoverable VAT cost to the landlord.

15   Redevelopment of the Property

The Finance Act 1997 changes apply to second leases provided the property is not redeveloped. If the property is redeveloped it is a new property for VAT purposes and a subsequent lease is treated as a first letting.

15.1   Example

A landlord granted a 35 year lease to a tenant who recovered the VAT and 10 years later surrendered the lease back to the landlord. The landlord redeveloped the property and granted a new 35 year lease. The second 35 year lease is treated as a first lease not as a second one.

16   Reverse Charge

VAT is a sales tax and normally it is the seller who has to collect the VAT from the customer and pass it on to the Revenue. Under the reverse charge, the reverse happens. The seller does not charge VAT but rather the purchaser is responsible to the Revenue for it. The purchaser accounts for the VAT to the Revenue by including the amount of VAT in the sales box of his return (T1). To the extent that he is entitled to recovery he claims back VAT by including the appropriate amount in box T2 of the return.

The reverse charge applies to the majority of surrenders and assignments after 26 March 1997. That means in the case of surrender or assignments that it is usually the landlord or assignee who accounts for the VAT and the tenant/assignor does not.

Full details on the reverse charge are set out in Part A.9

17   Key points/Conclusion

Where a lease of more than 10 years is created, the vatable interest is the reference point for all future transactions in the property until either:

1.   The lease terminates or

2.   The Revenue gets the entire amount of VAT due in respect of the leasehold interest. For example, if the lease is granted to a bank - which is not entitled to any recovery or

3.   The property is redeveloped.

PART D

THE DETAILED ASPECTS OF SHORT LETTINGS

1.   Rental Income

A short letting is a letting of less than 10 years.

Under VATA 1972 First Schedule paragraph (iv) the letting of immovable goods is exempt with the exception of:

(a) letting of machinery or business installations when let separately from any other immoveable goods of which such machinery or installations form part;

(b) letting of the kind to which *paragraph (ii) of the Third Schedule or *paragraph (xiii) of the Sixth Schedule refers;

(bi) provision of facilities of the kind to which *paragraph (viia) of the Sixth Schedule refers;

(c) provision of parking accommodation for vehicles by the operators of car parks; and

(d) hire of safes;

*Paragraph (ii) of the Third Schedule is transitional for the Finance Act 1993 and is of little relevance now. The lettings which paragraph (xiii) of the Sixth Schedule covers are hotel, guesthouse lettings etc. The facilities covered by paragraph (viia) of the Sixth Schedule are facilities for taking part in sporting activities.

The activities of squash, tennis, golf clubs etc. are regarded as the letting of immoveable goods and are exempt from VAT when they are provided by non profit making organisations (eg. members golf clubs). However where they are provided by a profit making or commercial organisation they are treated as the provision of facilities for taking part in sporting activities and are liable to VAT @ $12^1/2\%$ (eg. commercial golf clubs). Green fees of members golf clubs are chargeable to VAT.

The lettings covered by the exemption are those of less than 10 years.

2.   The meaning of the word letting

In many cases there will be no doubt that there is a letting as in, for example, a 2 year 9 month lease. But in the case of licences and easements it is less certain whether they are lettings. The problem is the term "letting" is not defined in the VAT Act. It is not defined in the EU 6th Directive. It's not a term used in property law.

However, there is an indication of its meaning in VATA 1972 First Schedule paragraph (iv). That paragraph gives an umbrella exemption to the "letting of immovable goods" and then goes on to exclude certain lettings of immovable goods from the exemption. It excludes room lettings by hotels and guest houses. It excludes allowing a golfer play on a commercial course for a green fee. Since in the eye of the legislation room lettings by hotels and golfing come within the umbrella exemption and needed to be specifically excluded, I conclude that the term letting of immovable goods is very broad. It means allowing another to use one's property.

3. Licences

A licence is an authority to do something which would otherwise be illegal.

For example, the entitlement to operate a shop within a hospital might be given by the hospital by way of a licence to occupy land rather than by lease. A licence is usually given instead of a lease when it is desired to avoid giving rights that accrue under a lease. In my opinion a licence is a letting of immovable goods even though the licensee does not have an interest in the property. It is an exempt letting (see British Airports Authority v C & E. Commrs. 1975 IBVC 59).

4. The impact of a short letting on inputs

Since a short letting is an exempt activity there is no entitlement to input credit and VAT is not chargeable on the rent.

4.1 Impact on inputs – example

Property Owner Limited purchased a freehold for £1m plus VAT of £125,000. It let it on 2 year 9 month lease. This was a short term letting which is VAT exempt with the result that Property Owner Limited was not entitled to recovery of the £125,000 VAT on the purchase of the freehold nor did it have to charge VAT on the rent.

4.2 Impact on inputs – example

Alpha Limited and Beta Limited are in group relationship but are not group registered for VAT. Alpha Limited purchases a property out of which Beta Limited trades. Alpha Limited has allowed Beta Limited a tenancy at will. It is a short term letting which is exempt. Alpha Limited is not entitled to input credit.

5. Surrender of possession

This is a concept closely allied to short-term letting above. A surrender of possession arises where a person who has been entitled to input credit later lets the property short term. For VAT purposes it results in the inputs already claimed being clawed back. It is known in VAT terms as a self-supply.

5.1 Meaning of Surrender of possession

The phrase "surrender of possession" is used in VATA 1972 Section 4(3). It is not defined in the VAT Act nor is it a term used in the EU 6th Directive. In property law it means the yielding of the residue of a term of interest in land as when a tenant surrenders possession of his interest to the landlord.

The problem with this undefined term is that possession could mean

1. Actual physical occupation of the property or

2.   Possession in law which is the right to the enjoyment thereof irrespective of whether the person in possession has taken occupation.

For example, if a tenant has taken a lease on a premises but not yet moved in, he would be in possession in law but not in physical possession.

In my opinion, the surrender takes place when the tenant gets the right to the enjoyment whether or not he takes physical occupation or not. Obviously if the tenant takes physical occupation he must at that stage have legal possession.

In the practical application of the tax, it is taken as meaning a lease (formal or not) of less than 10 years.

5.2   Example of surrender of possession

Chartered Accountants & Co. purchased a premises for £500,000 plus VAT of £50,000 (the rate at the time was 10%). The firm recovered the £50,000 VAT. Some years later the firm moved to a new premises and let the old one on a short lease. Letting the old premises on a short lease was a self-supply chargeable to VAT. The view of the Revenue is that as a matter of correct interpretation this is a supply chargeable to VAT at market value in accordance with VATA 1972 10(9)(b). There is another view that it is chargeable to VAT on the cost (VATA 1972 Section 10(4)). In practice the inputs already claimed are clawed back See however late waiver below.

5.3   Conclusion on surrender of possession

The foregoing is the current wisdom on surrender of possession which is accepted by the Revenue Commissioners and practitioners. I think it is not quite as clear as is generally accepted. There are good arguments that the surrender of possession does not give rise to an irrecoverable VAT cost.

6.   Waiver of exemption

The problems caused to the owner of a property by a short term letting or a surrender of possession can be overcome quite simply by waiving entitlement to exemption (VATA 1972 Section 4(3)(b)(i), Section 7 and VAT regulations 1979 No. 4). A waiver of exemption results in VAT inputs being allowed and VAT being chargeable on the rents. A waiver of exemption sounds more complicated than it is. It is simply a letter to the Inspector giving him the following details:

(a)   the client's name and address,

(b)   the client's VAT number,

(c)   a statement that the client wishes to waive exemption in respect of services specified in VATA 1972 First Schedule paragraph (iv) and

(d)   the VAT period from which it is desired that the waiver will have effect. This cannot be earlier than VAT period in which the waiver is being submitted.

In short a waiver of exemption is a letter to the Inspector stating that VAT will be charged on all short term rents.

A waiver of exemption may also be put in place when registering for VAT by answering yes on part E of the registration form to the question:

"Exemption waiver

Does the applicant wish to waive exemption from VAT in respect of letting of property?"

6.1 Example of waiver of exemption

Property Owner Limited purchased a property for £1m plus VAT of £125,000. It let the property on 2 year 9 month lease. This was a short term letting exempt from VAT with the result that Property Owner Limited was not entitled to recovery of the £125,000 VAT nor did it have to charge VAT on the rents. However, Property Owner Limited wrote to the Revenue Commissioners waiving its exemption with the result that it was entitled to recover the VAT of £125,000 and was obliged to account for VAT on the rents. If the tenant was entitled to recovery, he would presumably not object to the VAT charge.

6.2 Example of waiver of exemption

A property owner had the following rents:

Apartments	— yearly tenancies	£24,000
Shop Unit	— yearly tenancy	£12,000
Pre '72 building	— 35 year lease	£10,000
Pre '72 shop	— yearly tenancy	£ 8,000
Total		54,000

He is not registered for VAT. He acquired a unit in a shopping centre for £150,000 plus £18,750 VAT. He let the unit for 2 years 9 months. In order to reclaim the £18,750 he waived his entitlement to exemption from VAT in respect of the rents. The result of waiving his exemption was:

	Gross	**VAT (21%)**	**Net**
Apartment Rents	24,000	4,165	19,835
Shop Unit	14,520	2,520	12,000
Pre '72 Building 35 yr. lease	10,000	—	10,000
Pre '72 Shop – yearly	9,680	1,680	8,000
Total			49,835

His rental income dropped by £4,165 which was the amount of VAT on the apartment rents which could not be passed on to the tenants.

> **TAX TIP: Check if there are other short term rents before waiving an exemption.**

6.3 What is covered by the waiver

The Revenue Commissioners have confirmed that a waiver of exemption extends only to all short term lettings. In practice it does not extend to long leases of undeveloped property.

6.4 Waiving exemption on time on letting before 26 March 1997

The Revenue view is that a waiver of exemption on a letting before 26 March 1997 should not be allowed earlier than the taxable period in which the application for waiver is made.

6.4.1. Example of late waiver on letting before 26 March 1997

A property owner purchased a freehold office block in January 1994 for £2m plus VAT of £250,000. He let it on a short term lease from 1 February 1994. He applied for a waiver of exemption on 10 March 1994 in order to get his entitlement to input credit. His application was too late. It should have been with the Inspector within the VAT period January\February 1994. He was not entitled to input credit. Inspectors are very strict on this.

6.4.2. Questionable rigidity on time limit for waiver

This rigid time limit is not a requirement of the VAT Act itself but rather is an imposition by the secondary legislation (VAT Regulations 1979 Regulation 4). It seems to me an unduly harsh snare for the unwary and is more than a mere giving effect to the principles and policies which are contained in the statute itself. It contrasts with other time limits which are set down in the statute e.g. the time limit for refunds is 10 years under VATA 1972 Section 20(4). If you have a client who is a victim of this time limit, I suggest you consider the appropriateness of the time limit in the light of the case City View Press Limited and Another v An Comhairle Oíluna 1980 IR 398 which deals with the limits on regulations.

6.4.3 Lettings from 26 March 1997 – back dated waiver

Under new regulations effective from 26 March 1997 a person who misses sending the waiver of exemption to the Inspector on time may in certain circumstances be allowed a back-dated waiver. To get a back-dated waiver the landlord must apply in writing to the Inspector stating:

1. His name
2. His address
3. His VAT registration number
4. The tenant's name
5. The tenant's address
6. The tenant's VAT registration number
7. Details of the letting agreement
8. The date from which the waiver should have effect (this cannot be earlier than 26 March 1997)

The landlord should attach a letter from the tenant stating:

1. That he (the tenant) is entitled to full recovery of VAT on the rents

2. That he (the tenant) agrees to the back-dating

The effect of a back-dated waiver is as follows:

1. No adjustments are required for the past. The landlord is deemed to have paid the VAT and the tenant is deemed to have deducted it and all obligations such as invoicing are deemed to have been complied with. Any other short-term rents are unaffected as regards the past.

2. The application for back-dating is treated from the date of application (or an agreed later date) as a waiver of exemption in respect of all short-term lettings from then on. A back-dating is only allowed where a person was in the first instance entitled to the input credit and subsequently short term lets the property. It is not allowed where the property is let short term from the beginning and the waiver is not sent on time.

7. Cancellation of waiver of exemption

Under Regulation 4, a person who waives the exemption may later cancel the waiver and, if they do, they must repay the excess of VAT repayments received over VAT payments made during the period of the waiver or the previous 10 years whichever is the shorter.

> **TAX TIP: Where there are substantial up-front VAT costs, consider if it is advantageous to waive the exemption and later cancel the waiver.**

7.1 Example of waiver and cancellation of waiver

Patrick Kelly purchased a number of apartments which he intended to let on short term leases. He purchased the apartments on 1st May 1993 and registered for VAT. He waived his entitlement to exemption in respect of short term lettings. He has no other lettings.

Patrick Kelly was entitled to recover the VAT charged to him on the purchase of the apartments but he must account for VAT @ 21% on the rental income he receives. He will remain registered for VAT until such time as the VAT payable on the rental income equals the VAT he has recovered on the purchase price and maintenance expenses of the apartments. At that point he can cancel his VAT registration without penalty.

There is also sometimes Income Tax advantage to be gained by waiving exemption and later cancelling the waiver. The advantage can be illustrated by comparing what A and B did in the following example:

A bought a house for £112,500 VAT inclusive. He did not waive entitlement to exemption. His investment cost him £112,500. His rental income for Income Tax purposes was say £12,100.

B bought a similar house for the same price (£112,500) and let it for the same rent, £12,100. B waived exemption thus reducing the cost of his investment to £100,000. In addition his rental income for income tax purposes was reduced to £10,000.

The inter-action of VAT and Income Tax resulted in B having the cash flow advantage of the VAT element in the cost paid back to him and when repaying that VAT B in effect got an Income Tax deduction for the VAT. It was the equivalent for B of getting an interest free loan of £12,500 and also getting an income tax deduction for the repayments.

7.2   Calculation of VAT repayable on cancellation post 26 March 1997

The regulation which set out how to calculate how much had to be paid back to the Revenue had some gaps in it. The legislation was amended with effect from 26 March 1997. For example, if an export company acquired a property, VAT free under VATA 1972 Section 13A prior to 26 March 1997 the VAT element on the purchase of the property was not taken into account in calculating the VAT due to Revenue on cancellation. It will be taken into account for cancellations from 26 March on.

7.2.1   Example

Ms. Jane Eyre ran a clothes manufacturing business at Carraroe, Co. Galway. All the product was exported to the U.S. with the result that she had a 13A authorisation permitting her to buy goods and services VAT free. She purchased a premises for £400,000 VAT free. She acquired another clothes manufacturing business VAT free under the transfer of business provision (VATA 1972 3(5)(b)(iii). A factory premises was acquired under the transfer for £320,000.

She later fell into bad health and closed down the factories. She let both factories short term at a total rent of £50,000 per annum. She waived her entitlement to exemption. After four years she cancelled her waiver of exemption and repaid £44,000 to the Revenue calculated as follows:

VAT on 13A premises	£50,000
VAT on 3(5)(b)(iii) premises	£30,000
Input tax deducted in respect rents say	£6,000
Total £	86,000
VAT on rents £50,000 x 4 x 21%	£42,000
Amount paid on cancellation	£44,000

8.   The rate of VAT on short term lettings

VAT is charged at 21% on short term lettings and not at the 12^1/$_2$% rate that applies to long leases and sales of freeholds.

9.   The VAT clause in a short lease

An example of a VAT clause in a short lease is as follows:

> *"and the lessee hereby covenants with the lessor in the manner following that is to say:*
>
> *To pay and discharge all Value Added Tax payable in respect of this lease and to keep the lessor indemnified against payment thereof"*

Where a landlord has waived exemption he will charge the tenant VAT on the rent in accordance with this clause and the tenant will claim it back if entitled to recovery. However if the landlord has recovered VAT and does not waive his exemption he will suffer VAT on a self-supply. Under the above clause he will be entitled to recoup the VAT on the self-supply from the tenant who in turn cannot reclaim it.

10.   Short lettings within a VAT Group

It is not uncommon within a VAT Group to have one company owning a property and another company using it without there being any formal lease i.e. a short letting.

Concern has been expressed whether such a short letting has adverse VAT consequences. In the absence of a waiver of exemption is this a surrender of posession that gives rise to disallowable VAT or a VAT claw back? In my opinion the correct treatment of inter-VAT group short lettings is as follows:

(1) The short term lettings are a non event for VAT purposes.

(2) The entitlement to inputs is not affected by the short term letting. Inputs will be determined as if all companies in the Group were one, ignoring the short term letting.

(3) There is no need for a waiver of exemption. The need for a waiver would only arise if the letting was to someone outside the VAT group. However a waiver by any one company within the group extends to all companies within the group making all the groups short term lettings chargeable to VAT.

11. Income Tax/Corporation Tax deduction for irrecoverable VAT

Irrecoverable VAT is allowable or not for Income Tax and Corporation Tax depending on the expense. For example, VAT on stationery purchased by a lending company becomes part of the cost of stationery and is thus deductible for Income Tax or Corporation Tax. The true cost of the disallowable VAT in such circumstances is mitigated by the Income Tax or Corporation Tax deduction.

VAT on entertainment is not recoverable. Entertainment expenses are not allowable for Income Tax or Corporation tax. Thus the disallowable VAT on entertainment costs is not mitigated by a Corporation Tax or Income Tax deduction. The same applies to VAT or capital costs that do not rank for capital allowances.

In short disallowable VAT follows the cost from which it springs.

12. Time share

I am of the opinion that the sale of time share which in total is less than 10 years (i.e. 520 weeks) cannot be a disposal of an interest in immovable goods in view of the definition in VATA 1972 Section 4(1)(b) and in line with the judgement in the U.K. case of Cottage Holiday Associates Limited V.C. & E Commrs (1982) (IBVC) 527. In that case a lease for one weeks occupation each year for 80 years was a term certain for 80 weeks, not 80 years, and did not therefore amount to a major interest. It follows that if the total term is for more than 520 weeks there is a disposal of an interest in immovable goods.

However, in practice the Revenue Commissioners treat holiday time share as the provision of holiday accommodation within VATA 1972 Sixth Schedule paragraph (xiii) (b) irrespective of whether the total term is more or less than 10 years. A time share for more than 10 years is not treated as a disposal.

PART E

REGISTRATION, RECOVERY, REPAYMENT AND RELIEF

1. Registration

1.1 Register on time

It is important to register on time. Since many building projects take a good deal of time to complete, registration is often an election to register (VAT Act 1972 Section 8(3)). There is provision in the relevant regulation (Regulation 3 of the VAT Regulations 1979) that an election cannot be back-dated to a date before the VAT period in which the election is made. Therefore, if the election is not made on time, the VAT on the earlier inputs could be lost.

1.2 Thresholds

The threshold of £40,000 which applies to those selling goods does not apply to those selling immovable goods, which includes the creation of a lease of more than 10 years, (VATA 1972 Section 4(7)). Any transaction in developed property, irrespective of the amount involved, brings with it a requirement to register for VAT.

It is somewhat different for short leases. A short term letting is the supply of a service which is exempt. The landlord may waive the entitlement to exemption. If the turnover from short lettings is £20,000 or less and the landlord wishes to be taxable, he should, as well as waiving his entitlement to exemption, make an election to be a taxable person.

In summary the thresholds are:

Sale of Property or Long Lease	— Nil threshold
Short term lettings	— £20,000 threshold

Normally, there is no difficulty in getting a VAT registration provided there is a clear intention to make vatable sales, albeit at some future time.

1.3 Standard Enquiry

The Taxes Central Registration Office (TCRO) in Dublin send a standard letter, on receipt of an application to register for VAT in respect of property, a copy of which is set out on the next page.

Office of the Inspector of Taxes,
Taxes Central Registration Office,
9/15 Upper O'Connell Street,
Dublin 1
Telephone -(01) 874 6821 Extn.
Fax   -(01) 874 6078

Reference Number

This matter is dealt with by:

Dear Sirs,

Re: **Subject:**

VAT

Ref:-

I refer to your recent application to register for VAT and I note that the activity being carried on relates to property development and/or property rental.

I shall be obliged, therefore, if you will let me have the following information:

1. The address of the property.

2. The date on which it was purchased or when development commenced.

3. The planning permission reference number, if applicable.

4. A copy of the minutes of the board meeting/meeting of the partners, whereby it was resolved that the property in question would be purchased and/or developed and would be disposed of or utilised in a manner which would give rise to a VAT liability i.e.

(a) by outright sale of the property

(b) by creation of a long term lease in excess of ten years or

(c) by waiver of exemption in respect of short term lettings

(Note: the waiver of exemption applies to all rents receivable from short term lettings including those from properties other than that mentioned above).

The minutes should show the date of the meeting, the names of all those present at the meeting and should be signed by the company secretary or precedent acting partner in the case of a partnership.

Yours faithfully,

This is not a standard practice in all districts. Those applying to TCRO will find it speeds registration, if the information sought above is sent with the application for registration (Forms TR1 or TR2).

If the clear intention is to make a non-vatable supply, registration is not appropriate and will not be granted. Otherwise there is normally no difficulty in getting a registration.

Example

The ubiquitous, Joe Bloggs inherited his grandmother's house on her death. He intended to sell it without doing any development work to it. The intended sale is not chargeable to VAT and so his application for VAT registration was not appropriate and was not allowed.

1.4 Time taken to get a VAT number

It usually takes about 10 working days to get a VAT number from the day the application is received by the VAT office.

2. Recovery

2.1 General Rules

The general rules as regards entitlement to recovery of VAT on purchases and expenses are as follows:

1. Input VAT on goods and services which are used to make sales chargeable to VAT is allowed in full.

2. Input VAT on goods and services which are used to make sales which are not chargeable to VAT is not allowed at all.

3. Input VAT on goods and services which are used partly to make sales which are chargeable to VAT and partly to make sales which are not chargeable to VAT is allowed in part.

This can be illustrated as follows:

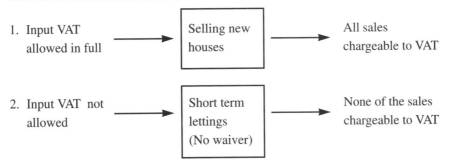

1. Input VAT allowed in full → Selling new houses → All sales chargeable to VAT

2. Input VAT not allowed → Short term lettings (No waiver) → None of the sales chargeable to VAT

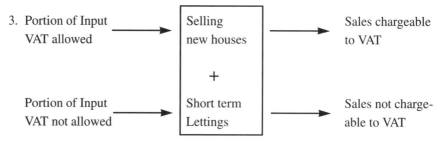

| 3. Portion of Input VAT allowed | → | Selling new houses | → | Sales chargeable to VAT |

Selling new houses + Short term Lettings

| Portion of Input VAT not allowed | → | Short term Lettings | → | Sales not chargeable to VAT |

2.2 VAT on pre-trading costs

As regards VAT on costs preparatory to carrying on an economic activity, the European Court of Justice found that the input VAT, in respect of transactions preceding making taxable supplies, was allowable. The administration, however, was entitled to require that the declared intention be supported by objective evidence, such as proof that the premises it was proposed to construct were specifically suited to commercial exploitation. (Rompelman -v- Minister van Financien 1985 3CMLR 202).

This case acts as a precedent in interpreting Irish·VAT law. Therefore, the distinction in Corporation Tax and Income Tax between engaging in activities preliminary to trading and actual trading, is not usually a problem in VAT.

While registration will be granted from the very beginning, Inspectors sometimes hold VAT repayments until they are satisfied that vatable sales will be made. The most common reason for holding repayment is that planning permission has not been granted. In my opinion this is not an adequate reason for holding repayment and is contrary to the principles established in the precedent cases (see below).

2.2.1. Example of VAT on pre-trading costs

Thomas Quinn was considering building a hotel in Westport, Co. Mayo. From 1 January 1993 to 31 December 1993, he incurred VAT on legal costs, on the costs of a feasability report and on the cost of a planning appeal. In January 1994 building commenced. He was granted registration from 1 January 1993 but repayments were held until building commenced in January 1994. The Inspector's reason for holding repayments was that he was not satisfied that vatable supplies would be made. For example, planning permission might not have been granted.

2.2.2. Precedent cases

If you have a case in which you wish to argue for earlier repayment of VAT on pre-trading costs, I recommend you read the following cases:

Rompleman -v- Minister van Financien 1985 3 CMLR 202 – See above.

Merseyside Cablevision Limited -v- Commrs. of Customs and Excise [1987] V.A.T.T.R. 134.

Fishguard Bay Developments Limited Lon\87\625x Nov. 89 4549.

2.2.3 An alternative to withholding VAT repayments

An alternative to withholding VAT repayments which is available to the Revenue Commissioners, is that they make repayment from the date of registration and obtain from the taxpayer a bank guarantee to the extent of the repayment made (VATA 1972 Section 23A). The cost of the guarantee to the taxpayer would be considerably less than the cost of the VAT repayments withheld. It does not increase the overall amount of funds at the taxpayers disposal because financial institutions include guarantees as part of their exposure.

3. Development by subsidiary

H Limited owned a premises which it allowed S Limited (its subsidiary) use for the purposes of its (S's) vatable supplies. There was no formal lease agreement. S Limited had development work carried out to the premises which it paid for and charged to the inter-company account between it and H.

On appeal against the inspector's refusal to allow S input credit the Circuit Court held:

(1) S was entitled to input credit as the expenditure was incurred for its taxable supplies.

(2) There was no requirment for S to have an interest in the property

(3) S was not obliged to account for output VAT. The judge held that the inter-company amount was compensation not consideration. [*International VAT Moniter* July/August 1995, Page 257]

I understand the case is not being appealed.

4. VAT on post-letting expenses

The question of entitlement tax input credit on post letting expenses was considered in case of Erin Executor and Trustee Company Limited (as trustee of Irish Pension Fund Property Unit Trust) v Revenue Commissioners [1993 No. 414 R] usually referred to as the IPFPUT case. The High Court decision was that the property went out of the VAT net for the duration of the lease and therefore VAT on expenses arising from any convenant, clause or term of the lease during the currency of the lease could not be recovered. If the inputs were incurred during the currency of the lease but for the purpose of making a new taxable supply then the inputs can be recovered. The case is, I understand, under appeal to the Supreme Court and is set down for hearing in October 1997.

5.   Repayment to farmers

Unregistered farmers are entitled to a repayment of the VAT suffered in relation to outlay on farm buildings and structures and land drainage and reclamation, provided the total amount of VAT claimed is more than £100.

VAT on mobile equipment or machinery is not refunded.

Included in the entitlement are fencing, well drilling, video observation units, dairy building and fixtures therein.

The subsequent sale by a farmer of a property on which he has got a VAT repayment as an unregistered farmer is not chargeable to VAT. The repayment does not arise because he was "entitled to input credit".

6.   Relief for Bad Debts

6.1   No Bad Debt Relief on Long Leases

For example, Shopping Developments Limited granted a 35 year lease of a unit to a tenant, at a rent of £10,000 p.a. It issued a VAT invoice to him for £14,675 (£10,000 x 11.74 x $12^1/_2$%). The tenant never paid the VAT and absconded shortly afterwards.

Shopping Developments Limited triggered a VAT liability of £14,675 on the creation of the lease, but was not entitled to bad debt relief.

In the past there was doubt whether bad debt relief extended to lessors who failed to collect from their tenants.

The Finance Act 1994 section 95 has fairly sealed the matter by adding a proviso to the section dealing with bad debts (VATA 1972 Section 10(3)(c)), as follows:

> *"Provided that in any event this paragraph shall not apply in the case of the letting of immovable goods which is a taxable supply of goods in accordance with Section 4".*

To my mind, it is harsh piece of legislation and the moral seems to be——let the lessor beware.

If the shift mechanism referred to in Part A had been used the problem would not have arisen.

6.2   Bad Debt relief on Sales of Freeholds and Short Lettings

The legislation is very specific in its exclusion from bad debt relief. The exclusion applies to long leases. This means that relief is available should a bad debt arise for VAT on the sale of a freehold or on a short lease based on the maxim- expresso unius personae vel rei, est exclusio alterius. That is, the expression of one person or thing, is the exclusion of another.

A bad debt on the sale of a freehold could arise where the vendor granted the purchaser credit with regard to payment of the VAT. It would be unusual for that to happen. The usual practice is that the purchaser pays the vendor the purchase price plus VAT on closing.

PART F

A BRIEF OUTLINE ON U.K. VAT ON PROPERTY

> **CAUTION:** U.K. VAT law relating to property is extremely complex. This brief outline merely gives a flavour of what is involved.

1.   Introduction

The law on VAT on property in the United Kingdom is different from the law on VAT on property in Ireland. The purpose of this part of the book is to give a non-technical summary on VAT on property in the U.K. Because it is a summary it is by definition incomplete. I will consider VAT on property in the U.K. under 6 headings:

1. The *zero-rated* supply of new buildings

2. The *standard rated* supply of new buildings

3. The *exempt* supply of buildings

4. The option to tax

5. Transfer of a business as a going concern (TOGC)

6. Capital goods adjustment scheme

2.   The zero-rated supply of new or converted buildings

The supply by a builder of a major interest in a residential building or a charitable non-business building is zero-rated. A major interest is a freehold or a lease of more than 21 years.

This means that the purchaser of a new house in the United Kingdom benefits from the zero VAT rate in contrast with the purchaser of a new house in Ireland who bears VAT at $12^1/_2\%$ on the purchase price. The zero-rating extends to other types of residential property such as a children's home, a hospice and residential accommodation for students. The zero-rating does not extend to all types of residential accommodation. For example, the sale of newly developed hotels, prisons or hospitals are not zero-rated.

A charity in the United Kingdom benefits from zero rating on the purchase of a new non-business premises in contrast with VAT at $12^1/_2\%$ borne by an Irish charity purchasing a new premises.

Zero rating extends to the grant of a major interest by a person reconstructing a listed building which is intended for use after reconstruction as a dwelling or for a charitable non-business purpose.

The grant of a major interest in a dwelling converted from a non-residential building is also zero-rated. For example, a warehouse converted into apartments.

3.   The standard rated supply of new buildings

The sale of the freehold of a new building other than a residential or charitable building is chargeable to VAT in the United Kingdom at $17^1/_2\%$. For example, the sale of a new office block to a bank in the United Kingdom gives rise to an irrecoverable VAT cost at $17^1/_2\%$. There are special rules for determining what is a new building. Broadly it is a building which is less than 3 years old.

4.   The exempt supply of buildings

Supplies of property which are neither zero-rated nor standard rated as set out above are exempt.

5.   The option to tax

Property owners may elect to charge VAT on most supplies of commercial property which would otherwise be exempt. The election enables them to recover input tax and makes the consideration on the sale of the freehold or the rent under a lease liable to VAT at the standard rate.

The rules relating to the election to waive exemption are intricate. The election to waive may be made in respect of any land or building specified (with some exceptions) and when made, it refers to the entire interest the owner\landlord has in that particular building. In contrast with the Irish option to tax (i.e. waiver of exemption on short lettings) an election to waive exemption in the U.K. is made on a building by building basis.

Also, in contrast with the Irish legislation a waiver of exemption once made is irrevocable for 20 years. A waiver by a company in a group registration also binds other members of that group.

6.   Transfer of a business as a going concern (TOGC)

The transfer of a business as a going concern is not chargeable to VAT in the U.K..

Many sales between landlords are within the ambit of the TOGC provisions with the result that VAT is not chargeable. There are certain specific criteria that must be satisfied for TOGC to apply.

7.   Capital Goods Adjustment

In accordance with Article 20 of the EU 6th Directive on VAT the U.K. operates a capital goods adjustment to input credits. The Irish legislation does not provide for a capital goods adjustment.

The capital goods adjustment is an adjustment made to input credit on capital goods (eg. premises) each year for 10 years in line with the entitlement to input each year.

Example

A UK Bank purchased a new premises for Stg£10m plus Stg£1.75m VAT. Its entitlement to input credits for the first four years was as follows:

	Leasing *Activity* *(vatable)*	*Lending* *Activity* *(exempt)*
Year 1	40%	60%
Year 2	50%	50%
Year 3	30%	70%
Year 4	90%	10%

The bank's entitlement to input credit in year one was £700,000 (Stg£1.75m x 40%).

Each year thereafter for the next nine years additional input was allowed or input was clawed back to the extent that taxable use varied from the initial 40%. The entitlement for years 2, 3 and 4 was as follows:

Year	*Calculation*		*Input*	
2	Stg. £1.75m x 10% x 1/10	=	£17,500	Additional input
3	Stg. £1.75m x 10% x 1/10	=	(£17,500)	Clawback of inputs
4	Stg. £1.75m x 50% x 1/10	=	£87,500	Additional input

8.   Summary

A very broad summary of VAT on Property in the United Kingdom is as follows:

New houses and new premises for charities are zero rated while new commercial buildings are chargeable at $17\frac{1}{2}$%. Other supplies of property are exempt with the option to tax.

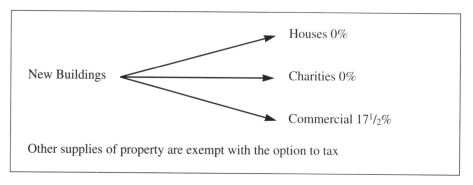

New Buildings → Houses 0%

New Buildings → Charities 0%

New Buildings → Commercial $17\frac{1}{2}$%

Other supplies of property are exempt with the option to tax

PART G

VAT ON PROPERTY UNDER THE E.U. 6TH DIRECTIVE

1. Article 4

Article 4 of the E.U. 6th Directive defines the term "taxable person". It includes a person who exploits tangible property for the purpose of obtaining an income therefrom on a continuing basis. It also permits Member States to treat as taxable, a person who carries out a property transaction on an occasional basis. The article then goes on in paragraph 3(a) to set out suggested criteria which Member States may use in deciding whether a once-off transaction makes an otherwise non-taxable person taxable. One of the criteria is the supply before first occupation. This means that if a person purchased a house and sold it again before he occupied it, Member States are permitted to treat that person as a taxable person.

The article is so broad and permissive I do not see anything in it with which the domestic legislation is in conflict.

2. Article 5

Article 5.1 defines supply of goods. Paragraph 3 of article 5 allows Member States to treat certain interests in immovable goods and rights in rem as supplies of goods.

The Irish legislature has availed of this permission by treating leases of 10 years or more as supplies of goods.

3. Article 13(B)(b)

The exemption for letting immovable property is contained in article 13(B)(b) as are the exclusions from the exemption, such as the provision of accommodation by hotels. VAT Act 1972 First Schedule paragraph (iv) is in harmony with article 13(B)(b).

The article allows discretion to Member States to apply further exclusions to the exemption. Our legislature has availed itself of this permission by making facilities for taking part in sporting activities chargeable to VAT.

4. Article 13(B)(g)

This article exempts buildings no longer considered to be new where such buildings are supplied by a taxable person. Ireland has derogated from this exemption (see later). The question of the interaction of article 13(B)(g) with article 4(3) was raised in a written question from MEP Mr. Fernand Herman to the European Commission on 27 October 1992.

Question from Mr. Fernand

(27 October 1992)

> *Council Directive 77/388/EEC on the harmonization of the laws of the Member States relating to turnover taxes contains the phrase 'the supply....of buildings or parts of buildings and the land on which they stand' in Articles 4(3) and 13(B)(g). Can the interpretation and meaning of this phrase differ, depending on whether it relates to taxable activity (Article 4) or VAT exemption (Article 13)?*

Answer given by Mrs. Scrivener

on behalf of the Commission

(16 December 1992)

> *There is no contradiction between Article 4(3)(a) and Article 13(B)(g) of the Directive, as the Honourable Member's question implies. These two provisions relate to entirely different concepts. The first is designed to enable Member States to treat as a taxable person anyone, e.g. a private individual, who supplies a new building, a taxable person being anyone who carries out an economic activity, irrespective of the arrangements (taxation or exemption) which otherwise apply to his activity. The second provision merely exempts the supply of buildings no longer considered to be new, where such buildings are supplied by taxable persons.*

5.   Article 13(B)(h)

This paragraph exempts undeveloped land but excludes building land from the exemption thus making building land chargeable to VAT. Under the Directive building land includes both improved and unimproved land. Our legislation is different in that it only includes improved (i.e. developed) land except under VATA 1972 Section 4(5) under which undeveloped land is chargeable.

6.   Article 13 C Options

Under article 13C Member States may give taxpayers the right to choose to have rental income chargeable to value added tax. This is reflected in our legislation in what is known as the waiver of exemption on short term rents.

7.   Article 28 and Annex E

Under this article with the accompanying Annex E, Ireland is entitled to require those who have been entitled to input credit to charge VAT on a subsequent sale. In some other EU countries, once the building is no longer considered new its sale is not chargeable to VAT.

PART H

REVENUE PUBLICATIONS AND STANDARD CONTRACT FOR SALE

V.A.T LEAFLET NO. 2
(July, 1980)

V.A.T.
ON
PROPERTY
TRANSACTIONS

[The views of the Revenue Commissioners stated in this part are their views at July 1980. Some parts of this leaflet have been superseded by the Finance Act 1997 changes. It would be prudent to check with your local Inspector before coming to a conclusion on any particular aspect]   F.G.

REVENUE COMMISSIONERS
DUBLIN CASTLE

CONTENTS

121

VALUE-ADDED TAX

PROPERTY TRANSACTIONS

Introduction

1.   This leaflet deals with the application of VAT to dealings in immovable goods, that is, land and buildings and goods which have become fixtures in the legal sense. For the sake of convenience, land, buildings and fixtures are referred to as "property" throughout the leaflet.

2.   The special provisions of VAT law relating to property are contained in section 4 and in paragraphs (8) and (9) of section 10 of the Value-Added Tax Act, 1972, as amended. Regard should also be had to the Value-Added Tax Regulations, 1979, and in particular to regulation 7(8) (which modifies the cash receipts basis of charge on the disposal of interests in property) and regulation 19 (which sets out the manner in which interests in property are to be valued). The general effect of the legal provisions is that in the normal way VAT is effectively suffered once and once only by any one taxpayer in relation to any particular development of any property.

3.   Nothing in this leaflet should be taken as overriding the legal provisions or requirements.

Taxable persons

4.   Any person who in the course or furtherance of business supplies taxable interests in developed property is a taxable person for the purposes of VAT. The only exceptions to this rule are the State and local authorities who can be taxable persons only when the Minister for Finance so provides by order. No such order has yet been made. The meaning of "supply" in relation to property is given in paragraphs 10 and 11 and the meaning of "taxable interest" in paragraph 16.

5.   Taxable persons are required to register for VAT, keep records, issue VAT invoices to other registered persons, make returns of their purchases and sales every two months and pay whatever VAT is due by them. Details of all these matters will be found in the "Guide to the Value-Added Tax" which is available from the Office of the Revenue Commissioners (VAT), Castle House, South Great George's St., Dublin 2, or from inspectors of taxes.

6.   The turnover limits which govern the question of registration for traders generally do not apply to persons dealing in property and such persons have an obligation to register regardless of their turnover. Registration is normally allowed in advance of trading, that is, before taxable disposals of property are made.

Taxable transactions

7.   In the circumstances described in paragraphs 29-31 undeveloped property is treated for VAT purposes as developed property. Otherwise, the rule is that

123

a *supply* of property (other than a *self-supply* — see paragraph 11) can be liable to VAT *only* if all the following conditions are satisfied:

   (i) the property must have been actually *developed or re-developed* (see paragraphs 13-15) in whole or in part after 31 October, 1972;

   (ii) *the person making the supply must hold the freehold interest in, or a leasehold interest of at least ten years in,* the property; (a "taxable interest" — see paragraphs 16-19); and

   (iii) the person making the supply must dispose of *the freehold interest or an interest of ten years or more* (a "taxable interest" — see paragraphs 16-19).

8.   Even when all these three conditions are satisfied there is, in fact, no liability unless the following conditions are also satisfied:

   (i) the person making the supply must dispose of the interest referred to at paragraph 7(iii) *in the course or furtherance of business* (see paragraphs 20-25); and

   (ii) the person making the supply must have been *entitled to (as distinct from having received) a VAT credit or deduction* (see paragraphs 26 and 27) in respect of the development of the property or the acquisition of the interest referred to at paragraph 7(ii) above.

9.   The various conditions mentioned in paragraphs 7 and 8 above are discussed in the following paragraphs.

Meaning of "supply"

10.   A "supply" in relation to property means a disposal of a taxable interest in property. For VAT purposes, a supply of property takes place when a person who has a taxable interest in the property (see paragraphs 16-19) disposes of that interest in its entirety or creates a lesser taxable interest in favour of another while retaining the reversion on that interest. Thus, a supply takes place —

   (a) when a person who has a freehold interest either transfers that interest in its entirety or grants a lease for a term of at least 10 years, or

   (b) when a person who has a leasehold interest, which at the time of its creation was for a term of at least 10 years, assigns his interest under the lease or grants a sub-lease for a term of at least 10 years.

It is specifically provided by section 4(1)(b) of the VAT Act that the creation of an interest is to be regarded as the disposal of that interest.

Meaning of "self-supply"

11.   A self-supply is liable to VAT and occurs when —

   (a) a person who has a taxable interest (see paragraphs 16-19) in property and who was entitled to a tax deduction in respect of the purchase or development of that property either converts it to some private use or parts with possession in circumstances which do not amount to a supply as described in paragraph 10. Thus, a builder would be regarded as having made a self-supply if he were to occupy as a private residence a house he had himself built. He would, similarly, be regarded, unless he elected to be taxable on the rent receivable (see paragraph 47), as having made a self-supply if he were to let or lease for a term of less than 10 years a house he had himself built; or

(b) a person who has disposed of a taxable interest in property retains the reversion on that interest. Thus, if a person who holds a freehold interest in property grants a lease, for, say, 12 years, he will be regarded as having made a supply to the lessee of the leasehold interest and as having made a technical supply to himself (a "self-supply") of the freehold, reversionary interest in the lease.

12.   An interest in property which is regarded as self-supplied is treated as having passed out of the business area. Tax is not chargeable on a subsequent disposal of that interest unless the person making the disposal has taken a credit or deduction for any tax charged or has incurred further expenditure on development in relation to which a tax credit or deduction can be claimed. Thus, a builder who constructs a house which he uses as a private residence will be chargeable on the self-supply of the house. He would not, however, be chargeable again on a subsequent sale of the house unless he had incurred further capital outlay on the house in relation to which he was entitled to a tax credit or deduction.

Meaning of "development"

13.   Property is regarded as developed when —

(a) a new building is constructed; or

(b) an existing building is extended, altered or reconstructed; or

(c) an existing building is demolished; or

(d) some engineering or other work is carried out which adapts the property for materially altered use.

The fact that planning permission has been obtained for development does not, of itself, constitute development for VAT purposes.

14.   In most cases it will be possible to determine without difficulty whether or not a property has been developed or re-developed but where it is not possible regard should be had to the following considerations:

(a) Work which is not designed to make a material alteration in the use to which the property is to be put is not a development. Thus, no account is taken of fencing, land drainage, laying of roads for agricultural purposes and so on.

(b) The exact area which has been developed can be determined only by considering all the material circumstances. Thus, if a site is prepared for building work by having roads and sewers laid, the entire area which would reasonably be regarded as served by the roads and sewers would be regarded as developed. On the other hand, if a single house is built in the corner of an area consisting of, say, 100 acres of agricultural land, the area regarded as developed would be the land on which the house stands together with a reasonable plot surrounding the house.

(c) Work on maintenance and repairs, that is, work which leaves the property essentially as it was, does not constitute development.

15.   In determining whether or not a property was developed after 31 October, 1972, or subsequent to its acquisition after that day, relatively small outlay on additions or alterations may be ignored notwithstanding that a tax credit or deduction may have been claimed in relation to such outlay. In practical terms, this may be taken as meaning that, where there is no essential change in the use of the property, such outlay may be ignored if it is reasonably clear that its cost would not exceed 10 per cent. of the total amount on which tax would be chargeable if the work in question were treated as a development.

Example

	Property A	Property B
	£	£
Cost to person making the supply	100,000	150,000
Outlay on alterations subsequent to acquisition by the person making the supply	12,000	30,000
Sold for (or capitalised value of rent if not sold but taxable interest created)	150,000	200,000

Property A would be regarded as not having been developed subsequent to its acquisition by the person making the supply and, consequently, would be outside the scope of VAT because the outlay on development was less than 10 per cent. of the selling price or value. Property B would be regarded as developed and, consequently, liable to tax on supply provided all the other requirements for chargeability are satisfied. Tax would be chargeable by reference to the full supply value of £200,000 and not by reference to the cost of development after acquisition.

Meaning of "taxable interest"

16.   For VAT purposes a taxable interest in property means "an estate or interest therein which, when it was created, was for a period of at least ten years". The meaning does not include a mortgage. A freehold interest (or fee simple interest) is, therefore, a taxable interest, as is a leasehold interest of ten years or more.

17.   A lease under the terms of which the lease itself may be terminated by either party within ten years or the rent may be revised at intervals of less than

ten years is regarded as creating a taxable interest once the lease itself is for a term of ten years or more. Likewise a lease granted for an initial term of less than ten years is regarded as creating a taxable interest if, under the terms of the lease, the lessee, at his option, can extend the term of the lease to ten years or more.

18.   A lease granted for a term of less than ten years which the lessee can extend beyond ten years by invoking statutory rights outside the terms of the lease would not be regarded as creating a taxable interest.

19.   A mortgage does not create a taxable interest; but if a mortgagee should foreclose and the mortgagor should lose his equity of redemption (that is, if his right to have his interest in the property transferred back to him is extinguished) there is at that point a transfer to the mortgagee of the mortgagor's interest. If that interest is a taxable interest and if the other conditions for liability are satisfied tax would be payable by the mortgagor.

Meaning of "in the course or furtherance of business"

20.   It will be recalled that one of the several conditions governing the liability to VAT of property transactions is that they be carried out "in the course or furtherance of business".

"Business" is defined, in part, in section 1 of the VAT Act as follows:

> "'business' includes . . . any trade, commerce, manufacture, or any venture or concern in the nature of trade, commerce or manufacture, . . . whether for profit or otherwise".

21.   Any person who engages in the exploitation of developed property, whether by way of the creation or disposal of taxable or other interests is regarded as carrying on a business activity which, subject to the other conditions governing liability, is within the scope of VAT. It is immaterial whether the person carries out the development himself or engages another person, for example, a builder, to do the work on his behalf. It is likewise immaterial whether the person disposes or intends to dispose of his entire interest in the property when the development work is completed or uses the property to provide himself with an income from lettings. Whichever of these courses he pursues he is regarded as pursuing it in the course or furtherance of business.

22.   In the practical application of the position outlined in the previous paragraph it will be accepted that a person who is not a property dealer for income tax purposes will not be subject to VAT in respect of property which he acquires with all tenants already signed up, whether on long or short leases. If he acquires a property and has himself to secure the tenants he will be subject to VAT. If he acquires a property with some tenants signed up and some still to be signed up he will also be subject to VAT unless the lettings still to be made can be regarded as insignificant in relation to the property as a whole.

23.   No difficulty is likely to arise when a property disposed of has formed a business asset of a taxable business. The fact that the property has been treated as a capital asset is immaterial and, consequently, provided the other essential conditions for liability are satisfied, the disposal of a taxable interest in a shop or factory will be regarded as made in the course or furtherance of business. It is relevant to mention in this connection that it is specifically provided by section 3(5)(b)(iii) of the VAT Act, that, even when all the other essential conditions for liability are satisfied, tax will not be chargeable in respect of the transfer of ownership of property or other goods if the transfer is made in connection with the transfer of a business or part thereof to another taxable person.

24.   If a property has formed a business (as distinct from an investment) asset of an exempt business, say, the business premises of an unregistered bank or the offices of an unregistered insurance concern, no liability will arise when the bank or insurance concern disposes of its interest assuming it was not at any time entitled to a credit or deduction in respect of any tax invoiced in respect of the acquisition or development of the property.

25.   In regard to the disposal of a property for which all the other conditions for liability are satisfied and which has not formed part of the business assets of a trader engaged in taxable activities other than property dealing, whether the disposal in question was made in the course or furtherance of business depends on the facts of the case. It may be that it has already been established for income tax purposes that the person making the disposal is carrying on a business of dealing in property and that the property in question forms part of the assets of that business. In that case, the disposal will be regarded for VAT purposes as made in the course or furtherance of business but the fact that a particular transaction does not attract liability to income tax does not necessarily mean that it is also exempt from VAT.

Meaning of "entitled to a VAT credit or deduction"

26.   If a person is not entitled to a VAT credit or deduction in respect of the purchase or development of property he cannot have a VAT liability in relation to a disposal of such property. If a person is entitled to a credit or deduction which, for whatever reason, he does not claim or receive, this does not exempt him from liability if all the other conditions for liability are satisfied.

27.   A person who makes a self-supply of developed property is entitled to a credit or deduction in respect of the acquisition of the property or of its development in the same way as if it were an ordinary supply. He may not invoice the tax on a self-supply to another registered person, for example, on the creation of a lease of less than ten years.

A guide to whether or not any particular supply of property is taxable

28.   It will be seen that whether or not any particular supply of property is taxable depends on the facts of each case and no general rule can be relied on

to determine the question in every case but the following question and answer system may be helpful. The system should not be used in cases of building licenses and similar arrangements (see paragraph 30). If the answer to *any* of the following questions is "NO" there can be no VAT liability; there can only be a VAT liability if the answer to *every* question is "YES".

(i) Was the property developed (see paragraphs 13-15) after 31 October, 1972?

(ii) Does the person supplying the property hold the freehold interest in the property, or an interest of ten years or more (see paragraphs 16-19)?

(iii) Was the person supplying the property entitled to relief from VAT on his acquisition or development of the property? (Relief might have been obtained by means of a tax credit or deduction — see paragraphs 26 and 27; or by tax-free acquisition under the provision of section 3(5)(b)(iii) of the VAT Act — see paragraph 23).

(iv) Is the person supplying the property registered for VAT or ought he to be registered?

Where the answer to *each* of these questions is "YES" and there is, therefore, a liability, this liability arises in relation to either

(a) the supply to the purchaser or tenant, if the interest granted is ten years or more (see paragraphs 10 and 16-19)

or

(b) the self-supply, if the interest granted is less than ten years (see paragraphs 11, 12).

Building licences and similar arrangements

29. When a supply of property is liable to tax the charge extends to the whole of the property, including the site. No difficulty should arise in this regard when a purchaser is dealing with a single seller. A difficulty could arise when a purchaser acquires his interest in the site from one person and has contracted with another person to carry out the building work on the site.

30. To meet this situation, it is specifically provided (section 4(5) of the VAT Act) that a landowner who does not himself engage in any development work can, nevertheless, be treated as a taxable person in certain circumstances. The most common example of the application of this provision relates to the granting of building licences. Under such an arrangement, a landowner, in consideration of the payment of a site fine by a builder, permits the builder to erect a building on the site and undertakes to convey an interest in the site to the builder's nominee (for example, a house purchaser). In those circumstances, the landowner is regarded as a taxable person and is accountable for tax, firstly, on the site fines, and secondly, on the value of any interest conveyed to the purchaser.

31. The special provision referred to is designed to prevent evasion and secure a uniform tax incidence as between different methods of dealing in property. The provision would not be invoked, for example, in the case of an unregistered landowner who disposed of interests in his land solely to registered builders.

Sale and leaseback arrangements

32. Development projects are commonly financed by means of sale and leaseback arrangements. Under such arrangements a developer purchases a site and sells his interest in it to a financial concern. He then has the site leased back to him and at the same time grants a mortgage on his interest in the lease to the financial concern as security for future borrowing to meet the cost of development. The treatment for VAT purposes is as follows: —

(a) If the site is undeveloped at the time of its sale by the developer to the financial concern or if no development has been carried out subsequent to 31 October, 1972, neither the sale nor the leaseback attracts liability to VAT;

(b) If development has been carried out subsequent to 31 October, 1972, (for example, if an existing building has been demolished) the sale would, technically, be taxable and the leaseback would also be taxable. The value of the lease would in normal circumstances be the same as the consideration for the sale and, consequently, any liability on the sale on the part of the person making the supply would be offset by the credit on the leaseback. In such circumstances, a sale and leaseback between persons who could both be technically taxable may be ignored for VAT purposes even in regard to developed property, provided the leaseback is for a term of at least 10 years and the value of the lease corresponds, at least approximately, to the value of the interest which was sold.

Amount on which VAT is chargeable

33. In the case of a taxable supply of property the amount on which VAT is chargeable is the amount which the supplier becomes entitled to receive "including all taxes, commissions, costs and charges whatsoever, but not including value-added tax chargeable in respect of the supply". There must, therefore, be included any payment such as a site fine or building licence fee and the capital value of any rent created under a lease for 10 years or more. (State grants should not be included). The manner in which a rent is to be capitalised is discussed in paragraphs 36 and 37.

34. For the purposes of calculating the tax chargeable, the various elements of consideration are added together and taxed at an effective rate of 3 per cent. (see paragraphs 44-46).

35. In the case of a taxable self-supply of property, the tax is calculated at the effective rate of 3 per cent. on the tax-exclusive cost of development plus the cost of the site.

Valuation of interest in property

36.   The capital value of a rent created in connection with the disposal of an interest in property is the price, excluding tax, which the right to receive the rent would fetch in the open market. The price may be ascertained in any one of the following ways and the taxpayer may adopt whichever valuation he wishes:

(a) On a valuation made by a competent valuer.

(b) By multiplying three-quarters of the annual rent by the number of complete years in the term of the lease. On this method, the value of an annual rent of £1,000 under a lease for 12 years would be ¾ × £1,000 × 12 = £9,000.

(c) By regarding the capital value as the nominal amount of the most recent National Loan which would yield annually the equivalent of the annual rent taking the *redemption* rate of interest as the rate of yield. On this basis, if the redemption rate were 16.10 per cent., an annual rent of £1,000 would be valued at £6,210 (that is £1,000 × 6.21 — see table below). For the purposes of this method only National Loans which mature no earlier than 5 years from the date of issue may be taken into account.

Methods (b) and (c) may not be used if the terms of the lease provide for an increase in the rent within five years of the grant of the lease. If, for example, there is provision for an increase in the rent after, say, three years, or the rent is calculated yearly by reference to profits, the interest disposed of must be valued by method (a).

In connection with the valuation of interests by method (c) above, the following are the appropriate multipliers for the various National Loans issued up to 1979: —

Date of issue	Redemption yield	Multiplier $\left(\dfrac{100 \div}{\text{redemption yield}} \right)$
10 Nov. 1971	9.35 per cent.	10.69
24 Nov. 1972	9.91 per cent.	10.09
16 Nov. 1973	12.01 per cent.	8.32
15 Nov. 1974	12.55 per cent.	7.96
7 Nov. 1975	14.67 per cent.	6.81
1 March 1977	12.24 per cent.	8.17
26 April 1977	14.01 per cent.	7.14
4 Oct. 1977	8.77 per cent.	11.40
7 Feb. 1978	11.88 per cent.	8.41
15 Aug. 1978	11.08 per cent.	9.025
1 Feb. 1979	13.04 per cent.	7.67
15 Sept. 1979	13.39 per cent.	7.47
20 Dec. 1979	16.10 per cent.	6.21

37.   The value of a reversionary interest is ascertained by deducting the value of the interest actually disposed of from the value of the full interest. If the lessor's full interest was the fee simple, the value of the fee simple would have to be established on the basis of a valuation by a competent valuer. If the value of the interest disposed of should exceed the value of the full interest (this might happen if the value of the interest disposed of was calculated according to a different method from the calculation of the full interest) the reversionary interest would have no value. In any event the value of the reversionary interest should be ignored if the property cannot revert to the lessor within 20 years of granting the lease.

Time when tax becomes due

38.   As already explained, a supply of property takes place only when certain conditions are satisfied. One of these is that the person supplying the property must dispose of a taxable interest. For practical purposes the date of supply is the date on which the purchaser or lessee acquires a taxable interest himself. If he takes occupation of the property or otherwise acquires an equitable interest before he acquires a legal interest (that is, before the lease is drawn up and signed), the supply takes place on the date on which he takes occupation or otherwise acquires an equitable interest, whichever is the earlier.

39.   The date on which tax falls due varies according to whether or not the purchaser or lessee is a taxable person. If he is not a taxable person the tax falls due on the date of the supply. If he is a taxable person the tax falls due not later than the 10th day of the month following the month in which the supply takes place. For example, if, say, a taxable interest in a residential flat was supplied to an unregistered person on 1st January the tax would fall due on that date (although it would not be payable until between 10th and 19th March); and if a registered shopkeeper was supplied with a taxable lease on a shop on 1st January the tax would fall due on the date on which the supply was invoiced or ought to have been invoiced (that is, not later than 10th February) although it would not be payable until between 10th and 19th March.

40.   If a lease of ten years or longer is granted, the whole of the tax falls due by reference to the date on which the purchaser or lessee acquires a taxable interest, or takes occupation or otherwise acquires the equitable interest, whichever of these events is the earlier (see paragraph 38). Irrespective of whether or not the lessor has been authorised to calculate his VAT liability on the basis of cash actually received, there are no provisions whereby the liability to pay tax may be spread forward over the term of the lease.

41.   In the case of a self-supply of property, tax falls due on the date on which the self-supply takes place. If, for example, a registered builder occupies on 1st January a house he has built himself, tax is due on 1st January (although it would not be payable until between 10th and 19th March). If a registered lessor creates a short lease (less than 10 years) on 1st January, tax falls due on 1st January or earlier if the lessee is given occupation or an equitable interest before 1st January.

Time when tax becomes payable

42.   Tax is payable between the 10th and 19th day of the month following the end of the taxable period within which the tax became due. The tax falling due within the taxable period January/February is payable between the 10th and 19th March; that falling due within March/April between 10th and 19th May; and so on.

43.   If tax is not paid within the proper time interest will be charged at the rate of 1¼ per cent. for each calendar month or part of a month. There is a minimum interest charge of £5.

Invoicing tax on property

44.   A taxable person who has become liable for tax on a property transaction may issue a tax invoice in respect of the interest of which he has disposed. He may not issue a tax invoice in repect of any reversion retained by him or in respect of any other self-supply although he is liable for tax on these supplies also.

45.   Invoices to lessees in respect of supplies of taxable interests should be made out as follows: —

		£
Value of interest disposed of, say,		5,000
70 per cent. chargeable at zero per cent.		3,500
Balance of 30 per cent.	=	1,500
VAT @ 10 per cent.	=	£150

46.   A taxable person may claim a credit or deduction in the normal way for tax properly invoiced to him in respect of the acquisition of a taxable interest in property. It is entirely a matter for the parties to any such transaction to determine the manner in which the tax is passed on to the purchaser. No matter what may be agreed in this regard the obligation remains on the person disposing of a taxable interest to issue an invoice showing VAT on the value of the full interest disposed of and not merely on the payments received or receivable from the purchaser.

Rents

47.   In general, tax is not chargeable on rents of property unless the person in receipt of the rents elects to be taxable on them. If he does elect he becomes taxable on all such rents excluding those payable under taxable leases (see paragraph 50). Rents of property, when chargeable to tax, are chargeable in full at the low rate unlike taxable supplies of property where only a fraction of the consideration is taxable.

48.   A person who waives his exemption and elects to be taxable on rents receivable and who subsequently wishes to cancel his waiver may do so only by refunding any excess of tax repaid to him over tax paid by him.

49. The following rents are taxable whether or not an election for taxability has been made: —

   (a) Rents of machinery or business installations, when let separately from the premises of which they form part. Thus, a rent charged for, say, a lift would be taxable even though the lift would technically be regarded as a fixture in the premises in which it was installed;

   (b) The letting of rooms, garage space, parking space or other accommodation in the course of carrying on a hotel business;

   (c) The provision of parking accommodation for vehicles by the operators of car parks; and

   (d) The hire of safes.

50. A rent (including a ground rent) under a lease for a term of 10 years or more is regarded as part of the consideration for disposing of an interest in the property. The interest disposed of is required to be valued for tax purposes as described in paragraphs 36 and 37 and the rents under such leases should, therefore, be excluded in computing liability under an election to be taxable on rents receivable.

51. If a lease provides for a separate payment of a specified amount for services to be supplied by a landlord, such payment should be treated as part of the rent if the services are of a kind which are commonly provided by a landlord for his tenants in relation to lettings of premises of the kind in question. Where, under a lease, a landlord agrees to arrange for the supply of certain services to his tenants and recovers the cost from them on an apportioned basis he is not liable in respect of the services in question. However, should he supply any of the services using his own labour or other resources he would become liable in respect of the supply of that service regardless of whether he was liable in respect of the letting of the premises.

Cash basis of accounting

52. A person who deals almost exclusively with unregistered customers may be authorised to calculate his tax liability by reference to cash actually received. When this basis is used, cash received in respect of rents arising from the supply of taxable interests should be ignored. Such rents must be valued and the amounts so obtained treated as if they were cash receipts. (It will be seen that the supply of taxable interests is taxable by reference to the capitalised value of rents no matter which basis of accounting a trader adopts. See also paragraph 40). Cash receipts relating to properties on which no development work was carried out on or after 1 November, 1972 may also be ignored.

Auction and agency sales of property

53. Property sold by auction or through agents is treated for VAT purposes as having been simultaneously supplied to and by the auctioneer or agent if the interest disposed of is *not* a taxable interest. The effect of this treatment is

that an auctioneer or agent has no liability on his commission from such transactions. In relation to taxable interests, and leases and lettings of less than ten years (including lettings of undeveloped land) the auctioneer or agent is liable on his commission or fees.

D.I.Y. housebuilders

54.   There is no provision for repayment or relief from tax for persons building houses for their own occupation. Building materials are generally liable to VAT at the low rate but certain goods are liable at the standard rate. These rates compare with an effective rate of 3 per cent. on houses built by contractors. The excess of the rates of tax chargeable on the materials over the rate chargeable in the case of contractors is not repayable or otherwise relieved.

Typical cases

55.   Company A owns the freehold of a plot of undeveloped land and creates a 99 year lease in favour of company B. Company B builds an office block and sells its entire 99 year interest to company C. Company C disposes of its interest by 21 year leases.

Company A has no liability since the interest it sold was not an interest in developed land. Neither has it a liability on the ultimate reversion of the property to it. Company B has a liability and the tax for which it is liable may be invoiced in the normal way to company C. Company C can take a credit or deduction for the tax invoiced by company B. It has a liability on the interests it creates but not on the reversionary interests, since the leases are over 20 years.

56.   Company D, a bank not carrying on any taxable activities, purchases an undeveloped plot on which it has built for its own use by contractor E an office premises. The premises having more capacity than the bank needs, the bank leases the excess by long leases (that is, leases of ten years and more).

The bank becomes taxable in relation to the entire building. It is liable on the part it uses itself as a self-supply and on the part it leases out as a supply.

57.   Company F, registered for VAT, leases a shop under a 10 year lease but while planning how it will use the premises sub-lets the shop on a monthly basis to trader G, also registered. Company F does not elect to pay tax on the rent.

Company F is liable on the self-supply of the shop. No credit is available to trader G.

58.   After a year company F, referred to in the previous paragraph, commences to use the shop itself.

It cannot then make an adjustment for the tax on the self-supply.

59. Insurance company H buys the freehold of undeveloped land, develops part of the land by building an office block and leaves the remainder undisturbed. It disposes of the office block by 21 year leases and sells the balance of the freehold to another company.

The insurance company is liable on the leases created on the developed part of the property only. It has no liability on the disposal of the freehold of the undeveloped land. The exact area which has been developed will be determined on the facts of each particular case (see paragraph 14(b)).

60. A superannuation fund purchases a newly developed block of flats with *all* tenants already signed up.

The superannuation fund is not a taxable person. It has no liability on its receipts from the tenancies whether these are received from the tenants, the developer or someone else.

61. Company J acquires a 35 year interest in a developed building, claims the VAT credits and subsequently creates a five year lease in favour of company K. It elects to account for VAT on the rent received from company K. At the end of the five years company J sells the balance of its leasehold interest to company L.

The sale of the balance of the leasehold interest is taxable. Had company J not elected to account for VAT on the rent received on the original five-year lease there would have been a self-supply of the property which would have taken the property outside the scope of VAT unless there was further development.

62. A private individual buys, but does not occupy, a new house. He holds the property for a year and then sells it.

He has no liability since (a) he cannot have been entitled to a VAT credit or deduction or, alternatively, (b) he did not, presumably, sell the house in the course or furtherance of business. If he sold the house through an auctioneer or agent the latter's commission would not be taxable.

63. A property, re-developed after 31 October, 1972, has been occupied by the same tenants since before 1 November, 1972, under agreements dated January, 1972. On the expiration of the agreements the freehold of the property is sold.

There is no VAT liability since the supplier was not a taxable person for VAT. The letting of immovable goods, which was the only activity engaged in by the supplier, is exempt. The supplier, therefore, had no right to a tax credit or deduction and consequently no liability on the disposal of the freehold.

64. Company M has excess warehouse space and lets the excess on monthly tenancies. The warehouse was not developed after 1 November, 1972.

The lettings are exempt. A distinction should be made between letting which is exempt and the provision of storage, which is taxable.

65. Company N grants a lease in developed property to company O. Subsequently, by agreement between the parties, the lease is vacated by the lessee and a new lease is drawn up between company N and company P.

The second lease is not taxable since there was no development of the property after the vacation of the lease. In practice the position would be much the same in the event of the abandonment of a lease by a lessee, without agreement.

66. Company Q leases two floors of a new building to company R. Subsequently a third floor of the same building is leased to the same company.

The second lease is treated as a separate lease and is taxable as such. It would not be correct to ''cancel'' the first lease and grant a new lease in respect of the three floors.

67. A VAT-registered property developer owns an old building which he develops and leases on an annual basis. He does not elect to pay VAT on the rents.

The developer is liable for VAT on the basis of a self-supply, the chargeable amount being the actual (that is, the historic) cost of acquisition of the building, increased by the tax-exclusive development costs.

Inquiries

68. A person requiring more information about VAT on property should address his inquiry in writing to the local inspector of taxes (see list of offices in the ''Guide to the Value-Added Tax'') or to the Revenue Commissioners (VAT), Castle House, South Great George's Street, Dublin 2.

INDEX

2. Guide to Value Added Tax

CHAPTER 15

BUILDING AND ASSOCIATED SERVICES

[The following pages are from the Revenue Commissioners Guide to Value Added Tax dated June 1988. The issued a revised Guide in December 1994 but it did not deal with property. It would be prudent to check with your local Inspector before coming to a conclusion on any particular aspect.]   F.G.

REVENUE COMMISSIONERS

JUNE 1988

Building and other contractors

15.1   Building contractors and other contractors operating in the building sector (such as electrical, plumbing, plastering, heating, painting, roofing and flooring contractors) are carrying on taxable activities and they are obliged to register for VAT if their annual turnover is in excess of £12,000.

15.2   When registered for VAT purposes, contractors are liable for tax at 10 per cent on most activities in the building sector (see paragraph 15.3). Contractors are entitled, like other taxable persons, to set off against their liability most of the tax properly invoiced to them by their suppliers. The result of this sometimes is that the tax on a contractor's purchases exceeds liability. In these circumstances the difference is refunded direct to the registered contractor following receipt by the Collector-General of his VAT return.

Where 10 per cent rate of VAT applies

15.3   The 10 per cent rate of VAT applies to most activities carried on by building contractors and other contractors operating in the building sector. It normally applies, therefore, to housebuilding and construction work generally; to building renovation and demolition; to building maintenance and repair; to the installation of plumbing, heating and electrical services; and to the supply, installation, maintenance and repair of fixtures. The 10 per cent rate also applies, subject to certain conditions, to the supply and placing in a fixed position of garden sheds, greenhouses and similar structures.

15.4   The 10 per cent rate of VAT does not apply to the supply only of any building materials other than ready-mixed concrete and concrete blocks, nor does it apply to the supply and installation, or installation only, of fittings, as distinct from fixtures.

Fixtures

15.5   Fixtures are goods which have become attached to buildings in such a way that they cannot be removed without substantial damage being caused to the goods themselves or to the building to which they are attached. In the case of houses, fixtures could, as a general rule, be said to include the basic structural items (excluding carpets and other floor coverings, cookers, hobs, gas and electric fires and the like) normally to be found in a new, unfurnished, standard house.

15.6   It is important to note that, apart from ready-mixed concrete and concrete blocks, the supply only of goods never qualifies for the 10 per cent rate of VAT even though the goods may eventually become fixtures. For example, the supply only of kitchen units to a builder is chargeable at 25 per cent even though the units, when installed in a building by the builder, may be chargeable at 10 per cent. The builder, of course, is entitled to full deduction for the tax charged to him on the units, subject to the usual conditions. The installation only or the maintenance and repair and decoration of fixtures is normally taxable at 10 per cent.

15.7   The following is a list of goods which are regarded as qualifying for the 10 per cent rate of VAT once they have been permanently installed as fixtures and subject, of course, to the two-thirds rule (see paragraphs 15.11, 15.12).

Advertising hoardings
Airconditioning equipment
Airdomes
Attic insulation
Attic ladders
Baths
Burglar alarms
Canopies (at filling stations)
Central heating systems
Cold rooms (excl. free-standing type)
Counters (excl. free-standing type)
Curtain rails (fixed)
Double glazing
Electrical wiring down to and including lampholders, power points and fuse boards
Fencing posts
Fire escapes
Fireplaces
Fitted kitchen units
Fitted wardrobes and presses
Floor covering stuck down over its entire surface
Foam insulation (injected into cavity walls)
Gates
Generators
Headstones
Immersion heaters
Lifts and associated machinery
Milking parlour equipment
Mirrored tiles and similar fixed wall-coverings
PABX telephone systems
Partitioning
Pelmets (fixed)
Prefabricated buildings (subject to conditions)
Recessed lighting (excl. light tubes and lamps)
Roller shutters
Sewerage treatment plants
Sinks
Sliding door gear
Slurry tanks
Storage heaters/radiators
Storage tanks for oil or water for heating etc. systems
Strong rooms (in banks)
Switchgear
Traffic signalling equipment

Weighbridges
Window cleaning rails (for cradle)
Window guards (wire mesh)

15.8   The following goods are not regarded as fixtures, whether or not they are installed:-
Blinds
Clocks including time clocks such as flexitime equipment
Cooker hoods
Curtains
Electric and gas fires
Exhibition stands
Fitted carpets and lino, other than floor covering stuck down over its entire surface
Free-standing shop counters
Kitchen cookers
Lighting other than recessed lighting
Mirrors (see paragraph 15.7 regarding mirrored tiles and similar fixed wall-coverings)
Most shelving
Refrigeration units, including deep freezes
Safes (certain)
Seating, including cinema and church seating whether or not secured to the floor
Snooker tables and other games tables
Washing machines and dishwashers, including plumbed-in machines

The supply, or supply and installation for a single inclusive charge, of these goods is chargeable to VAT at 25 per cent. It is open to a contractor to charge separately for supply and for installation in which case the supply element will be liable at the 25 per cent rate and the installation element at 10 per cent, to the extent, if any, that the installation element itself involves the installation of a fixture. For example, the supply and installation of an electric cooker for an inclusive charge are liable at 25 per cent. If, in connection with the installation, it was necessary to re-wire for a power supply point and a separate charge was raised for such work, the 10 per cent rate would apply to this charge. The connection of the cooker to the power supply would be liable at 25 per cent.

15.9   It is important for main contractors to understand that, while it may generally be so, charges invoiced by sub-contractors do not always or necessarily qualify for the 10 per cent rate. In some circumstances the 25 per cent rate may apply (see, for example paragraph 15.8). While tax invoiced by a sub-contractor at 25 per cent would be deductible by the main contractor, the latter, in turn, would be liable at the same rate in some circumstances (if, for example, goods such as those mentioned in paragraph 15.8 were involved) but not in others (see last sentence of paragraph 15.12).

VAT on a typical building job

15.10   The following sets out in very general terms how VAT applies at the various stages of building contracts. The rate of VAT on building jobs is generally 10 per cent. The rate of VAT on non-fixtures is generally 25 per cent.

Sequence of Events	VAT Liability
(i) Tender	Not governed by VAT law. Obviously the contractor, in his own interests, should make it clear whether his tender price is inclusive or exclusive of VAT. The customer, especially if he is not registered for VAT, will probably wish to know how much, in total, he is being quoted and accordingly it may be advisable to give the rate and amount of VAT if tendering on a tax-exclusive basis. While the rate of VAT will generally be 10 per cent there are circumstances in which this is not so.
(ii) Award of Contract	——
(iii) Deposit (or payment in advance)	Tax payable by reference to taxable period within which payment is received, whether the contractor is on the sales or the moneys received basis.
	Invoice. A VAT invoice in respect of payments received must be issued within the time limit (see Chapter 10.5) to customers who are registered for VAT. It does not have to be issued to unregistered customers but may be if it suits the contractor's business convenience.
(iv) Contractor's progress account	Tax not payable at time of issue. Account does not rank as VAT invoice.
(v) Certificate from architect, engineer, etc.	Certificate does not rank as VAT invoice.
(vi) Progress payment to contractor	Tax payable by reference to taxable period within which payment is received, whether the contractor is on the sales or the moneys received basis.
	Invoice must be issued as in (iii).
(vii) Contractor's final account	Tax not payable at time of issue (assuming there is a guarantee period).
	Account does not rank as VAT invoice.
(viii) Certificate from architect, engineer, etc.	Certificate does not rank as VAT invoice.
(ix) Final payment to contractor (excl. retention money)	Tax payable by reference to taxable period within which payment is received, whether the contractor is on the sales or the moneys received basis.
	Invoice. A VAT invoice must be issued within the time limit to customers who are registered for VAT. It does not have to be issued to unregistered customers but may be if it suits the contractor's business convenience.
(x) Retention money	(a) Tax payable by reference to the taxable period within which the guarantee period expires if contractor is on sales basis.
	Invoice. A VAT invoice must be issued when guarantee period expires if customer is registered.
	(b) Tax payable by reference to the taxable period within which money is received if contractor is on the moneys received basis.
	Invoice. A VAT invoice must be issued when guarantee period expires if customer is registered.

The two-thirds rule

15.11   *The rate of tax applying to services, including building services, depends on the "two-thirds rule". This provides that a transaction is liable for VAT as a sale of goods at the appropriate rate and not as a service if the value of the goods (that is, their cost, excluding VAT, to the service contractor) used in providing the service exceeds two-thirds of the total charge to the customer.*

15.12   *The two-thirds rule does not usually affect building services in which the labour element is substantial. It would be likely to come into operation in the case of a service consisting of the supply and installation of, say, a transformer or a strong room. The possibility of its application should never be overlooked and contractors should consult the Revenue Commissioners or the Inspector of Taxes if there is any doubt about the correct liability to tax. Sub-contractors, in particular, may find that the 25 per cent rate may apply to their portion of a main contract even though the main contract may itself be liable at the 10% rate.*

Do-it-yourself

15.13   Building materials, with the exception of ready-mixed concrete and concrete blocks to which the 10 per cent rate applies, are liable at 25 per cent. There is no provision for the repayment to private individuals who do their own building work of any excess of tax charged on building materials over the 10 per cent rate which would be chargeable if the work was done by a contractor registered for VAT.

Property transactions

15.14   VAT on dealings in land and buildings (property) is the subject of a separate leaflet entitled "Property Transactions" which may be obtained from the Revenue Commissioners (VAT), Castle House, South Great George's Street, Dublin 2 or from Inspectors of Taxes.

15.15   As a general rule property does not attract liability to VAT unless all the following conditions are satisfied:-

(a)   the property must have been developed in whole or part after 31 October, 1972;

(b)   the vendor must have a taxable interest in the property;

(c)   the vendor must have disposed of a taxable interest in the property;

(d)   the disposal must have been made in the course or furtherance of business;

and

(e)   the circumstances must have been such that the person disposing of the interest was entitled to a tax credit for any tax suffered in relation to the development or the acquisition of his interest.

All these matters and others, including the valuation of interests, are discussed in "Property Transactions" which should always be consulted in relation to this subject.

Note for Reader

The 10% rate was increased to 12.5% from 1 March 1993.

The 25% rate was reduced to 23% from 1 March 1990 and further reduced to 21% with effect from 1 March 1991.

3. SERVICE CHARGES

OFFICE OF THE REVENUE COMMISSIONERS,
VALUE ADDED TAX BRANCH,
CASTLE HOUSE,
SOUTH GREAT GEORGE'S STREET,
DUBLIN 2.

OIFIG NA gCOIMISINEIRI-IONCAIM,
BRAINSE CHAIN BHREISLUACHA,
TEACH AN CHAISLEAIN,
SRAID SAN SEOIRSE THEAS,
BAILE ATHA CLIATH, 2.

(01) 792777 Ext2440\2441
May 30 1985

VAT on goods and services supplied to property lessees
through landlords ("service charges")

Dear Sir,

I refer to our recent discussion and confirm that, having regard to the special features of the application of VAT to property, the Revenue Commissioners are prepared, *as a concession*, to agree to the following arrangements for the transmission to VAT-registered lessees of a deduction for VAT charged on these goods and services.

(1) A landlord who is not registered for VAT and who is not obliged to register may seek the agreement of his Inspector of Taxes (VAT) to become registered by concession. The application should be made by letter to the Inspector and should give the address(es) of the property(ies), a list of the registered tenants, the accounting year/s and quote the registered VAT number of the landlord, if already registered. On being satisfied regarding the circumstances of the case the Inspector will register the landlord. A landlord whom an Inspector agrees to register will be allocated a VAT number which will enable the landlord to issue to his registered lessees *once a year*, directly or through his management agents, invoices bearing this number and showing VAT, where appropriate. Such invoices will enable the registered lessees to take a deduction for the VAT invoiced, subject to the usual conditions.

(2) Landlords who are registered for VAT in accordance with the procedure described above will have the same obligations as persons who are obliged to be registered. They will, therefore, be obliged to keep records in sufficient detail to enable their VAT returns to be checked and validated. In the following instances their obligations will be somewhat modified.

(i) *Invoices*

The landlords will not be obliged to issue invoices showing VAT as they receive payments from their lessees. Only *one* invoice showing VAT should be issued to the lessee and this at the end of the landlord's accounting year. Any difficulties in this regard (e.g. changes in VAT rates during the year, end of an accounting year not co-inciding with the end of a VAT taxable period) will be settled by the Inspector.

(ii) *Returns*

Unless a landlord has several properties to which different accounting years apply, only one VAT return per year will be required. Although a VAT return form is intended to cover a taxable period of two months only (January/February, March/April and so on) the entry in the return should cover the accounting year of the property in question. This will mean that five "NIL" returns will have to be made each year. *If "NIL" returns are not made, computer-operated follow-up procedures will be automatically activated.*

If a landlord has several properties and different accounting years apply to different properties, as many "positive" returns as there are accounting years will be required each year. "NIL" returns will also be required as appropriate.

The returns should show no net liability or repayment since they will merely represent the appropriate values of liable considerations invoiced to land-lords by suppliers and the same values invoiced by the landlords to their VAT-registered lessees. The returns should show the precise values involved, segregated as between the different tax ratings.

Conditions

(3) It is a condition of the concession that it be kept within the strictest bounds and be subject to the following conditions in particular:

(i)   it will operate from accounting years ended March 1985 and later;

(ii)   it will be subject to regular review;

(iii)   it will be subject to withdrawal in any particular case at the discretion of the Inspector if he ceases to be satisfied that the conditions of the scheme are met or where he discovers that the limits of the Scheme are exceeded;

(iv)   it may not result in repayments to participating landlords or in relief for input VAT to which these landlords would not otherwise be entitled.

Exclusions

(4) The concession will not extend to the supply of services/goods by landlords using their own labour or other resources. Such supplies are taxable in the ordinary way. This is so whether or not a landlord was liable in respect of the letting of the premises in question.

(5) The arrangement likewise does not apply to other expenses incurred on a joint basis by lessees, for example, staff employed jointly by a number of lessees subject to re-imbursement by the others.

VAT-registered landlords

(6) Landlords who are already registered for VAT may also avail themselves of this concession once they obtain the agreement of their Inspector of Taxes. Such landlords continue to be obliged to make VAT returns in respect of those activities for which they are already registered or obliged to be registered. Details of the transactions covered by the concession should be included, at the appropriate time, in such a landlord's ordinary VAT returns.

Payments on account

(7) A VAT deduction may <u>not</u> be taken by VAT-registered lessees in respect of VAT included in demands for payments on account made by a landlord or his management agent and VAT should not be separately shown on such demands for payment since a deduction may only be claimed by lessees in respect of VAT shown on the end of the year final invoices.

Any problems arising out of the operation of the concession should be addressed to the appropriate Inspector of Taxes (VAT). An example of the operation of the concession is attached.

Yours faithfully,

D. Dempsey.

EXAMPLE

A company develops a site as an office/shop complex and creates 35 year leases in favour of 10 lessees. The company undertakes, as landlord, to provide insurance, security and cleaning services and heat and light and the lessees covenant to re-imburse the company for such cost. The complex is managed by a property management agent on behalf of the company. The lessees undertake to re-imburse the company for the agent's fees also. Each lessee makes a quarterly payment on account of £2,500. At the end of the year the landlord or his agent calculates each lessee's liability as £10,175 made up as follows:

	Charge excl. VAT	VAT	Total	Each lessee's share (1/10th)
	£	£	£	£
Insurance (exempt)	50,000	-	50,000	5,000
Electricity (zero)	10,000	-	10,000	1,000
Heating Oil, Gas (10%)	10,000	1,000	11,000	1,000 + 100 VAT
Cleaning Security (23%)	20,000	4,600	24,600	2,000 + 460 VAT
Management (23%)	5,000	1,150	6,150	500 + 115 VAT
	£95,000	£6,750	£101,750	£9,500 + 675 VAT (Total £10,175)

A landlord, or the management agent on the landlord's behalf, who has made the necessary arrangement with his Inspector of Taxes should issue an itemised invoice (see specimen attached) showing the consideration excluding VAT and indicating separately the VAT on each liable charge. This will enable a VAT-registered lessee to take the appropriate deduction in his VAT return.

SPECIMEN INVOICE

From: A. Landlord

To: A. Lessee

VAT No. 123456 A

Unit 14(b), XYZ Shopping Centre

Date

To "service charges" for
year ended 31 March 1985
as follows:

Insurance	£5,000 + Nil VAT (exempt)
Electricity	£1,000 + Nil VAT (0%)
Heating Oil, Gas	£1,000 + £100 VAT (10%)
Cleaning and Security	£2,000 + £460 VAT (23%)
Management Agent's Fees	£ 500 + £115 VAT (23%)
	£9,500 + £675 VAT
Total	£10,175
Less: Paid on Account	£10,000
Balance	£ 175

4. ENQUIRY LETTER ON REGISTRATION

Office of the Inspector of Taxes,
Taxes Central Registration Office,
9/15 Upper O'Connell Street,
Dublin 1

Telephone -(01) 874 6821 Extn.

Fax   -(01) 874 6078

Reference Number

This matter is dealt with by:

Dear Sirs,

Re: Subject:
**   VAT**
**   Ref:-**

I refer to your recent application to register for VAT and I note that the activity being carried on relates to property development and/or property rental.

I shall be obliged, therefore, if you will let me have the following information:

1. The address of the property.

2. The date on which it was purchased or when development commenced.

3. The planning permission reference number, if applicable.

4. A copy of the minutes of the board meeting/meeting of the partners, whereby it was resolved that the property in question would be purchased and/or developed and would be disposed of or utilised in a manner which would give rise to a VAT liability i.e.

    (a) by outright sale of the property

    (b) by creation of a long term lease in excess of ten years or

    (c) by waiver of exemption in respect of short term lettings

    (Note: the waiver of exemption applies to all rents receivable from short term lettings
             including those from properties other than that mentioned above).

The minutes should show the date of the meeting, the names of all those present at the meeting and should be signed by the company secretary or precedent acting partner in the case of a partnership.

Yours faithfully,

5. LIQUIDATORS AND RECEIVERS

VAT

Liquidators and Receivers

General

1. The combined effects of Sections 78, 80 and 84 of the Finance Act, 1983, are to extend and alter the accountability of liquidators (including court liquidators) and receivers in relation to VAT by requiring them to make returns and pay tax on the disposal by them of goods owned by "taxable persons" (see paragraph 5). This is so whether or not the business of a company in liquidation continues to be carried on and whether or not a receiver is appointed under a floating (general) or fixed (specific) charge.

2. These legal provisions come into operation on 1 September 1983 and apply to disposals made by liquidators and receivers on or after that date including disposals made by them on or after that date which arise out of liquidations and receiverships which commenced before that date.

3. The provisions are not regarded as applying to the Official Assignee in connection with bankrupts, arranging debtors or insolvent persons.

4. The accountability provided for in the Finance Act 1983 is in addition to such accountability and responsibility as liquidators and receivers already have under the VAT law in force prior to the passing of this Act. The purpose of this note is to describe how it is envisaged that liquidators and receivers should in practice discharge their functions in relation to VAT on disposals on and after 1 September 1983. All references throughout this note to liquidators should be understood as including court liquidators.

Taxable Disposals

5. Subject to the exceptions listed below, the disposals for which liquidators and receivers are accountable are disposals of goods forming part of the business assets of a VAT-registered person or of a person who ought to have been VAT-registered. Accountability does not arise in respect of the disposal of the business assets of persons who are properly not VAT-registered persons. Even where goods which are disposed of by a liquidator or receiver are the assets of a VAT-registered person (or a person who ought to have been VAT-registered person) the following are not taxable:

    a) goods including goodwill or other intangible assets disposed of in connection with a transfer of a business or part of a business to another VAT-registered person;

    b) zero rated and exempt goods (for example, certain food, drink, clothing, horses and greyhounds). The supply of stocks, shares and other securities is exempt;

    c) exported goods;

    d) business goods in respect of which the company in liquidation or receivership was not entitled to a VAT deduction (for example, cars acquired otherwise than as stock-in-trade, and certain land and buildings. As a general rule only land and buildings which have been developed in whole or part after 31 October 1972 and which meet certain other conditions are taxable. For full details see the leaflet entitled "Property Transactions");

161

    (e) sale of debts;

    (f) moneys received in respect of pre-liquidation or-receivership transactions. There are some exceptions (see paragraph 7) and

    (g) goods returned to supplier under reservation of title arrangements. (If these goods were invoiced to the company in liquidation or receivership and a VAT deduction was taken the supplier is required to issue a credit note. This will have the effect of cancelling the deduction – see also paragraph 15).

6.   Where a liquidator or receiver has difficulty in establishing whether or not he is accountable on any particular disposal he should consult the appropriate Inspector of Taxes (see Foreword to the "Guide to the Value-Added Tax" for addresses and telephone numbers). Such a difficulty might be encountered in the case of land and buildings where it might not be possible for a liquidator or receiver to establish independently if the several conditions governing liability had been met (see "Property Transactions").

Receivers appointed under a fixed charge, only

7.   In the case of receiverships in which a receiver is appointed under a fixed (specific) charge, the receiver is accountable on disposals of the specific asset only. The company itself (not the receiver) is liable on moneys received in respect of transactions (sales of goods and services) whether pre or post-receivership, if it is accounting on the cash basis. (The company is, in any event, liable on transactions not covered by the terms of the receiver's appointment no matter what basis of accounting it is using).

Registration

8.   All liquidators and receivers who dispose of any taxable goods (including immovable, goods – see paragraph 5) forming part of the business assets of a VAT-registered person, or a person who ought to have been registered, must, *regardless of the value of their disposals*, register for VAT in respect of each liquidation or receivership. Application for registration should be made on form VAT 1 in the name of the company with the suffix "in liquidation or in receivership (as appropriate) per A.B.". A new VAT number will be allocated to each such registration. If companies in liquidation or receivership were, prior to liquidation or receivership, registered as a group for VAT purposes, the liquidators or receivers may, if they wish, apply for a corresponding group registration. (see paragraphs 5.9, 5.10 of Guide).

Returns

9.   Although, strictly speaking, they are not taxable persons in respect of goods disposed of by them, liquidators and receivers are obliged to make periodic returns and remit tax on such disposals. No special form of return is contemplated, the general return form (VAT 3) being considered adequate for the purpose. The returns require to be made at the usual times, that is, by the 19th day of the "uneven" months January, March and so on).

10. Goods disposed of by liquidators or receivers should be excluded from any separate return a taxable person may be obliged to make (for example, in the case of a receivership over a specific charge, where the company might sell goods not covered by the charge).

VAT Payable

11. The amount of VAT payable by liquidators and receivers in respect of goods (including immovable goods) disposed of by them is the VAT content, at whichever VAT rate is appropriate, in the amount received from the disposal. The proceeds of all disposals are regarded as being tax-inclusive. Where no money is paid in respect of a disposal of goods (for example, in the case of goods distributed in specie among creditors or shareholders) an amount equivalent to the VAT, at the appropriate rate, on the value of the goods is payable.

VAT Deductible

12. Claims for deductions are subject to the ordinary rules governing deductions (see Chapter 8 of the "Guide to the Value-Added Tax"). Claims should be segregated between pre- and post-liquidation/receivership transactions as follows:

    a) VAT incurred by a liquidator or receiver on goods and services purchased by him in connection with a liquidation or receivership should be claimed in the returns which he is required to make of goods disposed of by him. Claims for VAT charged on a liquidator's or receiver's professional services may, provided the company in liquidation or receivership is a taxable person, be included in these returns also; and

    b) VAT adjustments arising out of pre-liquidation and pre-receivership transactions should be claimed under the company's original VAT number not the VAT number of the company in liquidation or receivership.

Bad Debts

13. Relief for bad debts is allowable, subject to the usual conditions. Claims for relief should be made on a supplementary VAT return under the company's original VAT number.

Invoices, Credit Notes, Settlement Vouchers

14. Liquidators and receivers should issue invoices and credit notes on the same basis as taxable persons, the name of the person issuing the document being "Company X in liquidation/receivership per A.B.", the VAT number on the document being the number allocated for that purpose.

15. Goods returned to a company in liquidation or receivership should be treated as having been bought back by the liquidator or receiver. If the person returning the goods does not issue a VAT invoice, the liquidator or receiver should issue a settlement voucher and take the appropriate deduction in his VAT return.

Preferentiality

16. There is no change in this regard.

Statement by liquidator or receiver to owner of goods

17. A copy of the invoice issued to purchasers of goods disposed of suffices for this purpose.

    Issued by the Revenue Commissioners.

    September, 1983.

6. CLAIM BY AN UNREGISTERED FARMER FOR REFUND OF VALUE ADDED TAX – FORM NO. VAT 58

BEFORE COMPLETING THIS FORM PLEASE READ PAGE 4

FORM NO. VAT 58   CLAIM BY UNREGISTERED FARMER FOR REFUND OF VALUE-ADDED TAX

CLAIMANTS FULL NAME

ADDRESS (BLOCK LETTERS)

TELEPHONE NO. _____

TAX REFERENCE No. _____
(THIS CAN BE OBTAINED FROM YOUR LOCAL TAX OFFICE)

AMOUNT CLAIMED £ _____
(GIVE DETAILS ON PAGE 3)

DO YOU CARRY ON ANY TRADE, PROFESSION OR VOCATION APART FROM YOUR FARMING ACTIVITIES?   YES
                                                                (TICK BOX)   NO

I/WE CLAIM REFUND OF THE ABOVE-MENTIONED AMOUNT IN ACCORDANCE WITH THE PROVISION OF THE VALUE-ADDED TAX (REFUND OF TAX) (NO. 1) ORDER, 1972, AS AMENDED.

I/WE DECLARE THAT:-

(1)   I AM NOT/WE ARE NOT REGISTERED FOR VALUE-ADDED TAX NOR AM I/ARE WE OBLIGED TO REGISTER

(2)   THE OUTLAY IN RELATION TO WHICH THIS CLAIM ARISES WAS INCURRED SOLELY

(a)   ON THE CONSTRUCTION, EXTENSION, ALTERATION OR RECONSTRUCTION OF A BUILDING OR STRUCTURE DESIGNED FOR USE SOLELY OR MAINLY FOR THE PURPOSE OF A FARMING BUSINESS,
OR

(b)   ON THE FENCING, DRAINAGE OR RECLAMATION OF ANY LAND INTENDED FOR USE FOR THE PURPOSES OF A FARMING BUSINESS.

(3)   I/WE HAVE COMPLIED WITH ALL THE OBLIGATIONS IMPOSED ON ME/US BY THE VALUE-ADDED TAX ACT, THE INCOME TAX ACTS, THE CORPORATION TAX ACTS OR THE CAPITAL GAINS TAX ACT OR ANY INSTRUMENTS MADE THEREUNDER, IN RELATION TO:-

(a)   THE REPAYMENT OR REMITTANCE OF THE TAXES, INTEREST AND PENALTIES REQUIRED TO BE PAID OR REMITTED THERE UNDER,
AND

(b)   THE DELIVERY OF RETURNS.

(CLAIMANTS WHO WISH TO HAVE THE AMOUNT DUE OFFSET AGAINST OUTSTANDING TAX LIABILITIES FOR PAST YEARS SHOULD ENCLOSE A SIGNED STATEMENT TO THAT EFFECT GIVING DETAILS OF THE RELEVANT PERIODS, AMOUNTS DUE, ETC.)

THERE ARE PENALTIES FOR CLAIMING REPAYMENT OF TAX TO WHICH YOU ARE NOT ENTITLED.

SIGNATURE _____
(OF EACH CLAIMANT)
_____

DATE _____

OFFICIAL USE ONLY	
CASE NO. _____	WS NO _____
EXAMINED _____	DATE _____
CHECKED _____	DATE _____
AUTHORISED _____	DATE _____
AMOUNT ALLOWED £_____	

N.B.   THESE DETAILS MUST BE COMPLETED AND INCLUDE A FULL DESCRIPTION OF WORK
CARRIED OUT.

(I)   <u>Buildings or Structures</u>

      (a)   Type of building or structure: _____

_____

_____

_____

_____

      (b)   Dimensions: _____

      (c)   Date of commencement of work: _____

      (d)   Date of completion of work: _____

      (e)   Fixed equipment - if included in
claim state type and where
installed: _____

(ii)   <u>Land Improvement</u>

      (a)   Nature of improvement
(drainage, etc.): _____

      (b)   Acreage improved: _____

DETAILS OF AMOUNT CLAIMED

(if there is insufficient space please attach separate list)

Supplier	Amount of VAT shown on invoice*		Supplier	Amount of VAT shown on invoice*	
	£	P		£	P
			BROUGHT FORWARD		
CARRIED FORWARD			TOTAL		

<u>INVOICES</u>

* <u>Original invoices</u> must be submitted in support of the claim. **Repayment will not be made on delivery dockets, statements or photocopy invoices.**

Invoices must show the VAT content separately and also your supplier's VAT Number. They must contain an adequate description of the goods/services involved e.g. "miscellaneous hardware" is not sufficient description.

Supporting invoices will be retained in this Office with the paid claim. If required for farm records please take copies <u>before</u> submitting the originals.

An explanation is required where invoices are not in the name of the claimant(s).

<u>(THESE NOTES DO NOT PURPORT TO BE A LEGAL INTERPRETATION OF THE RELEVANT ORDER)</u>

VAT IS REFUNDABLE <u>ONLY</u>:-

- IF THE CLAIMANT IS NOT REGISTERED FOR VAT OR REQUIRED TO REGISTER FOR VAT

- IF THE CLAIMANT IS UP TO DATE IN RELATION TO INCOME TAX, CORPORATION TAX AND CAPITAL GAINS TAX.

- ON OUTLAY ON

  - THE CONSTRUCTION, EXTENSION, ALTERATION OR RECONSTRUCTION OF FARM BUILDINGS AND CERTAIN FIXED EQUIPMENT WHICH IS INSTALLED IN A FARM BUILDING.

  - FENCING, LAND DRAINAGE AND RECLAMATION.

- IF THE TOTAL AMOUNT OF VAT CLAIMED IS £100 OR MORE.

- IF THE CLAIM IS MADE WITHIN TEN YEARS FROM THE END OF THE TAXABLE PERIOD TO WHICH IT RELATES.

<u>VAT IS NOT REFUNDABLE ON</u>:-

MOBILE EQUIPMENT AND MACHINERY.
ROUTINE MAINTENANCE AND SERVICING OF MACHINERY.
OUTLAY ON TOOLS OR PARTS FOR TOOLS E.G. SHOVELS, CUTTING DISCS, DRILL BITS ETC.
FUEL, OIL, DIESEL ETC.
SILAGE COVERS, ANIMAL FEEDS, MEDICINES, FERTILIZER ETC.

<u>CLAIMS MUST BE SUPPORTED BY</u>:-

- INVOICES FOR ALL GOODS AND SERVICES IN THE CLAIM - SEE NOTE REGARDING INVOICE ON PREVIOUS PAGE.

- FULLY COMPLETED CLAIM FORM INCLUDING TAX REFERENCE NUMBER AND SIGNATURE OF EACH NAMED CLAIMANT.

CLAIMS AND SUPPORTING DOCUMENTS SHOULD BE SENT TO

Revenue Commissioners,

Accountant General's Office,

Government Buildings,

Kilrush Road,

Ennis,

Co. Clare.

Telephone: (065) 41200

7. TAX REGISTRATION FORMS TR1 AND TR2

TAX REGISTRATION   TR1

FOR PERSONS OTHER THAN COMPANIES AND PAYE TAXPAYERS

* Companies requiring to register should complete Form TR2.
* PAYE employees taking up their first employment should complete Form 12A

To register for Income Tax (non-PAYE), Employer's PAYE/PRSI or VAT please complete the relevant parts (Parts A, B, C, D, E) of this form and return it to:

       Taxes Central Registration Office (TCRO)
       Arus Brugha,
       9/15 Upper O'Connell Street,
       Dublin 1.
       Tel. (01) 874 6821

PART A

FOR WHICH TAXES DO YOU REQUIRE REGISTRATION ? *[Note 1]*
[Tick (✓) appropriate box(es)]

Income Tax (non-PAYE)	**Employer's PAYE/PRSI**	**Value Added Tax**
Complete Parts A, B + C	Complete Parts A, B + D	Complete Parts A, B + E

The tax office may, in some circumstances, ask for additional information in relation to an application for VAT registration.

If you have been previously registered for any tax and hold Tax Reference Numbers, please quote them in the following box(es)

      RSI Number* (Income Tax (non-PAYE))

      Employer (PAYE/PRSI)

      Value Added Tax

* Individuals only - If you are unable to trace your RSI Number or have never previously been registered for any tax please state:

(i)   If married, your pre-marriage name
       (where different)

(ii)   Your date of birth

(iii)   Your mother's surname at birth

IF YOU REQUIRE YOUR TAX AFFAIRS TO BE DEALT WITH IN IRISH, PLEASE TICK (✓) HERE

DECLARATION - which must be made in every case

I declare that the particulars supplied by me in this application are true in every respect.

NAME (in BLOCK LETTERS)

SIGNATURE

Capacity (Individual, Secretary, Partner, Trustee etc.)

DATE

TELEPHONE NUMBER   FAX NUMBER

PART B
BASIC INFORMATION

Name or Title
[Note 2]
Business Address

Telephone No

Fax No

Private Address
(if different to
Business
Address)

Telephone No

Fax No

Partnership, Trust or other body - Give the following additional information in respect of each partner, trustee or other officer:

Name	Private address	Capacity	RSI Number *

(If necessary, use a separate sheet for details of any further names)

* Partners in a
Partnership Only.

Details of Accountant/Tax Adviser, if any *[Note 3(a)]*

Name

Address

Tel. No.

Fax No.

SUB-CONTRACTORS
If the business is that of Building/Construction/Forestry/Meat Processing, do you use Sub-contractors ?

Tick (✓) appropriate box   **YES**   **NO**

WHAT IS YOUR MAIN BUSINESS OR ACTIVITY ? Please give a precise description of the business/activity carried on/ about to be carried on, for example "Draper", "Hairdresser", "Textile Manufacturer", "Property Letting", "Investment Income" etc. (Do not use general terms such as "Shopkeeper", "Manufacturer" etc.)]

Please also tick (✓) one of the following nine boxes to indicate the one which most closely classifies the business/activity

Retailing	Wholesaling	Manufacturing
Building and Construction	Banking, Insurance and Building Society	Hotel and Catering
Other Private Business	Public Body	Other Activity

WHEN DID THE BUSINESS OR ACTIVITY COMMENCE ?

TO WHAT DATE WILL ANNUAL ACCOUNTS BE MADE UP ?

PART C
REGISTRATION FOR INCOME TAX (NON-PAYE)

If you wish to register for Income Tax (non-PAYE) please tick (✓) here

PART D
REGISTRATION AS AN EMPLOYER FOR PAYE/PRSI

DATE
State
(a) the date from which Registration is required

(b) the date the first employee commenced or will commence

EMPLOYEES
State number of employees in the business or activity

If you wish to register for ONE employee only, enter a tick (✓) if

homehelp   childminder

housekeeper   substitute teacher

PAYROLL AND PAYE / PRSI RECORDS SYSTEM
Enter a tick (✓) for System used

Tax Deduction Cards
(Official)   Other Manual System*   Computer System*

*Note: If you intend to use a manual or computerised system you will be contacted by the Revenue Commissioners
(P35 Section), Government Offices, Nenagh, Co. Tipperary, to ensure that the system you intend to use satisfies
Revenue requirements. You should not use such a system without getting Revenue approval.

CORRESPONDENCE ON PAYE/PRSI *[Note 3(b)]*
If correspondence relating to PAYE/PRSI is being dealt with by an agent, please (✓) this box. Please give the agent's
name and address if different to the Accountant/Adviser named in Part B

REGISTRATION

(i)   State the date from which Registration is required

(ii)   Is registration being sought because turnover exceeds, or is likely to exceed, the limits prescribed by law for registration?   Tick (✓) appropriate box   Yes   No

(iii)   If the answer to (ii) is "Yes", please enter estimated turnover for the next 12 months   £

(iv)   Is registration being sought only in respect of European Union (EU) acquisitions   Yes   No
(farmer/non-taxable entity)?

ELECTION TO BE A TAXABLE PERSON *[Note 4]*
Is the applicant electing to be a taxable person?   Tick (✓) appropriate box   Yes   No

EXEMPTION WAIVER *[Note 5]*
Does the applicant wish to waive exemption from VAT in respect of the letting of property?:
Tick (✓) appropriate box   Yes   No

MONEYS RECEIVED BASIS OF ACCOUNTING - GOODS AND SERVICES *[Note 6]*
Is application being made for the "moneys received" basis ? Tick (✓) appropriate box   Yes   No
If the reply is "Yes", is it being made because expected turnover
(a) will be less than £250,000   Tick (✓)
or   appropriate
(b) to non-registered persons will exceed 90% of total turnover   box

EUROPEAN UNION/NON-EUROPEAN UNION TRADE
Does the applicant anticipate being engaged in
TRADE WITHIN THE EU: ACQUISITIONS   SUPPLIES   [If the answer
is "yes" tick (✓)
NON-EU TRADE: IMPORTS   EXPORTS   appropriate box(es)]

RELATED BUSINESS(ES) *[Note 7]*
If the secretary or any director of the applicant company is now or has been involved as secretary/director/sole proprietor/partner in any other VAT-registered business, during the last two years,tick (✓) appropriate box   Yes   No

If the answer is "Yes", state   (a) the name of the business
and
(b) the VAT registration number(s).

IF A FOREIGN BUSINESS REGISTERING IN THIS STATE:-
State the anticipated annual turnover from supplies of taxable goods or services
within the State £

PRINCIPAL BANK ACCOUNT
Bank and Branch
Account Number

DO YOU OWN OR RENT YOUR BUSINESS PREMISES ?   Tick (✓) appropriate box Owned   Rented
If the business premises are rented, please state:
The name and address of the Landlord
(not an estate agent or rent collector)
The amount of rent paid £   per week, month, year (state which)
The date on which you started paying the rent
The length of the agreed rental/lease period

IS THE BUSINESS NEW or ACQUIRED FROM A PREVIOUS OWNER ? Tick (✓) appropriate box New   Acquired
If acquired from a previous owner, please state:
The name of the person from whom you acquired it and
the present address of that person

The VAT number of that person

CORRESPONDENCE ON VAT MATTERS *[Note 3(b)]*
If correspondence relating to VAT is being dealt with by an agent,
please (✓) this box   and give the name and address if
different to the Accountant/Adviser named in Part B.

NOTES TO ASSIST YOU IN COMPLETING FORM TR1

GENERAL

This Form can be used to register a person (other than a company or a PAYE employee) for Income Tax (non-PAYE), as an employer and/or VAT, in one operation. [Companies requiring to register should complete Form TR2. PAYE employees taking up their first employment should complete Form 12A.]
Please read the Form through **BEFORE** completing any of the Sections in it. You may find that only part of it will need to be filled up.

NOTE 1 REGISTRATION

To register for Income Tax (non-PAYE) only   - Please complete Parts A, B + C
To register for PAYE/PRSI only   - Please complete Parts A, B + D
To register for VAT only   - Please complete Parts A, B + E
To register for ALL taxes   - Please complete Parts A, B, C, D + E

NOTE 2 NAME

The name to be entered here is the full name of the person (including a trust, club or society) wishing to be registered.

NOTE 3 ACCOUNTANT / TAX ADVISER

(a)   The entry here is in respect of the applicant's accountant/tax adviser who will prepare the trading accounts and tax returns of the business.

(b)   Where a different person from the accountant etc. at (a) handles matters relating to PAYE and/or VAT, please supply the name(s) and address(es) in the space(s) provided under the PAYE & VAT sections of the form. This will enable the tax office to direct relevant correspondence to the appropriate person.

NOTE 4 ELECTION TO BE A TAXABLE PERSON

A person can choose to be a taxable person for VAT, even though not obliged by law to become registered. (Registration is required when turnover has exceeded, or is likely to exceed, the limits prescribed by law.)

NOTE 5 EXEMPTION WAIVER

A person can choose to become a taxable person for VAT in respect of certain lettings of property even though the services provided are normally exempt from VAT.

NOTE 6 MONEYS RECEIVED BASIS OF ACCOUNTING - GOODS AND SERVICES

If at least 90% of the applicant's turnover comes from supplying goods or services to persons who are NOT registered - for example hospitals, schools or the general public - the applicant can be authorised to calculate the VAT payable on the basis of moneys actually received during the taxable period involved.

NOTE 7 RELATED BUSINESSES

If the applicant has been a non-proprietary director only, it will suffice to give the name(s), without the VAT number, of the company or companies concerned.

DECLARATION - Part A

Whatever Sections of the Form have been completed, the Declaration in Part A **MUST** be signed before an applicant may be registered for any tax

TAX REGISTRATION
FOR COMPANIES
TR2

*Persons, other than companies, requiring to register should complete Form TR1.
*PAYE taxpayers should complete Form 12A.
To register a company for Corporation Tax, Employer's PAYE/PRSI, or VAT please complete the relevant parts
(Parts A, B, C, D, E) of this form and return it to :

PART A

FOR WHICH TAXES DO YOU REQUIRE REGISTRATION ?   *[Note 1]*

[Tick (✓) appropriate box(es)]

Corporation Tax		**Employer's PAYE/PRSI**		**Value Added Tax**	
Complete Parts A, B + C	☐	Complete Parts A, B + D	☐	Complete Parts A, B + E	☐

The tax office may, in some circumstances, ask for additional information in relation to an application for VAT registration.

**If you have been previously registered for any tax and hold Tax Reference Numbers please
quote them in the following box(es)**

Tax reference (Corporation Tax) ⬚

Employer (PAYE/PRSI) ⬚

Value Added Tax ⬚

IF YOU REQUIRE YOUR TAX AFFAIRS TO BE DEALT WITH IN IRISH, PLEASE TICK (✓) HERE ☐

DECLARATION - which must be made in every case

I declare that the particulars supplied by me in this application are true in every respect.

NAME
(in BLOCK LETTERS)

SIGNATURE
*(To be signed by company secretary
or other officer authorised)*

DATE

PART B
BASIC INFORMATION

Name of Company *[Note 2]*
Business Address

Registered Office Address

Telephone No.

Telephone No.

Fax No.

Fax No.

IRISH REGISTERED COMPANY - Please give the following information:

Companies Registration Office Number

Date company was registered

Directors - Give the following information in relation to each director:

Name

Address

RSI Number

(If necessary, use a separate sheet for details of any further directors)

Does any shareholder have 50% or more beneficial interest in the issued capital ?

Tick (✓) appropriate box   **YES**   **NO**

If the answer is yes, state
Name of Shareholder
Address
(If already included above as a director, simply state the name here)

Percentage of Shareholding   %

RSI Number
(unless given above)

Company Secretary: State the company secretary's name address and RSI number (if already included above as a director, simply state the company secretary's name here.)

Name

Address

RSI Number

Details of Accountant, Tax Adviser, if any *[Note 3(a)]*

Name

Address

Tel. No.   **Fax No.**

SUB-CONTRACTORS
If the business is that of Building/Construction/Forestry/Meat Processing do you use Sub-contractors ?

Tick (✓) appropriate box   **YES**   **NO**

FOREIGN REGISTERED COMPANY - Please give the following information
(i)   Address in this State of Fixed Place of Business, if any
(ii)   Is Trading Stock held at this address ?   Tick (✓) appropriate box   **YES**   **NO**
(iii)   State at what address in this State the company's books and records will be produced for inspection by Revenue officials

PART B
BASIC INFORMATION (Contd.)

WHAT IS THE COMPANY'S MAIN BUSINESS OR ACTIVITY ? Please give a precise description of the business/activity carried on/about to be carried on, for example "Draper", "Hairdresser", "Textile Manufacturer" "Property Letting" "Investment Income" etc. (Do not use general terms such as "Shopkeeper", "Manufacturer" etc.)

Please also tick (✓) one of the following nine boxes to indicate the one which most closely classifies the business/activity:

Retailing		Wholesaling		Manufacturing	
Building and Construction		Banking, Insurance and Building Society		Hotel and Catering	
Other Private Business		Public Body		Other Activity	

WHEN DID THE BUSINESS /ACTIVITY COMMENCE ?

TO WHAT DATE WILL ANNUAL ACCOUNTS BE MADE UP ?

PART C
REGISTRATION FOR CORPORATION TAX

If you wish to register the company for Corporation Tax please tick (✓) here

PART D
REGISTRATION AS AN EMPLOYER FOR PAYE/PRSI

DATE
State:
(a) the date from which Registration is required

(b) the date the first employee commenced or will commence

EMPLOYEES (including Directors)
State:
(i) Number of Directors   (ii) Number of employees, other than Directors

PAYROLL AND PAYE / PRSI RECORDS SYSTEM
Enter a tick (✓) for System used

Tax Deduction Cards (Official)   Other Manual System   Computer System

Note: If you intend to use a manual or computerised system you will be contacted by the Revenue Commissioners (P35 Section), Government Offices, Nenagh, Co. Tipperary, to ensure that the system you intend to use satisfies Revenue requirements. You may not use such a system without getting Revenue approval.

CORRESPONDENCE ON PAYE/PRSI *[Note 3(b)]*
If correspondence relating to PAYE/PRSI is being dealt with by an agent, please tick (✓) this box and give the agent's name and address if different to the Accountant/Adviser named in Part B

PART E
REGISTRATION FOR VAT

REGISTRATION
(i)   State the date from which Registration is required

(ii)   Is registration being sought because turnover exceeds, or is likely to exceed, the limits
prescribed by law for registration?   Tick (✓) appropriate box   Yes   No

(iii) If the answer to (ii) is "Yes", please enter expected turnover for the next 12 months   £

(iv) Is registration being sought only in respect of European Union (EU) acquisitions   Yes   No
                                          (farmer/non-taxable entity)?

ELECTION TO BE A TAXABLE PERSON *[Note 4]*
Is the applicant electing to be a taxable person?   Tick (✓) appropriate box   Yes   No

EXEMPTION WAIVER *[Note 5]*
Does the applicant wish to waive exemption from VAT in respect of the letting of property?:
                                          Tick (✓) appropriate box   Yes   No

MONEYS RECEIVED BASIS OF ACCOUNTING - GOODS AND SERVICES *[Note 6]*
Is application for the "moneys received" basis being made?   Tick (✓) appropriate box   Yes   No
If the reply is "Yes", is it being made because expected turnover
   (a)   will be less than £250,000   Tick (✓)
               or   appropriate
   (b)   to non-registered persons will exceed 90% of total turnover   box

EUROPEAN UNION/NON-EUROPEAN UNION TRADE
Does the applicant anticipate being engaged in
    TRADE WITHIN THE EU: ACQUISITIONS   SUPPLIES   [If the answer is "yes"
                                                                 tick (✓) appropriate box(es)]
    NON-EU TRADE: IMPORTS   EXPORTS

RELATED BUSINESS(ES) *[Note 7]*
If the applicant is now (or has been during the last two years) a director, secretary,
sole proprietor or partner of any VAT-registered business tick (✓) appropriate box   Yes   No

If the answer is "Yes", state   (a) the name of the business
                           and
                           (b) the VAT registration number(s).

IF A FOREIGN BUSINESS REGISTERING IN THIS STATE :-
State the expected annual turnover from supplies of taxable goods or services
within the State £

PRINCIPAL BANK ACCOUNT
Bank and Branch
Account Number

DO YOU OWN OR RENT YOUR BUSINESS PREMISES ? Tick (✓) appropriate box   Owned   Rented
If the business premises are rented, please state:
    The name and address of the Landlord
    (not an estate agent or rent collector)

    The amount of rent paid £   per week, month, year (state which)
    The date on which you started paying the rent
    The length of the agreed rental/lease period

IS THE BUSINESS NEW or ACQUIRED FROM A PREVIOUS OWNER ? Tick (✓) appropriate box New   Acquired
If acquired from a previous owner, please state:
    The name of the person from whom you acquired it and
    the present address of that person

    The VAT number of that person

CORRESPONDENCE ON VAT MATTERS *[Note 3(b)]*
If correspondence relating to VAT is being dealt with by an agent,
please (✓) this box   and give the name and address if
different to the Accountant/Adviser named in Part B.

NOTES TO ASSIST YOU IN COMPLETING FORM TR2

GENERAL

This Form can be used to register a Limited company for Corporation Tax, Employer's PAYE/PRSI and/or VAT, in one operation. [Persons, other than companies, requiring to register should complete Form TR1. PAYE taxpayers registering for the **first time** should complete Form 12A.]

Please read the Form through **BEFORE** completing any of the Sections in it. You may find that only part of it will need to be filled up, to get the Registration you require.

NOTE 1 REGISTRATION

To register for Corporation Tax only   - Please complete Parts A, B + C
To register for Employer's PAYE/PRSI only   - Please complete Parts A, B + D
To register for VAT only   - Please complete Parts A, B + E
To register for All Taxes   - Please complete Parts A, B, C, D + E

NOTE 2 NAME

The name to be entered here is the full name of the company under which it is registered under the Companies' Acts.

NOTE 3 ACCOUNTANT / TAX ADVISER

(a)   The entry here is in respect of the accountant/tax adviser who will prepare the trading accounts and tax returns of the company.

(b)   Where a different person from the accountant etc. at (a) handles matters relating to Employer's PAYE/PRSI and/or VAT, please supply the name(s) and address(es) in the space(s) provided under the Employer's PAYE/PRSI & VAT sections of the form. This will enable the tax office to direct relevant correspondence to the appropriate person.

NOTE 4 ELECTION TO BE A TAXABLE PERSON

A company can choose to be a taxable person for VAT, even though not obliged by law to become registered. (Registration is required when turnover has exceeded, or is likely to exceed, the limits prescribed by law.)

NOTE 5 EXEMPTION WAIVER

A company can choose to become a taxable person for VAT in respect of certain lettings of premises even though the services provided are normally exempt from VAT.

NOTE 6 MONEYS RECEIVED BASIS OF ACCOUNTING - GOODS AND SERVICES

If at least 90% of the company's turnover comes from supplying goods or services to persons who are NOT registered - for example hospitals, schools or the general public - it can be authorised to calculate its own VAT payable on the basis of moneys received by it during the taxable period involved.

NOTE 7 RELATED BUSINESSES

If the secretary or any director of the company has been a non-proprietary director only, it will suffice to give the name(s), without the VAT number, of the company or companies concerned.

DECLARATION - Part A

Whatever Sections of the Form have been completed, the Declaration in Part A **MUST** be signed before a company may be registered for any tax.

8. STANDARD LAW SOCIETY CONTRACT FOR SALE
[1995 EDITION]

WARNING: IT IS RECOMMENDED THAT THE WITHIN SHOULD NOT BE
COMPLETED WITHOUT PRIOR LEGAL ADVICE

LAW SOCIETY OF IRELAND

GENERAL CONDITIONS OF SALE (1995 EDITION)

PARTICULARS
and
CONDITIONS OF SALE
of

*SALE BY PRIVATE TREATY
*SALE BY AUCTION

to be held at

on   the   day of,   , 199

at   o'clock

* Auctioneer:

Address:

Vendor:

Vendor's Solicitor:

Address:

Reference:

---
* Delete, if inappropriate

I   being the Spouse of the under-named Vendor hereby, for the purposes of Section 3, Family Home Protection Act, 1976, consent to the proposed sale of the property described in the within Particulars at the price mentioned below.

SIGNED by the said Spouse
in the presence of:

MEMORANDUM OF AGREEMENT made this   day of   199
BETWEEN

of

("VENDOR")

and

of

("PURCHASER")

whereby it is agreed that the Vendor shall sell and the Purchaser shall purchase in accordance with the annexed Special and General Conditions of Sale the property described in the within Particulars at the purchase price mentioned below.

Purchase Price   £   Closing Date:

less deposit   £ _____   Interest Rate: per cent per annum

Balance   £ _____

SIGNED   _____   SIGNED   _____

           _____   _____
                        (Vendor)   (Purchaser)

Witness   _____   Witness   _____

Occupation _____   Occupation _____

Address   _____   Address   _____

(for Sale by   As Stakeholder I/We acknowledge receipt of Bank Draft/Cheque for £
Auction)   in respect of deposit.

                        SIGNED   _____

PARTICULARS AND TENURE

DOCUMENTS SCHEDULE

SEARCHES SCHEDULE

1. Negative Search in the Registry of Deeds on the Index of Names only for all acts affecting the subject property by the Vendor fromthe   day of

   and

SPECIAL CONDITIONS

1. Save where the context otherwise requires or implies or the text hereof expresses to the contrary, the definitions and provisions as to interpretation set forth in the within General Conditions shall be applied for the purposes of these Special Conditions.

2. The said General Conditions shall:

    (a) apply to the sale in so far as the same are not hereby altered or varied, and these Special Conditions shall prevail in case of any conflict between them and the General Conditions

    (b) be read and construed without regard to any amendment therein, unless such amendment shall be referred to specifically in these Special Conditions.

(Delete if inappropriate)

3. In addition to the purchase price, the Purchaser shall pay to the Vendor an amount equivalent to such Value-Added Tax as shall be exigible in relation to the sale or (as the case may be) the Assurance same to be calculated in accordance with the provisions of the Value-Added Tax Act, 1972, and to be paid on completion of the sale or forthwith upon receipt by the Purchaser of an appropriate invoice (whichever shall be the later).

NOTE: These General Conditions are not to be altered in any manner. Any required variation or addition should be dealt with by way of Special Condition.

           Special Conditions should be utilised in instances where it is required to adopt Recommendations or Advices of the Law Society or of any Committee associated with it, where such Recommendations or Advices are at variance with provisions expressed in the General Conditions.

GENERAL CONDITIONS OF SALE

DEFINITIONS

1.   In these General Conditions:

"the Conditions" means the attached Special Conditions and these General Conditions

"the Documents Schedule", *"the Searches Schedule"* and *"the Special Conditions"* mean respectively the attached Documents Schedule, Searches Schedule and Special Conditions.

"the Memorandum" means the Memorandum of Agreement on Page 1 hereof

"the Particulars" means the Particulars and Tenure on Page 2 hereof and any extension of the same

"the Purchaser" means the party identified as such in the Memorandum

"the sale" means the transaction evidenced by the Memorandum, the Particulars and the Conditions

"the subject property" means the property or interest in property which is the subject of the sale

"the Vendor" means the party identified as such in the Memorandum.

2.   In the Conditions save where the context otherwise requires or implies:

"Apportionment Date" means either (a) the later of (i) the closing date (as defined hereunder) and (ii) such subsequent date from which delay in completing the sale shall cease to be attributable to default on the part of the Vendor or (b) in the event of the Vendor exercising the right referred to in Condition 25 (a) (ii) hereunder, the date of actual completion of the sale or (c) such other date as may be agreed by the Vendor and the Purchaser to be the Apportionment Date for the purpose of this definition

"Assurance" means the document or documents whereby the sale is to be carried into effect

"closing date" means the date specified as such in the Memorandum, or, if no date is specified, the first working day after the expiration of five weeks computed from the date of sale

"Competent Authority" includes the State, any Minister thereof, Government Department, State Authority, Local Authority, Planning Authority, Sanitary Authority, Building Control Authority, Fire Authority, Statutory Undertaker or any Department, Body or person by statutory provision or order for the time being in force authorised directly or indirectly to control, regulate, modify or restrict the development, use or servicing of land or buildings, or empowered to acquire land by compulsory process

"date of sale" means the date of the auction when the sale shall have been by auction, and otherwise means the date upon which the contract for the sale shall have become binding on the Vendor and the Purchaser

"development" has the same meaning as that conferred by the Local Government (Planning and Development) Act, 1963

"lease" includes (a) a fee farm grant and every contract (whether or not in writing or howsoever effected, derived or evidenced) whereby the relationship of Landlord and Tenant is or is intended to be created and whether for any freehold or leasehold estate or interest and (b) licences and agreements relating to the occupation and use of land, cognate words being construed accordingly

"purchased chattels" means such chattels, fittings, tenant's fixtures and other items as are included in the sale

"purchase price" means the purchase price specified in the Memorandum PROVIDED HOWEVER that, if the sale provides for additional moneys to be paid by the Purchaser for goodwill, crops or purchased chattels, the expression *"purchase price"* shall be extended to include such additional moneys

"Requisitions" include Requisitions on the title or titles as such of the subject property and with regard to rents, outgoings, rights, covenants, conditions, liabilities (actual or potential), planning and kindred matters and taxation issues material to such property

"stipulated interest rate" means the interest rate specified in the Memorandum, or, if no rate is so specified, such rate as shall equate to 4 per centum per annum over the rate (as annualised) of interest payable upon tax chargeable under the Capital Acquisitions Tax Act, 1976 and ruling at the date from which interest hereunder is to run

"working day" does not include any Saturday, Sunday nor any Bank or Public Holiday nor any of the seven days immediately succeeding Christmas Day.

INTERPRETATION

3. In the Conditions save where the context otherwise requires or implies:

Words importing the masculine gender only include the feminine, neuter and common genders, and words importing the singular number only include the plural number and vice versa

The words "Vendor" and "Purchaser" respectively include (where appropriate) parties deriving title under them or either of them and shall apply to any one or more of several Vendors and Purchasers as the case may be and so that the stipulations in the Conditions contained shall be capable of being enforced on a joint and several basis

Unless the contrary appears, any reference hereunder:

(a) to a particular Condition shall be to such of these General Conditions of Sale as is identified by said reference

(b) to a Statute or Regulation or a combination of Statutes or Regulations shall include any extension, amendment, modification or re-enactment thereof, and any Rule, Regulation, Order or Instrument made thereunder, and for the time being in force

Headings and marginal notes inserted in the Conditions shall not affect the construction thereof nor shall the same have any contractual significance.

AUCTION

4.   Where the sale is by auction, the following provisions shall apply:

    (a)   the Vendor may divide the property set forth in the Particulars into lots and subdivide, consolidate or alter the order of sale of any lots

    (b)   there shall be a reserve price for the subject property whether the same shall comprise the whole or any part of the property set forth in the Particulars and the Auctioneer may refuse to accept any bid. If any dispute shall arise as to any bidding, the Auctioneer shall (at his option) either determine the dispute or again put up the property in question at the last undisputed bid. No person shall advance at a bidding a sum less than that fixed by the Auctioneer, and no accepted bid shall be retracted. Subject to the foregoing, the highest accepted bidder shall be the Purchaser

    (c)   the Vendor may:

       (i)   bid himself or by an agent up to the reserve price

       (ii)   withdraw the whole of the property set forth in the Particulars or, where such property has been divided into lots, withdraw any one or more of such lots at any time before the same has been sold without disclosing the reserve price

    (d)   the Purchaser shall forthwith pay to the Vendor's Solicitor as stakeholder a deposit of ten per centum (10%) of the purchase price in part payment thereof, and shall execute an agreement in the form of the Memorandum to complete the purchase of the subject property in accordance with the Conditions.

PRIVATE TREATY SALE

5.   (a)   where the sale is by private treaty, the Purchaser shall on or before the date of the sale pay to the Vendor's Solicitor as stakeholder a deposit of the amount stated in the Memorandum in part payment of purchase price

    (b)   if notwithstanding Condition 5(a), a part of such deposit has been or is paid to any other person appointed or nominated by the Vendor that other person shall be deemed to receive or to have received said part as stakeholder

THE FOLLOWING CONDITIONS APPLY WHETHER THE SALE IS BY AUCTION OR BY PRIVATE TREATY

PURCHASER ON NOTICE OF CERTAIN DOCUMENTS

6.   The documents specified in the Documents Schedule or copies thereof have been available for inspection by the Purchaser or his Solicitor prior to the sale. If all or any of the subject property is stated in the Particulars or in the Special Conditions to be held under a lease or to be subject to any covenants, conditions, rights, liabilities or restrictions, and the lease or other document containing the same is specified in the Documents Schedule, the Purchaser, whether availing of such opportunity of inspection or not, shall be deemed to have purchased with full knowledge of the contents thereof, notwithstanding any partial statement of such contents in the Particulars or in the Conditions.

DELIVERY OF TITLE

7. Within seven working days from the date of sale, the Vendor shall deliver or send by post to the Purchaser or his Solicitor copies of the documents necessary to vouch the title to be shown in accordance with the Conditions.

TITLE

8. (a) The Title to be shown to the subject property shall be such as is set forth in the Special Conditions

    (b) Where the title to be shown to the whole or any part of the subject property is based on possession, the Vendor shall, in addition to vouching that title and dealing with such further matters as are required of him by the Conditions, furnish to the Purchaser on or before completion of the sale a certificate from the Revenue Commissioners to the effect (i) that the subject property or (as the case may be) such part of the same as aforesaid is not charged with any of the taxes covered by the provisions of Section 146, Finance Act, 1994 or (ii) that the Revenue Commissioners are satisfied that any such charge will be discharged within a time considered by them to be reasonable

    (c) Save as stipulated in the Special Conditions the Vendor shall, prior to or at the completion of the sale, discharge all mortgages and charges for the payment of money (other than items apportionable under Condition 27(b)) which affect the subject property.

9. Where any of the subject property is held under a lease, the Purchaser shall not call for or investigate the title of the grantor or lessor to make the same, but shall conclusively assume that it was well and validly made, and is a valid and subsisting lease.

10. Where any of the subject property is stated to be held under a lease or an agreement therefor then:

    (a) no Objection or Requisition shall be made or indemnity required on account of such lease or agreement being (if such is the case) a sub-lease or agreement therefor, or on account of any superior lease comprising other property apart from the subject property or reserving a larger rent, or on the ground of any superior owner not having concurred in any apportionment or exclusive charge of rent

    (b) no Objection or Requisition shall be made by reason of any discrepancy between the covenants, conditions and provisions contained in any sub-lease and those in any superior lease, unless such as could give rise to forfeiture or a right of re-entry

    (c) the production of the receipt for the last gale of rent reserved by the lease or agreement therefor, under which the whole or any part of the subject property is held, (without proof of the title or authority of the person giving such receipt) shall (unless the contrary appears) be accepted as conclusive evidence that all rent accrued due has been paid and all covenants and conditions in such lease or agreement and in every (if any) superior lease have been duly performed and observed or any breaches thereof (past or continuing) effectively waived or sanctioned up to the actual completion of the sale, whether or not it shall appear that the lessor or reversioner was aware of such breaches. If the said rent (not being a rack rent) shall not have been paid in circumstances where the party entitled to receive the same is not known to the Vendor, or if the subject property is indemnified against payment of rent, the production of a Statutory Declaration so stating shall (unless the contrary appears) be accepted as such conclusive evidence, provided that the Declaration further indicates that no notices or rent demands have been served on or received by the Vendor under the lease or agreement on foot of which the subject property is held; that the Vendor has complied with all the covenants (other than those in respect of payment of rent) on the part of the lessee and the conditions contained in such lease or agreement, and that he is not aware of any breaches thereof either by himself or by any of his predecessors in title

(d) if any of the subject property is held under a lease or agreement for lease requiring consent to alienation, the Vendor shall apply for and endeavour to obtain such consent, and the Purchaser shall deal expeditiously and constructively with and shall satisfy all reasonable requirements of the lessor in relation to the application therefor, but the Vendor shall not be required to institute legal proceedings to enforce the issue of any such consent or otherwise as to the withholding of the same. If such consent shall have been refused or shall not have been procured and written evidence of the same furnished to the Purchaser on or before the closing date, or if any such consent is issued subject to a condition, which the Purchaser on reasonable grounds refuses to accept, either party may rescind the sale by seven days prior notice to the other.

PRIOR TITLE

11. (a) The title to the subject property prior to the date of the instrument specified in the Special Conditions as the commencement of title, whether or not appearing by recital, inference or otherwise, shall not be required, objected to or investigated.

(b) In the case of registered freehold or leasehold land registered under the Registration of Title Acts, 1891 to 1942 or the Registration of Title Act, 1964 the provisions of subparagraph (a) of this Condition shall apply without prejudice to Sections 52 and 115 of the last mentioned Act and shall not disentitle the Purchaser from investigating the possibility of there having been a voluntary disposition on the title within the period of twelve years immediately preceding the date of sale or a disposition falling within Section 121, Succession Act, 1965 and the Vendor shall be required to deal with all points properly taken in or arising out of such investigation.

INTERMEDIATE TITLE

12. Where in the Special Conditions it is provided that the title is to commence with a particular instrument and then to pass to a second instrument or to a specified event, the title intervening between the first instrument and the second instrument or the specified event, whether or not appearing by recital, inference or otherwise, shall not be required, objected to or investigated.

REGISTERED LAND

13. Where all or any of the subject property consists of freehold or leasehold registered land registered under the Registration of Title Acts, 1891 to 1942 ("the Acts of 1891 to 1942") or the Registration of Title Act, 1964 ("the Act of 1964") then:

(a) if the registration is subject to equities under the Acts of 1891 to 1942, the Purchaser shall not require the equities to be discharged, but the Vendor shall, with the copy documents to be delivered or sent in accordance with Condition 7, furnish sufficient evidence of title prior to first registration or otherwise to enable the Purchaser to procure their discharge

(b) if the registration is with a possessory title under the Act of 1964 the Purchaser shall not require the Vendor to be registered with an absolute title, but the Vendor shall, with the copy documents to be delivered or sent in accordance with Condition 7, furnish sufficient evidence of the title prior to such registration or otherwise to enable the Purchaser to be registered with an absolute title

(c) the Vendor shall, with the copy documents to be delivered or sent in accordance with Condition 7, furnish to the Purchaser a copy of the Land Registry Folio or Folios relating to the subject property written up-to-date (or as nearly as practicable up-to-date), together with a copy of the relevant Land Registry map or file plan

(d) the Vendor shall furnish a Statutory Declaration, by some person competent to make it, confirming that there are not in existence any burdens which under the Act of 1964 affect registered land without registration, save such (if any) as are specifically mentioned in the Particulars or the Special Conditions

(e) if the Land Certificate has been issued to the Land Commission or if no such Certificate has been issued, the Purchaser shall not be entitled to require such Certificate to be produced, handed over on completion or issued

(f) the Purchaser shall procure himself to be registered as owner of the subject property at his own expense

(g) In the event of the subject property being subject to a Land Purchase Annuity the Vendor shall, prior to completion, redeem the same or (as the case may be) such proportion thereof as may be allocated to the subject property

IDENTITY

14. The Purchaser shall accept such evidence of identity as may be gathered from the descriptions in the documents of title plus (if circumstances require) a Statutory Declaration to be made by a competent person, at the Purchaser's expense, that the subject property has been held and enjoyed for at least twelve years in accordance with the title shown. The Vendor shall be obliged to furnish such information as is in his possession relative to the identity and extent of the subject property, but shall not be required to define exact boundaries, fences, ditches, hedges or walls or to specify which (if any) of the same are of a party nature, nor shall the Vendor be required to identify parts of the subject property held under different titles.

RIGHTS - LIABILITIES - CONDITION OF SUBJECT PROPERTY

15. The Vendor shall disclose before the sale, in the Particulars, the Special Conditions or otherwise, all easements, rights, reservations, privileges, taxes and other liabilities (not already known to the Purchaser or apparent from inspection) which are known by the Vendor to affect the subject property or which are likely to affect it.

16. Subject to Condition 15, the Purchaser shall be deemed to buy:

(a) with full notice of the actual state and condition of the subject property

and

(b) subject to (i) all leases (if any) mentioned in the Particulars or in the Special Conditions and (ii) all easements, rights, reservations, privileges, liabilities, covenants, rents, outgoings and all incidents of tenure.

REQUISITIONS

17.   The Purchaser shall, within fourteen working days after the delivery of the copy documents of title in accordance with Condition 7, send to the Vendor's Solicitor a written statement of his Objections (if any) on the title and his Requisitions. Any Objection or Requisition not made within the time aforesaid and not going to the root of the title shall be deemed to have been waived. The Vendor's Replies to any Objections or Requisitions shall be answered by the Purchaser in writing within seven working days after the delivery thereof and so on toties quoties, and, if not so answered, shall be considered to have been accepted as satisfactory. In all respects time shall be deemed to be of the essence of this Condition.

18.   If the Purchaser shall make and insist on any Objection or Requisition as to the title, the Assurance to him or any other matter relating or incidental to the sale, which the Vendor shall, on the grounds of unreasonable delay or expense or other reasonable ground, be unable or unwilling to remove or comply with, the Vendor shall be at liberty (notwithstanding any intermediate negotiation or litigation or attempts to remove or comply with the same) by giving to the Purchaser or his Solicitor not less than five working days notice to rescind the sale. In that case, unless the Objection or Requisition in question shall in the meantime have been withdrawn, the sale shall be rescinded at the expiration of such notice.

SEARCHES

19.   The Purchaser shall be furnished with the searches (if any) specified in the Searches Schedule and any searches already in the Vendor's possession, which are relevant to the title or titles on offer. Any other searches required by the Purchaser must be obtained by him at his own expense. Where the Special Conditions provide that the title shall commence with a particular instrument and then pass to a second instrument or to a specified event, the Vendor shall not be obliged to explain and discharge any act which appears on a search covering the period between such particular instrument and the date of the second instrument or specified event, unless same goes to the root of the title. Subject as aforesaid the Vendor shall explain and discharge any acts appearing on Searches covering the period from the date stipulated or implied for the commencement of the title to the date of actual completion.

ASSURANCE

20.   Subject to the provisions of Paragraph 11, Schedule 4, Capital Gains Tax Act, 1975 (as substituted), and (if relevant) to those contained in Section 107, Finance Act, 1993 (in relation to Residential Property Tax) on payment of all moneys payable by him in respect of the sale, the Purchaser shall be entitled to a proper Assurance of the subject property from the Vendor and all other (if any) necessary parties, such Assurance to be prepared by and at the expense of the Purchaser. The draft thereof shall be submitted to the Vendor's Solicitor not less than seven working days, and the engrossment not less than four working days, before the closing date. The delivery of the said draft or engrossment shall not prejudice any outstanding Objection or Requisition validly made.

VACANT POSSESSION

21.   Subject to any provision to the contrary in the Particulars or in the Conditions or implied by the nature of the transaction, the Purchaser shall be entitled to vacant possession of the subject property on completion of the sale.

LEASES

22.   Where the subject property is sold subject to any lease, a copy of the same (or, if the provisions thereof have not been reduced to writing, such evidence of its nature and terms as the Vendor shall be able to supply) together with copies of any notices in the Vendor's possession served by or on the lessee shall, prior to the sale, be made available for inspection by the Purchaser or his Solicitor.

23.   Unless the Special Conditions provide to the contrary, the Purchaser shall be entitled to assume that, at the date of sale, the Lessee named in any such Lease (as is referred to in Condition 22) is still the Lessee; that there has been no variation in the terms and conditions of said Lease (other than such as may be evident from an inspection of the subject property or apparent from the Particulars or the documents furnished to the Purchaser prior to the sale), and that the said terms and conditions (save those pertaining to the actual state and condition of the subject property) have been complied with.

COMPLETION AND INTEREST

24.   (a)   The sale shall be completed and the balance of the purchase price paid by the Purchaser on or before the closing date

       (b)   Completion shall take place at the Office of the Vendor's Solicitor.

25.   (a)   If by reason of any default on the part of the Purchaser, the purchase shall not have been completed on or before the later of (a) the closing date or (b) such subsequent date whereafter delay in completing shall not be attributable to default on the part of the Vendor

              (i)   the Purchaser shall pay interest to the Vendor on the balance of the purchase price remaining unpaid at the stipulated interest rate for the period between the closing date (or as the case may be such subsequent date as aforesaid) and the date of actual completion of the sale. Such interest shall accrue from day to day and shall be payable before and after any judgment and

              (ii)   the Vendor shall in addition to being entitled to receive such interest, have the right to take the rents and profits less the outgoings of the subject property up to the date of the actual completion of the sale

       (b)   If the Vendor by reason of his default shall not be able, ready and willing to complete the sale on the closing date he shall thereafter give to the Purchaser at least five working days prior notice of a date upon which he shall be so able ready and willing and the Purchaser shall not before the expiration of that notice be deemed to be in default for the purpose of this Condition provided that no such notice shall be required if the Vendor is prevented from being able and ready to complete or to give said notice by reason of the act or default of the Purchaser.

26.   The submission of an Apportionment Account made up to a particular date or other corresponding step taken in anticipation of completing the sale shall not per se preclude the Vendor from exercising his rights under the provisions of Condition 25 and in the event of such exercise the said Apportionment Account or the said other corresponding step shall (if appropriate) be deemed not to have been furnished or taken, and the Vendor shall be entitled to furnish a further Apportionment Account.

APPORTIONMENT AND POSSESSION

27.   (a)   Subject to the stipulations contained in the Conditions, the Purchaser, on paying the

purchase price, shall be entitled to vacant possession of the subject property or (as the case may be) the rents and profits thereout with effect from the Apportionment Date

(b)   All rents, profits, rates, taxes, outgoings and moneys (including rent, outgoings and money payable in advance but not including impositions derived from hypothecation) referable to the subject property shall for the purpose of this Condition, be apportioned (whether apportionable by law or not) on a day to day basis as at the Apportionment Date, up to which the liability for or the entitlement to the same shall (subject to apportionment as aforesaid to accord with the position obtaining as to moneys paid or due at such date) be for the account of the Vendor and thereafter for that of the Purchaser provided that if completion shall have been delayed through the default of the Vendor the Purchaser may opt for apportionment under this Condition as at the closing date or at the date at which the Purchaser (if also in default) shall have ceased to have been so in default whichever shall be the later

(c)   In the implementation of this Condition the Vendor shall be regarded as being the owner of the subject property until midnight on such date as is appropriate for apportionment purposes

(d)   The balance of the purchase price shall (where appropriate) be adjusted upwards or downwards to accommodate apportionments calculated pursuant to this Condition and the expression "balance of the purchase price" where used in the Conditions shall be construed accordingly

(e)   To the extent that same shall be unknown at the Apportionment Date (or shall not then be readily ascertainable) amounts to be apportioned hereunder - including any amount apportionable pursuant to Condition 27 (f) - shall be apportioned provisionally on a fair estimate thereof, and, upon ascertainment of the actual figures, a final apportionment shall be made, and the difference between it and the provisional apportionment shall be refunded by the Vendor or the Purchaser (as the case may be) to the other within ten working days of the liable party becoming aware of the amount of such difference

(f)   Excise and kindred duties payable in respect of the subject property or any licence attached thereto shall be apportioned on a day to day basis as at the Apportionment Date up to which the liability for the same shall be for the account of the Vendor and thereafter for that of the Purchaser and Condition 27 (c) shall apply for the purposes of such apportionment.

SECTION 45, LAND ACT, 1965

28.   Where Section 45, Land Act, 1965 applies, the Purchaser shall, at his own expense, procure any such Certificate or Consent as may be necessary thereunder for the vesting of the subject property in him or his nominee and the sale is not conditional upon such consent being obtained.

COMPULSORY REGISTRATION

29.   (a)   If all or any of the subject property is unregistered land the registration of which was compulsory prior to the date of sale the Vendor shall be obliged to procure such registration prior to completion of the sale

(b)   If all or any of the subject property is unregistered land, the registration of which shall become compulsory at or subsequent to the date of sale, the Vendor shall not be under any obligation to procure such registration but shall at or prior to such completion furnish to the Purchaser a Map of the subject property complying with the requirements of the Land Registry as then recognised and further the Vendor shall, if so requested within two years after completion of the sale, by and at the expense of the Purchaser, supply any additional information, which he may reasonably be able to supply, and produce and furnish any documents in his possession that may be required to effect such registration.

SIGNING "IN TRUST" OR "AS AGENT"

30.   A Purchaser who signs the Memorandum "in Trust", "as Trustee" or "as Agent", or with any similar qualification or description without therein specifying the identity of the principal or other party for whom he so signs, shall be personally liable to complete the sale, and to fulfil all such further stipulations on the part of the Purchaser as are contained in the Conditions, unless and until he shall have disclosed to the Vendor the name of his principal or other such party.

FAILURE TO PAY DEPOSIT

31.   The failure by the Purchaser to pay in full the deposit hereinbefore specified as payable by him shall constitute a breach of condition entitling the Vendor to terminate the sale or to sue the Purchaser for damages or both but such entitlement shall be without prejudice to any rights otherwise available to the Vendor.

32.   In case a cheque taken for the deposit (having been presented and whether or not it has been re-presented) shall not have been honoured, then and on that account the Vendor may (without prejudice to any rights otherwise available to him) elect either:

(a)   to treat the Contract evidenced by the Memorandum, the Particulars and the Conditions as having been discharged by breach thereof on the Purchaser's part

or

(b)   to enforce payment of the deposit as a deposit by suing on the cheque or otherwise.

DIFFERENCES - ERRORS

33.   (a)   In this Condition "error" includes any omission, non-disclosure, discrepancy, difference, inaccuracy, mis-statement or mis-representation made in the Memorandum, the Particulars or the Conditions or in the course of any representation, response or negotiations leading to the sale, and whether in respect of measurements, quantities, descriptions or otherwise

(b)   The Purchaser shall be entitled to be compensated by the Vendor for any loss suffered by the Purchaser in his bargain relative to the sale as a result of an error made by or on behalf of the Vendor provided however that no compensation shall be payable for loss of trifling materiality unless attributable to recklessness or fraud on the part of the Vendor nor in respect of any matter of which the Purchaser shall be deemed to have had notice under Condition 16(a) nor in relation to any error in a location or similar plan furnished for identification only

(c)   Nothing in the Memorandum, the Particulars or the Conditions shall:

(i)   entitle the Vendor to require the Purchaser to accept property which differs substantially from the property agreed to be sold whether in quantity, quality, tenure or otherwise, if the Purchaser would be prejudiced materially by reason of any such difference

or

(ii) affect the right of the Purchaser to rescind or repudiate the sale where compensation for a claim attributable to a material error made by or on behalf of the Vendor cannot be reasonably assessed

(d) Save as aforesaid, no error shall annul the sale or entitle the Vendor or the Purchaser (as the case maybe) to be discharged therefrom.

DOCUMENTS OF TITLE RELATING TO OTHER PROPERTY

34. (a) Documents of title relating to other property as well as to the subject property shall be retained by the Vendor or other person entitled to the possession thereof

(b) where the property is sold in lots, all documents of title relating to more than one lot shall be retained by the Vendor, until the completion of the sales of all the lots comprised in such documents, and shall then (unless they also relate to any property retained by the Vendor) be handed over to such of the Purchasers as the Vendor shall consider best entitled thereto

(c) the Vendor shall give to the Purchaser (and where the property is sold in lots, to the Purchaser of each lot) certified copies of all documents retained under this Condition and pertinent to the title to be furnished (other than documents of record, of which plain copies only will be given)

(d) subject as hereinafter provided, the Vendor shall give the usual statutory acknowledgement of the right of production and undertaking for safe custody of all documents (other than documents of record) retained by him under this Condition and pertinent to the title to be furnished. Such acknowledgement and undertaking shall be prepared by and at the expense of the Purchaser

(e) if the Vendor is retaining any unregistered land held wholly or partly under the same title as the subject property, the Assurance shall be engrossed in duplicate by and at the expense of the Purchaser, who shall deliver to the Vendor the Counterpart thereof, same having been stamped and registered and (if appropriate) executed by the Purchaser.

DISCLOSURE OF NOTICES

35. Where prior to the sale

(a) any closing, demolition or clearance Order

or

(b) any notice (not being of the contents of the Development Plan other than an actual or proposed designation of all or any part of the subject property for compulsory acquisition)

made or issued by or at the behest of a Competent Authority in respect of the subject property and affecting same at the date of sale has been notified or given to the Vendor (whether personally or by advertisement or posting on the subject property or in any other manner) or is otherwise known to the Vendor or where the subject property is at the date of sale affected by any award or grant which is or may be repayable by the Vendor's successor in title then if the Vendor fails to show

(i) that, before the sale, the Purchaser received notice or was aware of the matter in question

or

(ii) that same is no longer applicable or material

or

(iii) that same does not prejudicially affect the value of the subject property

or

(iv) that the subject thereof can and will be dealt with fully in the Apportionment Account

the Purchaser may by notice given to the Vendor rescind the sale.

DEVELOPMENT

36. (a) Unless the Special Conditions contain a provision to the contrary, the Vendor warrants:

In cases where property is affected by an unauthorised development or a breach of Condition/ Conditions in a Permission/ Approval amounting to a non-conforming development or where the Bye-Law Amnesty covered by Section 22(7), Building Control Act, 1990 is relevant, it is recommended that same be dealt with expressly by Special Condition.

(1) either

(i) that there has been no development (which term includes material change of use) of, or execution of works on or to, the subject property since the 1st day of October, 1964, for which Planning Permission or Building Bye-Law Approval was required by law

or

(ii) that all Planning Permissions and Building Bye-Law Approvals required by law for the development of, or the execution of works on or to, the subject property as at the date of sale, or for any change in the use thereof at that date were obtained (save in respect of matters of trifling materiality), and that, where implemented, the conditions thereof and the conditions expressly notified with said Permissions by any Competent Authority in relation to and specifically addressed to such development or works were complied with substantially

and

(2) that no claim for compensation has ever been made under Part III, Local Government (Planning and Development) Act, 1990

provided however that the foregoing warranty shall not extend to (and the Vendor shall not be required to establish) the obtaining of Approvals under the Building Bye-Laws or compliance with such Bye-Laws in respect of development or works executed prior to the 1st day of October, 1964.

(b) The Vendor shall, with the copy documents to be delivered or sent in accordance with Condition 7, furnish to the Purchaser copies of all such Permissions and Approvals as are referred to in Condition 36(a) other than in the proviso thereto, and (where relevant) copies of all Fire Safety Certificates and (if available) Commencement Notices issued under Regulations made pursuant to the Building Control Act, 1990 and referable to the subject property.

(c) The Vendor shall, on or prior to completion of the sale, furnish to the Purchaser

(i) written confirmation from the Local Authority of compliance with all conditions involving financial contributions or the furnishing of bonds in any such Permission or Approval (other than those referred to in the said proviso) or alternatively formal confirmation from the Local Authority that the roads and other services abutting on the subject property have been taken in charge by it without requirement for payment of moneys in respect of the same

(ii) a Certificate or Opinion by an Architect or an Engineer (or other professionally qualified person competent so to certify or opine) confirming that, in relation to any such Permission or Approval (other than those referred to in the proviso aforesaid) the same relates to the subject property; that the development of the subject property has been carried out in substantial compliance therewith and that all conditions (other than financial conditions) thereof and all conditions expressly notified with said Permission by any Competent Authority and specifically directed to and materially affecting the subject property or any part of the same have been complied with substantially (and, in the event of the subject property forming part of a larger development, so far as was reasonably possible in the context of such development).

(d) Unless the Special Conditions contain a stipulation to the contrary, the Vendor warrants in all cases where the provisions of the Building Control Act, 1990 or of any Regulations from time to time made thereunder apply to the design or development of the subject property or any part of the same or any activities in connection therewith, that there has been substantial compliance with the said provisions in so far as they shall have pertained to such design development or activities and the Vendor shall, on or prior to completion of the sale, furnish to the Purchaser a Certificate or Opinion by an Architect or an Engineer (or other professionally qualified person competent so to certify or opine) confirming such substantial compliance as aforesaid.

RESCISSION

37. Upon rescission of the sale in accordance with any of the provisions herein or in the Special Conditions contained or otherwise:

(a) the Purchaser shall be entitled to a return of his deposit (save where it shall lawfully have been forfeited) but without interest thereon

(b) the Purchaser shall remit to the Vendor all documents in his possession belonging to the Vendor and the Purchaser shall at his expense (save where Special Conditions otherwise provide) procure the cancellation of any entry relating to the sale in any register.

38. If any such deposit as is to be returned pursuant to Condition 37 shall not have been returned to the Purchaser within five working days from the date upon which the sale shall have been rescinded, the Purchaser shall be entitled to interest thereon at the stipulated interest rate from the expiration of the said period of five working days to the date upon which the deposit shall have been so returned.

39. The right to rescind shall not be lost by reason only of any intermediate negotiations or attempts to comply with or to remove the issue giving rise to the exercise of such right.

COMPLETION NOTICES

40. Save where time is of the essence in respect of the closing date, the following provisions shall apply:

    (a) if the sale be not completed on or before the closing date either party may on or after that date (unless the sale shall first have been rescinded or become void) give to the other party notice to complete the sale in accordance with this condition, but such notice shall be effective only if the party giving it shall then either be able, ready and willing to complete the sale or is not so able, ready or willing by reason of the default or misconduct of the other party

    (b) upon service of such notice the party upon whom it shall have been served shall complete the sale within a period of twenty-eight days after the date of such service (as defined in Condition 49 and excluding the date of service), and in respect of such period time shall be of the essence of the contract but without prejudice to any intermediate right of rescission by either party

    (c) the recipient of any such notice shall give to the party serving the same reasonable advice of his readiness to complete

    (d) if the Purchaser shall not comply with such a notice within the said period (or within any extension thereof which the Vendor may agree) he shall be deemed to have failed to comply with these Conditions in a material respect and the Vendor may enforce against the Purchaser, without further notice, such rights and remedies as may be available to the Vendor at law or in equity, or (without prejudice to such rights and remedies) may invoke and impose the provisions of Condition 41

    (e) if the Vendor does not comply with such a notice within the said period (or within any extension thereof which the Purchaser may agree), then the Purchaser may elect either to enforce against the Vendor, without further notice, such rights and remedies as may be available to the Purchaser at law or in equity or (without prejudice to any right of the Purchaser to damages) to give notice to the Vendor requiring a return to the Purchaser of all moneys paid by him, whether by way of deposit or otherwise, on account of the purchase price. Condition 38 shall apply to all moneys so to be returned, the period of five working days therein being computed from the date of the giving of such last mentioned notice. If the Purchaser gives such a notice and all the said moneys and interest (if any) are remitted to him, the Purchaser shall no longer be entitled to specific performance of the sale, and shall return forthwith all documents in his possession belonging to the Vendor, and (at the Vendor's expense) procure the cancellation of any entry relating to the sale in any register

    (f) the party serving a notice under this Condition may, at the request of or with the consent of the other party, by written communication to the other party extend the term of such notice for one or more specified periods of time, and, in that case, the term of the notice shall be deemed to expire on the last day of such extended period or periods, and the notice shall operate as though such extended period or periods, had been specified in this Condition in lieu of the said period of twenty-eight days, and time shall be of the essence in relation to such extended period

    (g) the Vendor shall not be deemed to be other than able, ready and willing to complete for the purposes of this Condition:

        (i) by reason of the fact that the subject property has been mortgaged or charged, provided that the funds (including the deposit) receivable on completion shall (after allowing for all prior claims thereon) be sufficient to discharge the aggregate of all amounts payable in satisfaction of such mortgages and charges to the extent that they relate to the subject property or

   (ii) by reason of being unable, not ready or unwilling at the date of service of such notice to deliver vacant possession of the subject property provided that (where it is a term of the sale that vacant possession thereof be given) the Vendor is, upon being given reasonable advice of the other party's intention to close the sale on a date within the said period of twenty-eight days or any extension thereof pursuant to Condition 40 (f), able, ready and willing to deliver vacant possession of the subject property on that date.

FORFEITURE OF DEPOSIT AND RESALE

41.   If the Purchaser shall fail in any material respect to comply with any of these Conditions, the Vendor (without prejudice to any rights or remedies available to him at law or in equity) shall be entitled to forfeit the deposit and shall be at liberty (without being obliged to tender an Assurance) to re-sell the subject property, with or without notice to the Purchaser, either by public auction or private treaty. In the event of the Vendor re-selling the subject property within one year after the closing date (or within one year computed from the expiration of any period by which the closing may have been extended pursuant to Condition 40) the deficiency (if any) arising on such re-sale and all costs and expenses attending the same or on any attempted re-sale shall (without prejudice to such damages to which the Vendor shall otherwise be entitled) be made good to the Vendor by the Purchaser, who shall be allowed credit against same for the deposit so forfeited. Any increase in price obtained by the Vendor on any re-sale, whenever effected, shall belong to the Vendor.

DAMAGES FOR DEFAULT

42.   Neither the Vendor nor the Purchaser, in whose favour an order for specific performance has been made, shall be precluded from an award of damages at law or in equity, in the event of such order not being complied with.

RISK

43.   Subject as hereinafter provided, the Vendor shall be liable for any loss or damage howsoever occasioned (other than by the Purchaser or his Agent) to the subject property (and the purchased chattels) between the date of sale and the actual completion of the sale BUT any such liability (including liability for consequential or resulting loss) shall not as to the amount thereof exceed the purchase price.

44.   The liability imposed on the Vendor by Condition 43 shall not apply:

   (a)   to inconsequential damage or insubstantial deterioration from reasonable wear and tear in the course of normal occupation and use, and not materially affecting value

   (b)   to damage occasioned by operations reasonably undertaken by the Vendor in his removal from, and vacation of the subject property, provided that the same are so undertaken with reasonable care

   (c)   where any such loss or damage has resulted from a requirement restriction or obligation imposed by a Competent Authority after the date of sale.

45.   Nothing in Conditions 43 and 44 shall affect:

   (a)   the Purchaser's right to specific performance in an appropriate case

(b) the Purchaser's right to rescind or repudiate the sale upon the Vendor's failure to deliver the subject property substantially in its condition at the date of sale (save where such failure shall have been occasioned by the Purchaser or his Agent)

(c) the operation of the doctrine of conversion

(d) the Purchaser's right to gains accruing to the subject property (or the purchased chattels) after the date of sale

(e) the Purchaser's right to effect on or after the date of sale his own insurance against loss or damage in respect of the subject property or any part of the same (or the purchased chattels)

(f) the rights and liabilities of parties other than the Vendor and the Purchaser

(g) the rights and liabilities of the Purchaser on foot of any lease subsisting at the date of sale, or of any arrangement whereby the Purchaser shall prior to the actual completion of the sale have been allowed into occupation of the subject property or any part thereof (or into possession of the purchased chattels).

CHATTELS

46. Unless otherwise disclosed to the Purchaser prior to the sale the Vendor warrants that, at the actual completion of the sale, all the purchased chattels shall be his unencumbered property and that same shall not be subject to any lease, rental hire, hire-purchase or credit sale agreement or chattel mortgage.

INSPECTION

47. The Vendor shall accede to all such requests as may be made by the Purchaser for the inspection on a reasonable number of occasions and at reasonable times of the subject property (and the purchased chattels).

NON-MERGER

48. Notwithstanding delivery of the Assurance of the subject property to the Purchaser on foot of the sale, all obligations and provisions designed to survive completion of the sale and all warranties in the Conditions contained, which shall not have been implemented by the said Assurance, and which shall be capable of continuing or taking effect after such completion, shall enure and remain in full force and effect.

NOTICES

49. Unless otherwise expressly provided, any notice to be given or served on foot of the Conditions shall be in writing, and may (in addition to any other prescribed mode of service) be given:

(a) by handing same to the intended recipient, and shall be deemed to have been delivered when so handed

(b) by directing it to the intended recipient, and delivering it by hand, or sending same by prepaid post to:

    (i) such address as shall have been advised by him to the party serving the notice as being that required by the intended recipient for the service of notices,

    or

    (ii) (failing such last mentioned advice) the address of the intended recipient as specified in the Memorandum,

    or

    (iii) (in the event of the intended recipient being a Company) its Registered Office for the time being,

    or

    (iv) the office of the Solicitor representing the intended recipient in relation to the sale

and any such notice shall be deemed to have been given or served, when delivered, at the time of delivery, and, when posted, at the expiration of three working days after the envelope containing the same, and properly addressed, was put in the post.

TIME LIMITS

50. Where the last day for taking any step on foot of the Conditions or any Notice served thereunder would, but for this provision, be a day other than a working day, such last day shall instead be the next following working day provided that for the purpose of this Condition the expression "working day" shall not be deemed to include (i) any Saturday, Sunday, Bank or Public Holiday nor (ii) any of the seven days immediately succeeding Christmas Day nor (iii) any day on which the registers or records wherein it shall be appropriate to make searches referable to the sale shall not be available to the public nor (iv) any day which shall be recognised by the Solicitors' Profession at large as being a day on which their offices are not open for business.

ARBITRATION

51. All differences and disputes between the Vendor and the Purchaser as to:

(a) whether a rent is or is not a rack rent for the purpose of Condition 10 (c), or

(b) as to whether any interest is payable pursuant to Condition 25 or as to the rate or amount thereof or the date from which it shall be exigible, or

(c) the identification of the Apportionment Date, or the treatment or quantification of any item pursuant to the provisions for apportionment in the Conditions, or

(d) any issue on foot of Condition 33, including the applicability of said Condition, and the amount of compensation payable thereunder, or

(e) the materiality of any matter for the purpose of Condition 36 (a), or

(f) the materiality of damage or any other question involving any of the provisions in Conditions 43, 44 and 45, including the amount of compensation (if any) payable, or

(g)   whether any particular item or thing is or is not included in the sale, or otherwise as to the nature or condition thereof

shall be submitted to arbitration by a sole Arbitrator to be appointed (in the absence of agreement between the Vendor and the Purchaser upon such appointment and on the application of either of them) by the President (or other Officer endowed with the functions of such President) for the time being of the Law Society of Ireland or (in the event of the President or other Officer as aforesaid being unable or unwilling to make the appointment) by the next senior Officer of that Society who is so able and willing to make the appointment and such arbitration shall be governed by the Arbitration Acts, 1954 and 1980 provided however that if the Arbitrator shall relinquish his appointment or die, or if it shall become apparent that for any reason he shall be unable or shall have become unfit or unsuited (whether because of bias or otherwise) to complete his duties, or if he shall be removed from office by Court Order, a substitute may be appointed in his place and in relation to any such appointment the procedures herein-before set forth shall be deemed to apply as though the substitution were an appointment de novo which said procedures may be repeated as many times as may be necessary.

LAW SOCIETY

OF

IRELAND

PARTICULARS

and

CONDITIONS OF SALE

(1995 Edition)

9. REQUEST FOR DEROGATION 4 MARCH 1997

Article 27 procedure
Request for derogation – Ireland
(97/C 67/04)

1. Introduction

1.1 This note deals with the major difficulties being encountered with VAT on property. To combat avoidance schemes, it seeks a derogation from the common VAT rules. Ireland has reviewed its system of VAT on property during 1996. The review shows that avoidance schemes are resulting in substantial amounts of VAT revenue being lost to the National Exchequer.

2. The Irish system of VAT on property

2.1 The short-term letting (that is of an interest of less than 10 years) of property is an exempt supply of services. The disposal of an interest (that is an interest of 10 years or more) in developed property is a taxable supply of goods. Where the disposal is by outright sale, the supplier must account for tax on the consideration payable. Sales of property do not usually give rise to avoidance schemes. Most of the avoidance schemes involve long-term leases.

2.2 Where a long-term lease (that is for 10 years or more) is created, the lease is treated as a supply of goods. VAT is chargeable on the market value of the lease. The lessor accounts for VAT on the market value. The lessee, if he is a taxable person, deducts this VAT in his VAT return. The lessor must also account for VAT on the value of his reversionary interest. The reversion of the property at the end of the lease is taxed as a self supply at the time of the creation of the lease. If the lease is for 20 years or more, the reversionary interest is valued at nil. The approach, therefore, is to treat the lessor as, in effect, totally disposing of his interest in the property. Any subsequent supply by the lessor of this property is not taxable unless it is re-developed.

2.3 Overall, the effect of Ireland's rules is that where a taxable person disposes of a developed building by long-term lease, VAT is chargeable on the open market value of the interest disposed of by him. If the person acquiring the interest is entitled to a deduction of the tax, he is liable to account for tax on any subsequent supply of that property.

2.4 As these taxation provisions were in place on 1 January 1977, Ireland was entitled to retain them in accordance with Article 27 (5) of the Sixth VAT Directive. In addition, Ireland implements the provisions of Article 28 (3) (a) to tax supplies of buildings in accordance with paragraph 11 of Annex E.

2.5 These special rules in relation to property were specifically introduced to prevent avoidance. Irish VAT law envisages that an exempt company needing new accommodation would contact a property developer to develop an office block. The developer develops a property and charges VAT on the development costs. As the client company is exempt, the VAT charge is a cost to it. It would be possible for the exempt company to minimize the up-front VAT charge by acquiring the office block by lease often from a related taxable company. Ireland's special VAT rules for property seek to prevent this by ensuring the VAT charge arises on the full value of the lease-hold interest at the time of the creation of the lease. This approach works perfectly where the lease runs its full course. However, the problem arise where the lease is 'broken' and a subsequent lease is created. It is this area, broken leases, which gives rise to the avoidance opportunities.

3. The avoidance schemes

3.1 The term 'broken' lease covers situations where the lessee opts out of the long-term lease through a variety of mechanisms. This allows the property to be disposed of to a third party. The avoidance schemes almost invariably mean that an exempt body takes possession of a VAT-free supply of property. This can best be illustrated by an example:

– a lessor develops property and claims back the VAT on the inputs,

– the lessor creates a 35-year lease to a taxable person,

– the lessor charges VAT on the open market value of the lease. The lessee deducts this VAT.

– after a year, the lessee abandons (one of the opt out mechanisms) the lease. Because the lessee has not met the terms of the lease, the lessor has vacant possession,

– the lessor sells the building to a fully exempt financial institution. Because he had fully disposed of the property when he created the original lease, this sale by him is not taxable and the lessee gets a developed property VAT free.

3.2 There are a number of variants of the avoidance schemes, but the common feature is the insertion of a taxable person with full deductibility between the lessor and the ultimate exempt company. This intermediate person usually has no assets. Frequently, the intermediary goes into liquidation as soon as the lease is broken. The actual surrender or assignment (other common opt-out mechanisms) of the lease is a taxable supply; and VAT should be charged on the open market value of the balance of the leasehold interest that is supplied.

3.3 Thus there are a number of ways in which a lessee can opt out of a lease:

– by assignment of the lease by the lessee to an assignee,

– by surrender of the lease by agreement between the lessor and the lessee. This would be followed by a disposal by the lessor through a further long-term lease, or by sake of the freehold, or

– by surrender of the lease without agreement. This could be by abandonment of the lease by the lessee or by ejection of the lessee by the lessor. Again, there would be a subsequent disposal of the interest by the lessor.

These circumstances can and do occur for valid commercial reasons. However, they are being artificially induced for VAT avoidance reasons.

4. The proposed solution

4.1 When a lease is broken the successful operation of the Irish VAT on property system requires that VAT is charged on the open market value of the balance of the leasehold interest that is supplied. However, as the supplier usually has no assets, a reverse charge mechanism on the recipient of the leasehold interest is essential for collection of the VAT debt.

4.2 A derogation is required from Article 21 (a) (a) which would provide for a reverse charge mechanism to apply to the surrender or assignment of a leasehold interest. The reverse charge would only apply where the recipient is:

(a) a taxable person with the rights of deduction;

(b) a person making exempt supplies in the course or furtherance of business;

and

(c) the State or local authorities.

5. Conclusion

5.1 The Irish request for a derogation accords with Article 27. It does not undermine the normal rules in Article 21 because our current valuation rules for property are themselves a derogation. The Irish authorities are aware that other Member States are experiencing difficulties in operating their systems of VAT on property. Ireland would welcome a review of the relevant provisions of the Sixth Directive and would participate actively in such a review. Pending an EU approach to the property issue, Ireland's main concern is to get the existing system to work as intended. To achieve this, the derogation measure is essential and, because of the losses to the national exchequer, the matter is urgent. Substantial amounts of tax revenue are being lost each year and this is likely to get worse unless action is taken.

5.2 Agreement to this request has no implications for other Member States in their treatment of property transactions for VAT.

10. DEROGATION
24 JULY 1997

COUNCIL DECISION OF 24 JULY 1997

authorising Ireland to apply a measure derogating from Article 21 of the Sixth Directive (77/388/EEC) on the harmonization of the laws of the Member States relating to turnover taxes

(97/510/EC)

THE COUNCIL OF THE EUROPEAN UNION

Having regard to the Treaty establishing the European Community,

Having regard to the Sixth Council Directive (77/388/EEC) of 17 May 1977 on the harmonization of the laws of the Member States relating to turnover taxes – Common system of value added tax: uniform basis of assessment[1], and in particular Article 27 thereof,

Having regard to the proposal from the Commission,

Whereas, under the terms of Article 27 (1) of Directive 77/388/EEC, the Council, acting unanimously on a proposal from the Commission, may authorize any Member State to introduce special measures for derogation from the provisions of that Directive in order to simplify the procedure for charging the tax or to prevent certain types of tax evasion or avoidance;

Whereas, by registered letter to the Commission dated 5 February 1997, Ireland requested authorization to introduce a measure derogating from Article 21 (1) of Directive 77/388/EEC;

Whereas, in accordance with Article 27 (3) of Directive 77/388/EEC, the other Member States were informed on 4 March 1997 of the request made by Ireland;

Whereas Ireland operates a specific system of applying VAT to property based, on the one hand, on the option under Article 5 (3) of Directive 77/388/EEC to treat the supply of certain interest (i.e. a lease of 10 years or more) in immovable property as a supply of goods and, on the other hand, on a derogation authorized under Article 27 (5) to treat the granting of such an interest by a lessor as a disposal of the lessor's entire interest in the property;

Whereas the Community law gives Member States a great deal of discretion in determining the VAT treatment to be applied to immovable goods, and its transposition has led to considerable variations in the national laws applied in this field.;

Whereas avoidance schemes have been set up, based on the use of surrender, including by way of abandonment of a leasehold interest or assignment of a leasehold interest, which result in the avoidance of the VAT where the ultimate acquirer of the property is not entitled to a full deduction of VAT;

Whereas it is also necessary to extend the derogation to the surrender or assignment of a leasehold interest to a taxable person having full right of deduction, as the surrender of the assignment of a leasehold interest will often arise due to financial difficulties of the lessee;

Whereas the measure envisaged is a derogation from Article 21 (1) (a) of Directive 77/388/EEC, whereby the person liable for the tax is the taxable person who carries out the taxable transaction;

---

(1) OJ No L 145, 13.6.1977, p. 1. Directive as last amended by Directive 96/95/EC, OJ No L 338, 28.12.1996, p. 89

Whereas the derogation provides that, where a surrender or assignment of a lease-hold interest is a taxable supply of goods, the person acquiring the interest is liable for the payment of the tax if that person is a taxable person or a non-taxable legal person;

Whereas this derogation should ensure a better functioning of the current VAT regime applied by Ireland on immovable goods;

Whereas, given the limited scope of the derogation, the special measure is proportionate to the aim pursued;

Whereas there exists a serious risk that use of the said VAT avoidance scheme will increase in the period between the request for a derogation and the authorization thereof; whereas at the latest since the publication on 26 March 1997 of the draft legislation which is the subject of the present request for a derogation, suppliers, lessors and lessees of property have no longer had a legitimate expectation of the continuation of the Irish legislation in force before that date; whereas it is therefore appropriate to authorize the derogation to take effect from 26 March 1997;

Whereas the Commission adopted on 10 July 1996 a work programme based on a step-by-step approach for progressing towards a new common system of VAT;

Whereas the tax treatment of immovable goods is an important issue to be reviewed in this programme;

Whereas the last package of proposals is to be put forward by mid-1999 and, in order to permit an evaluation of the coherence of the derogation with the global approach of the new common VAT system, the authorization is granted until 31 December 1999;

Whereas the derogation does not have a negative impact on the own resources of the European Communities accruing from VAT.

HAS ADOPTED THIS DECISION:

Article 1

By way of derogation from Article 21 (1) (a) of Directive 77/388/EEC, Ireland is hereby authorized, from 26 March 1997 until 31 December 1999, to designate the person to whom the supply is made as the person liable to pay the tax where the two following conditions are met:

– a surrender or assignment of a leasehold interest is treated as a supply of goods made by a lessee,

– the person acquiring the leasehold interest is a taxable person or a non-taxable legal person.

Article 2

This Decision is addressed to Ireland.

Done at Brussels, 24 July 1997.

For the Council
The President
M. FISCHBACH

11. V.A.T. ON PROPERTY

FINANCE ACT 1997
CHANGES

A Revenue Guide

REVENUE COMMISSIONERS
DUBLIN CASTLE

Introduction

1. Considerable changes were made to the provisions relating to VAT on property in the Finance Act 1997. This guide outlines those changes. The guide also outlines a new option for the back-dating of a waiver of exemption in relation to particular short-term lettings. The contents of VAT Leaflet No. 2 (July, 1980) 'VAT on Property Transactions' where it relates to matters covered by this guide should be disregarded.

2. This guide deals with: PARAGRAPH

3. These changes have effect from 26 March 1997.

4. Although these changes were introduced in the Finance Act, 1997 any references to sections in this guide are to sections in the Value-Added Tax Act, 1972 as amended by the 1997, and earlier, Finance Acts.

Assignments and surrenders from 26 March 1997 - an overview

5.   The main area of change introduced in the 1997 Finance Act is in the treatment of an assignment of an interest and the surrender of an interest. The treatment of such transactions is set out in greater detail in paragraphs 9 to 34. Charts A and B give an overview of the treatment of assignment and surrenders from 26 March 1997.

Chart A - VAT treatment of an assignment of an interest

Details of transaction :
- Landlord (L) creates 35 year lease.
- Annual rent £100,000, capitalised for VAT purposes at £1.44m.
- VAT is £180,000, deducted by tenant (T).
- After 1 year tenant assigns interest to assignee (A) - an exempt company for £10,000.

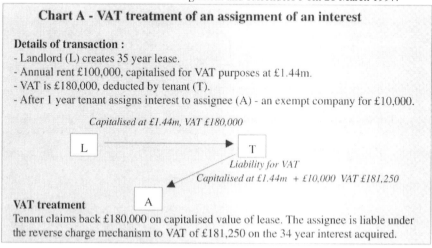

Capitalised at £1.44m, VAT £180,000

Liability for VAT
Capitalised at £1.44m + £10,000 VAT £181,250

VAT treatment
Tenant claims back £180,000 on capitalised value of lease. The assignee is liable under the reverse charge mechanism to VAT of £181,250 on the 34 year interest acquired.

Chart B - VAT treatment of a surrender of an interest

Details of transaction :
- Landlord (L) creates 35 year lease.
- Annual rent £100,000, capitalised for VAT purposes at £1.44m.
- VAT is £180,000, deducted by tenant (T).
- After 1 year tenant surrenders 34 year interest to landlord for £10,000

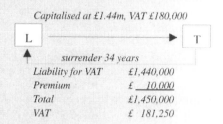

Capitalised at £1.44m, VAT £180,000

surrender 34 years

Liability for VAT	*£1,440,000*
Premium	*£ 10,000*
Total	*£1,450,000*
VAT	*£ 181,250*

VAT treatment
Tenant claims back £180,000 on capitalised value of lease. The landlord is liable under the reverse charge mechanism to VAT of £181,250 on the 34 year interest acquired. Subsequent supplies of the property will be liable to VAT subject to the rules as set out in paragraphs 35 to 48.

Interest

6. The definition of an interest in immovable goods for VAT purposes in sub-section 4(1)(b) has been amended. The amendment to the definition gives legal effect to the long-standing practice that a lease of less than ten years which contains, under the terms of the lease, an option for the tenant to extend the lease for a period of ten years or more, is an interest for VAT purposes.

7. The new sub-section 4(1)(c) follows on from 4(1)(b) and provides that a lease with an option, or indeed options, for the tenant to extend that lease, is treated as if it was a lease for the full extent of the original lease and options. For example, under the new sub-section, a lease for five years with an option for the tenant to extend the term of the lease for a further ten years is treated as if it were a lease for fifteen years and, therefore, as an interest for VAT purposes.

8. The status of a lease which contains a break-clause is unaffected by the new rules and continues to be treated as an interest if the lease is for a period of at least ten years. Therefore, a twenty year lease with a break-clause which can be exercised after five years is an interest for VAT purposes. (As this lease is for a term of at least twenty years the self-supply on the reversionary interest is valued at nil.) If the break-clause is exercised after the five years this is a surrender of an interest for VAT purposes.

Assignment of an interest/surrender of an interest

9. Section 1 has been amended to define an assignment of an interest in immovable goods as the transfer of an interest to a person other than the landlord.

10. Section 1 now also defines the surrender of an interest in immovable goods. The surrender of an interest means the return of the interest to the landlord. It includes the re-possession of the interest by ejectment or forfeiture or where the tenant abandons his or her interest. The failure of the tenant to exercise an option to extend the terms of his or her interest (see paragraphs 6 - 8 above) is also treated as a surrender. Where the landlord or the tenant invokes the terms of a break-clause, this is also a surrender of an interest for VAT purposes.

11. The amendment to sub-section 4(2) confirms that an assignment or a surrender is a supply of goods and is subject to VAT if the tenant who is making the assignment or surrender was entitled to a deduction of VAT on his or her acquisition of the interest. It should be noted that this is the case regardless of the length of time left in the interest. For example, in the case of a fifteen year lease which the tenant assigns or surrenders after six years the assignment or surrender is taxable although there are only nine years remaining in the lease.

12. Paragraphs 21 - 27 below set out the amount on which tax is chargeable on an assignment or surrender of an interest and paragraphs 28 - 30 below set out who is the person liable to pay the tax.

When is a supply of an interest in property taxable?

13. The first issue that must be settled with regard to VAT on property is whether a particular supply is taxable or not. This issue is the most common cause of queries in relation to VAT on property. Paragraphs 7 - 8 of VAT Leaflet No. 2 set out the basic rules in relation to whether a supply is taxable or not. These rules also apply to the surrender of an interest and to the assignment of an interest. The five conditions that must be met before tax is chargeable on a supply of an interest in property are:

    (i) the property must have been developed or redeveloped after 31 October, 1972;

    (ii) the person making the supply must hold the freehold interest in the property, or a leasehold interest in the property, which at the time the lease was created was for at least ten years;

    (iii) the person making the supply must dispose of the freehold interest or an interest which when it was created was for at least ten years;

    (iv) the person supplying the interest must be doing so in the course or furtherance of business; and

    (v) the person making the supply must have been entitled to a VAT credit or deduction in respect of the development of the property or the acquisition of the interest.

14. Whether or not some of these conditions are met will be more difficult to judge in the context of the new rules with regard to a surrender or an assignment. Also, given the new rules with regard to the valuation of a surrender or an assignment, the VAT implications of treating a surrender or an assignment incorrectly are more serious. Therefore, it is important to establish the VAT status of an interest at the time of its creation and its subsequent disposal. Essentially a disposal of an interest is taxable if it occurs within the 'VAT life' of the interest and the person disposing of the interest was entitled to deductibility in relation to the development of the property or the acquisition of that interest. **The VAT life is determined at the time of creation of an interest in the property.** If a landlord creates a thirty five year interest in property which is surrendered back to the landlord after five years, the landlord is treated for VAT purposes at the time of the surrender as if he or she has acquired a thirty year interest in the property.

15. While the term of the interest determines the VAT life of the interest, the person disposing of the interest (including by way of surrender or assignment) must have been entitled to a deduction of **all** or **part** of the VAT on the development or the acquisition of the interest for a particular disposal to be taxable. In the case of the sale of a freehold or the creation of an interest the person making the disposal is, subject to the application of section 4A, liable to the tax and can establish whether a deduction arose on the development or acquisition. However, in the case of a surrender or an assignment the person **receiving** the interest must in most instances account for the VAT liability under the reverse charge mechanism if the person **making** the surrender or assignment was entitled to deduct the VAT charged on the acquisition of the interest. Because of this it is recommended that a landlord

establishes at the time of the creation of an interest whether the tenant is entitled to a deduction. In many cases this will be obvious from the business activity involved. For example, retailers of goods are liable to VAT if their turnover exceeds the registration threshold, currently £40,000. Where the provisions of section 4A were applied to an original lease the surrender or assignment of that interest will always be taxable. Where there is any doubt in relation to a specific property the appropriate local tax office should be contacted.

Valuation of an interest - favoured rent

16.   There is no change in the methods of valuing a leasehold interest for VAT where a market rent is charged in a commercial arms-length transaction. Regulation 19 of the Value Added Tax Regulations, 1979 provides a number of methods of arriving at the open market value of a lease. These methods are set out in paragraph 36 of VAT Leaflet No. 2 and are as follows:

   (a)   valuation by a competent valuer;

   (b)   by multiplying three-quarters of the annual rent by the number of complete years in the term of the lease;

   (c)   by multiplying the annual rent by the multiplier (currently 14.43).

17.   However, sub-section 10(10), dealing with the definition of 'open market price' has been amended. The value of a leasehold interest is now based on the right to receive an open market rent assuming an unencumbered rent is charged in respect of that interest. The section also defines an 'unencumbered rent' as the rent that would be charged if the property was let on the open market free of restrictive conditions. This means that where a favoured rent is charged in respect of a leasehold interest the unencumbered rent will be substituted for the favoured rent in arriving at the open market price of the interest as set out in paragraph 18 below.

18.   In practice, the unencumbered rent will be substituted for the actual rent charged for the purposes of valuing an interest for VAT purposes where

   (i)   an exempt (or partially exempt) company or a non-taxable entity develops a property through a development company,

   (ii)   the conditions contained in a lease restrict the use of the property to a situation where there is effectively no open market for the interest and the exempt company or non-taxable entity or a related party to it is the only possible tenant, and

   (iii)   the cost of the development significantly exceeds the value of the interest, based on the actual rent charged, effectively confirming that a non-commercial rent is involved.

The situation involved is illustrated in example 1:

Example 1
A local authority owns a run-down property which it intends developing for the purposes of a sub-office/library. It sets up a development company which develops the property for £1 million. The development company creates a thirty-five lease in favour of the local authority at an annual rent of £10,000. The lease contains restrictive conditions in the clause which effectively limit the use of the building to local administration/library use.

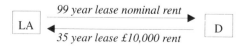

In this example the development company registers for VAT. It claims back the VAT of £125,000 on the development. It has a liability to VAT of £18,000 on the capitalised value of the thirty-five year lease resulting in a net repayment of £107,000. In effect the local authority has acquired a developed property at a VAT cost of £18,000 instead of £125,000.

19.   In this example the local authority acquired a developed property at a substantially reduced VAT cost. Under the new rules the Revenue will substitute the unencumbered rent for the favoured rent. This will mean that the prevailing market rent for a developed property in the particular location will be substituted for the favoured rent in valuing the lease for VAT purposes.

20.   It should be noted that in many circumstances where a favoured rent is charged the question of whether the lessor is making the supply in the course or furtherance of business will arise. If the supply is not made in the course or furtherance of business the development company will not be a taxable person and the lease will not be subject to tax nor will the lessor be entitled to deduct VAT on the development costs.

Valuation of an assignment

21.   As illustrated in chart A in paragraph 5 an assignment of an interest in immovable goods is valued as if it were the creation of an interest in those goods for a period equal to the unexpired portion of the lease. Therefore, if a landlord creates a thirty-five year lease at an annual rent of £100,000 this interest is valued, using the multiplier, at £1.44 million. If the tenant assigns his or her interest in the goods after a year then the assignment is valued as if it was the disposal of a thirty-four year interest in the property. At an annual rent of £100,000 and again using the multiplier, the value of the assignment for VAT purposes is £1.44 million.

22.   If an amount is payable by the assignee to the original tenant in respect of the assignment then this amount is treated in the same way for VAT purposes as a payment is treated on the creation of a lease. This means that any amount payable by the assignee is included in the taxable amount. However, if the tenant pays the assignee a reverse premium to take over the lease this amount is ignored for VAT purposes in valuing the assignment.

23.   Where there are less than ten years left in the term of interest that is assigned the assignment is taxable subject to the five conditions set out in paragraph 13 being met. In these cases the same options are available for valuing the assignment. For example, if a tenant assigns a seven year interest in a property with an annual rent of £100,000 any of the three methods may be used. However, the multiplier method will result in a significantly higher charge in this case.

24.   As is the case in relation to a valuation of an interest, valuation by a competent valuer will be required where the terms of a lease provide for a rent review within five years of the date of the assignment. For example, an interest is created for twenty years on 1 June 1997 and the terms of the lease provide for a rent review on 1 June 2001. The tenant, in turn assigns his or her interest to an assignee on 1 June 1998. Then, as the rent review will be due within five years of the assignment, the assignment must be valued by a competent valuer.

Valuation of a surrender

25.   As illustrated in Chart B in paragraph 5 a surrender of an interest in immovable goods is valued as if it were the creation of an interest in those goods for a period equal to the unexpired portion of the lease. Therefore, if a landlord creates a thirty-five year lease at an annual rent of £100,000 this interest is valued, using the multiplier, at £1.44 million. If the tenant surrenders back his or her interest in the goods after a year then the surrender is valued as if it was the disposal of a thirty-four year interest in the property. At an annual rent of £100,000 and again using the multiplier, the value of the assignment for VAT purposes is £1.44 million.

26.   If an amount is payable by the landlord to the tenant in respect of the surrender then this amount is treated in the same way for VAT purposes as a payment is treated on the creation of a lease. This means that any amount payable by the landlord is included in the taxable amount. However, if the tenant pays the landlord a reverse premium to take over the lease this amount is ignored for VAT purposes in valuing the surrender.

27.   For valuation purposes for VAT the market rent should be used in valuing the surrender. In many cases this will be the rent payable under the lease that is being surrendered.

The person liable to pay the tax

28.   Sub-section 4(8) provides for the introduction of a reverse charge mechanism in relation to the VAT payable on an assignment of an interest or a surrender of an interest in immovable goods. This means that where an assignment or a surrender of an interest is subject to tax, the tenant does not charge the tax but the person acquiring the interest accounts for the tax as if he or she made the supply. The reverse charge arises where the person to whom the interest is assigned or surrendered is one of the following:

    (a)   a taxable person,

(b)   the State or a local authority, which includes a health board;

(c)   a person who acquires the property for the purposes of making any of the following exempt supplies in the course or furtherance of business:
  - an exempt supply of property
  - financial services,
  - exempt lettings of property - short term,
  - agency services in relation to passenger transport, accommodation, insurance and other financial services,
  - insurance services,
  - public postal services,
  - public broadcasting services,
  - passenger transport.

29.   Where the person or entity acquiring the interest is not registered for VAT, that person or entity must register and account for VAT in respect of that transaction. The Appendix to this guide lists the addresses of the local tax offices.

30.   If a lease is assigned or surrendered by the tenant to a person other than those listed in paragraph 28 the tenant must account for the tax.

Invoicing and deductibility in relation to the reverse charge

31.   Where the reverse charge applies to an assignment or a surrender the recipient of the lease should prepare and retain in his or her records an invoice in respect of the transaction showing the date of the transaction, details of the property, the consideration and the VAT payable thereon. Any legal contracts should also be available for inspection by a Revenue official as required.

32.   The normal VAT deduction rules apply to VAT payable under the reverse charge. If a taxable person uses the premises to make taxable supplies the VAT charged may be deducted in the same period as the VAT is payable. If the premises is not intended to be used for the purposes of making taxable supplies then VAT on the assignment or surrender is not deductible.

33.   Sub-section 12(1)(a)(iiid) allows a tenant to deduct any VAT incurred in relation to the assignment or surrender which he or she would be entitled to deduct if the provisions of the reverse charge under sub-section 4(8) did not apply to the assignment or the surrender. This is a technical provision to ensure that the person assigning or surrendering a lease is subject to the normal rules with regard to deductibility.

34.   Tables 1 and 2 illustrate the various issues involved in the VAT treatment of an assignment and a surrender of an interest in immovable goods.

Table 1 - An assignment of an interest

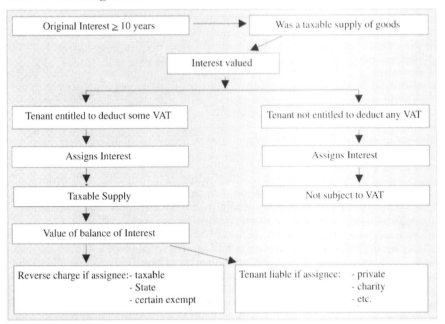

Table 2 - A surrender of an interest

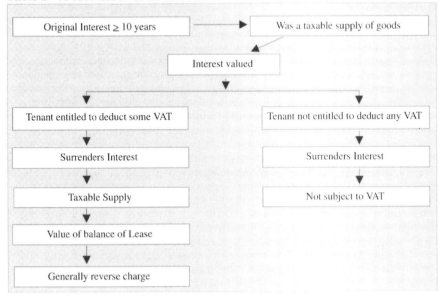

Surrender of an interest and subsequent supply

35.   The most complicated part of the 1997 provisions relate to a subsequent supply of an interest in a property following a taxable surrender. Prior to 26 March 1997 a subsequent supply of an interest in immovable goods following a surrender was not taxable. With the change in the treatment of the valuation of a surrender, as set out in chart B in paragraph 5, it was necessary to bring in new rules to deal with a subsequent supply of the property. Sub-sections 4(2A), 4(2B) and 4(2C) deal with the situations where the landlord makes a subsequent supply of the freehold or a leasehold interest in the property or lets the property on a short-term basis. (It should be noted that if the property has been redeveloped since the date of creation of the original interest then the provisions of these sub-sections do not apply to that property. Any supply of that property or an interest therein will be subject to VAT in accordance with the other provisions of section 4.)

36.   Before dealing with the treatment of the subsequent supplies it is useful to recap on the treatment of a lease and a surrender. A typical example is as follows:

Example 2
A landlord creates a twenty-five year lease on a retail outlet in a shopping centre at an annual rent of £50,000. This lease is capitalised using the multiplier of 14.43 at £721,500 plus VAT of £90,000 which, under the section 4A procedure, is self accounted for and deducted by the retailer. After two years the retailer, who is moving to a bigger unit, surrenders his interest to the lessor. There is no premium payable by either party. The surrender is taxable and as the annual rent for units in the centre is still £50,000, the capitalised value remains at £721,500 plus VAT. The landlord accounts for the VAT of £90,000 on the surrender under the reverse charge mechanism.

37.   The effect of the surrender of the interest in example 2 is that the landlord is treated for VAT purposes as if he or she is buying a twenty three year interest in that retail unit. The landlord had originally disposed of his or her full interest in that unit for VAT purposes when he or she disposed of the original interest. At that point the landlord had also accounted for VAT on the self-supply of the reversionary interest; but as the original lease was for a term of at least twenty years the value of the reversion was disregarded.

38.   Sub-section 4(2A) deals with the situation where the landlord supplies the freehold or creates a subsequent lease of ten years or more in the property. Again using the example above this can be illustrated as follows:

Example 3
Two months after the surrender the landlord creates a new twenty-five year lease in the unit to a second retailer. This lease is taxable as if it was a twenty two year and ten month lease, i.e. a lease for a period until the date of expiry of the original lease. This lease should be valued as if it was a twenty two year and ten months

lease and VAT charged. The section 4A mechanism may, if appropriate, apply to this lease.

39. As the subsequent interest in example 3 is a taxable supply, the lessor may deduct the VAT charged on the surrender. Indeed as the landlord intended making a taxable supply at the time of the surrender, he or she may deduct the VAT payable under the reverse charge mechanism in the same period as he or she accounts for the VAT on the surrender. In addition, any VAT incurred on expenses relating to the subsequent supply, for example, painting the premises after the surrender or legal or estate agency fees, may be deducted in the normal way. The position with regard to post-letting expenses is not affected by the 1997 changes. A VAT deduction is not allowed in respect of these expenses. However, in the case of services supplied to a property lessee through a landlord the existing concessionary treatment continues to apply. (Under this 1985 concession a landlord who is not registered for VAT and who is not obliged to register may seek the agreement of the local tax office to become registered. This type of registration allows the landlord to issue to each tenant, once a year, an invoice showing VAT charged to the tenant on services such as cleaning and security supplied through the landlord. A VAT-registered tenant can then take a deduction for VAT charged by the landlord on these 'service charges', subject to the usual rules.)

40. Where the period remaining in the surrendered interest is less than ten years at the time of the creation of the subsequent interest and this period is incorporated into a subsequent lease of at least ten years or into the sale of the freehold, the subsequent interest is treated as an exempt supply of goods. VAT is not chargeable on this new lease nor is the landlord entitled to deduct the VAT payable on the surrender of the interest. However, it is recognised that this could result in 'trapping' a substantial VAT charge in the hands of a landlord. To avoid this outcome sub-section 4(2A) provides that the landlord may opt to treat the lease of the subsequent interest as a taxable supply of goods. Where the landlord exercises this option, the open market price of the subsequent interest is valued as if it was a lease for the period from the date of creation of the subsequent interest to the date of the expiry of the interest that was surrendered. This can best be illustrated by an example:

Example 4
A landlord creates a ten year lease in a retail unit in a shopping centre. After one year the tenant surrenders the interest. As the tenant was entitled to deductibility on the acquisition of the lease the surrender is taxable and the open market price is valued as if it was the creation of a nine year lease. Assuming an annual market rent of £50,000 the open market price may be valued at:

$$\frac{£50,000 \times 3 \times 9}{4} = £337,500, \text{ giving a VAT liability of } £42,187.$$

(It may also be valued either using the multiplier or by a competent valuer.) The landlord accounts for the VAT on the reverse charge basis. As the landlord intends letting the unit on a long term lease and given that the tenant is likely to be a taxable person, the landlord opts to have the subsequent lease treated as a taxable supply of immovable goods. The landlord exercises this option by deducting the

VAT charged on the surrender. After three months the landlord creates a twenty year lease in favour of a second retailer at an annual rent of £60,000. This lease is taxable as a supply of goods but only to the extent of the eight years and nine months period. This is the period from the start of the subsequent lease to the expiry of the original lease. Again this may be valued as follows:

$$\frac{£60,000 \times 3 \times 8}{4} = £360,000, \text{ giving a VAT liability of £45,000.}$$

41.   The landlord exercises the option to treat a subsequent lease as taxable by deducting the VAT on the surrender. Before he or she deducts this VAT the intention must be to make a taxable supply and the Revenue may require evidence of this - in the case of a shopping centre this will be apparent from the nature of the property involved. If the landlord does not make a subsequent lease or if he or she changes his or her mind in relation to the subsequent lease, the VAT claimed must be refunded through the VAT return.

42.   The following table illustrates the various options set out in paragraphs 35 to 41 above.

Table 3: Sub-section 4(2A)

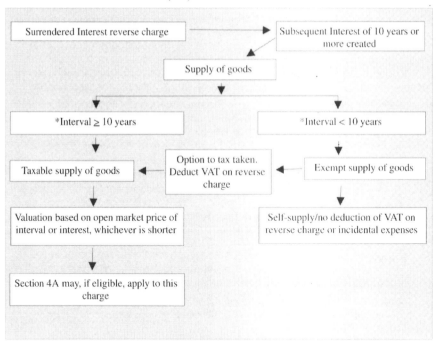

Note - interval means the period between the date of creation of the subsequent interest and the date of expiry of the interest that was surrendered.

43.   Sub-section 4(4) provides that where a person creates a taxable interest in a property he or she must also account for VAT on the reversionary interest in that property (see paragraphs 11 and 37 of VAT Leaflet No. 2). The new sub-section 4(2B) provides for the treatment of any reversionary interest on a subsequent lease. **The key issue which determines whether a taxable self-supply arises on the reversionary interest is whether the date of expiry of the subsequent interest is earlier than the date of expiry of the interest that was surrendered.** (Of course, in any situation where the subsequent interest is for a period of at least twenty years the value of the reversionary interest is disregarded.) If the date of expiry of the subsequent interest is later than the date of expiry of the original interest there is no taxable self-supply in relation to the reversionary interest. If the date is earlier, there is a taxable self-supply of the reversionary interest, but only in relation to the period from the date of expiry of the subsequent interest to the date of expiry of the original interest. This may be illustrated as follows:

Example 5
A landlord creates a taxable twenty year lease in a property. The landlord also accounts for VAT on the reversionary interest but because the lease was for twenty years the value of the reversion is nil. After one year the taxable tenant surrenders the interest. The landlord subsequently creates a fifteen year lease in the property. This fifteen year lease is taxable and the landlord must also account for VAT on the reversionary interest of four years as a self-supply.

44.   The following table illustrates the operation of sub-section 4(2B).

Table 4 : Sub-section 4(2B)

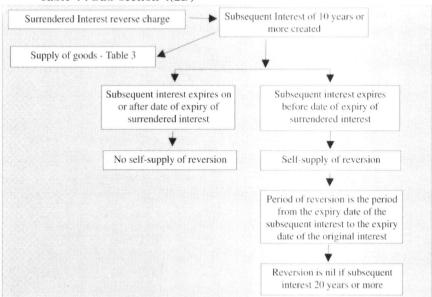

45. Sub-section 4(2C) deals with the situation where a landlord does not create a subsequent interest following a surrender but disposes of the property by a short-term letting. This is an exempt supply. The landlord must account for the VAT on the surrendered interest under the reverse charge mechanism but is not entitled to deduct this VAT. Sub-section 4(2C) and the amendment to sub-section 7(1) provide the landlord with an option to waive his or her exemption in respect of these short-term lettings. Where this waiver is exercised, the landlord can take credit on the surrender and VAT is chargeable at the standard rate on the rents.

46. Normally where a person waives his or her exemption the waiver applies to all of that person's rental income. However, sub-section 7(1) provides that where a person waives exemption in respect of a property which is let subsequent to a taxable surrender, the waiver applies to the property that was subject to the taxable surrender only. A person may apply to the appropriate tax office to waive his or her exemption. If the waiver specifically relates to a property which was acquired for VAT purposes by way of a surrender of an interest this should be stated on the application to the tax office.

47. If the interest in the property is disposed of in circumstances which are deemed, in accordance with sub-section 3(5), not to be a supply for VAT purposes then the disposal of the interest is not taxable nor is there a self-supply of the surrendered interest. This would arise, for example, where the interest is disposed of as part of a transfer of a business to a taxable person.

48. The following table illustrates the operation of sub-section 4(2C).

Table 5 : Sub-section 4(2C)

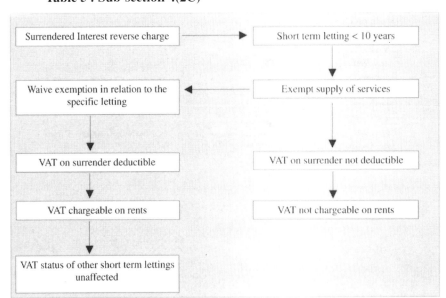

236

Self-Supplies

49.   Sub-section 10(4) is also amended to confirm that where a person self-supplies an interest in immovable goods the value of that interest forms the basis of the amount payable on the self-supply. In effect, the self-supply is a claw-back of the VAT deducted in relation to the acquisition of the interest (including VAT on expenses relating to the acquisition). This amendment confirms the Revenue view that the cost of acquiring the interest that is self-supplied includes the value of the interest and is not limited to the actual rent paid prior to the self-supply.

Example 6
A landlord creates a thirty five year lease in a property. The lease is capitalised at £1 million giving VAT of £125,000. The tenant is a taxable person who uses the property for his or her taxable business. He or she deducts the VAT. After one year the tenant puts the building to an exempt use. The self-supply is valued at the cost to the tenant which includes the capitalised value at which the tenant acquired the lease.

Cancellation of a waiver

50.   Prior to 26 March 1997, a landlord was required to refund to Revenue the net repayment (if any) received in respect of a waiver, on its cancellation. However, simplification schemes introduced over the years have given rise to situations where the review mechanism on cancellation did not give the required result. From 26 March 1997, this is corrected as follows. Sub-section 7(3) provides that where a person wishes to cancel his or her waiver of exemption in relation to the short-term letting of property, he or she must refund the excess of VAT deductible in relation to the property over the VAT payable on the rents. In calculating the VAT deductible for the property the person must now include:

- VAT charged by a supplier,
- any VAT accounted for by the person under the reverse charge mechanism in sub-section 4(8) or section 4A,
- any amount of VAT that would have been chargeable on the supply of the property if the supply was not zero-rated in accordance with section 13A (the zero-rating of supplies to exporters), and
- any VAT that would have been chargeable on the supply of property if the provisions of sub-section 3(5)(b)(iii) (transfer of business) did not apply to that supply.

If the person disposes of his or her interest in the property in circumstances where VAT is chargeable on the disposal, the VAT chargeable should be added to the VAT payable on the rents for the purposes of this calculation.

Technical self-supplies

51. Prior to 26 March, 1997 a waiver of exemption could only apply from the start of the period in which an application for a waiver was made or a later date as agreed between the applicant and the tax office. It is now permissible for the waiver to be back-dated in certain circumstances.

52. The waiver can be back-dated in respect of what has become known as a technical self-supply. A technical self-supply arises where a taxable person makes a short term letting of part of his or her commercial property to another taxable person but does not waive the exemption at that time. This usually happens where the business has excess space which it lets on a temporary basis or where the business is not ready to occupy the property and lets the property temporarily pending occupation. Due to lack of knowledge of the VAT rules, the person does not waive the exemption and must account for VAT on a self-supply.

53. The back-dating of the waiver is only possible where the tenant would be entitled to a full deduction of the tax charged on the rent.

54. Where a person wishes to back-date a waiver he or she must apply in writing to the appropriate tax office setting out the following details:

  * name, address and VAT registration number,
  * the tenant's name, address and VAT registration number,
  * details of the letting agreement,
  * the date from which the waiver should have effect.

The tax office will, where it is satisfied that the tenant would have been entitled to deduct all the VAT charged on the rents and subject to the above, notify the applicant of the date to which the back-dating applies. However, this date may not be earlier than 26 March, 1997.

55. Where a waiver is back-dated the **back-dated** waiver only applies to the specific letting which is the subject of the application referred to in paragraph 54. However, that application will be treated as if it were an application to waive the exemption in respect of **ALL** the applicant's short-term lettings from the start of the taxable period within which the application is made or a later date as agreed with the tax office.

56. Where the tax office approves the back-dating of the waiver, the tax payable on the rents by the landlord and the tax deductible by the tenant shall be deemed to have been both paid and deducted. The relevant obligations with regard to invoicing and returns shall also be deemed to have been complied with. In addition the landlord should incorporate the VAT chargeable for the back-dated period in any calculation of liability on cancellation of that waiver.

57.   The following example illustrates how the back-dated waiver will operate

Example 7

A taxable company has some spare office space which it lets on a short-term basis to a neighbouring company on 1 March 1998. It does not waive its exemption at the time. The tenant is fully taxable. In September 1998 the landlord company's accountant discovers the exempt short-term letting and advises the company that it has made an exempt supply for VAT purposes. The company must account for VAT on the self-supply or else it can apply to the tax office to back-date its waiver to 1 March 1998. As the tenant is fully taxable the company applies to backdate its waiver. The tax office allows the back-dating of the waiver to 1 March 1998. For the period from 1 March to 31 August 1998 the VAT on the rents is deemed to have been accounted for by the landlord and deemed to have been deducted by the tenant. In addition to its taxable business the company has another building let on short-term basis to a non business tenant. The back-dated waiver does not apply to this premises. However, from 1 September 1998 the waiver applies to all the company's short-term lettings and VAT is chargeable on all the rents in the normal way.

Queries

58.   Any queries in respect of the VAT treatment of a property transaction should be addressed to the appropriate tax office (see the Appendix attached).

Appendix

DISTRICT	ADDRESS	TELEPHONE	FAX
ATHLONE	Government Buildings, Pearse Street, Athlone, Co. Westmeath.	(0902) 92681	(0902) 92699
CASTLEBAR	Michael Davitt House, Castlebar, Co. Mayo.	(094) 21344	(094) 24221
CORK	Government Buildings, Sullivan's Quay, Cork.	(021) 966077	(021) 962141
DUBLIN	Dublin Audit District 1 & 2, *(Construction and Property),* Findlater House, 28/32 Upper O'Connell Street, Dublin 1.	(01) 8746821	(01) 8740284
	Dublin Audit District 3, *(Professions),* Hawkins House, Hawkins Street, Dublin 2.	(01) 6775004	(01) 6775003
	Dublin Audit District 4, *(Agribusiness and Fisheries),* Lansdowne House, Lansdowne Road, Dublin 4.	(01) 6689400	(01) 6684753
	Dublin Audit District 5, *(The Financial Sector),* Lansdowne House, Lansdowne Road, Dublin 4.	(01) 6689400	(01) 6689706
	Dublin Audit District 6, *(Groups, Foreign Branches and PLCs),* Lansdowne House, Lansdowne Road, Dublin 4.	(01) 6689400	(01) 6689706
	Dublin Audit District 7, *(Investment and Rental Income),* Lansdowne House, Lansdowne Road, Dublin 4.	(01) 6689400	(01) 6686512
	Dublin Audit District 8, *(Passenger and Goods Transport Services, Light Industry including Garages, Consumer Goods, Repair Services),* 4 Claremont Road, Sandymount, Dublin 4.	(01) 6607111	(01) 6606768

	Dublin Audit District 9, *(Hotel, Catering and Entertainment Industry, Personal* *Services and other Miscellaneous Service Activities),* 4 Claremont Road, Sandymount, Dublin 4.	(01) 6607111	(01) 6606768
	Dublin Audit District 10, *(Wholesalers and Retailers),* 4 Claremont Road, Sandymount, Dublin 4.	(01) 6607111	(01) 6606580
	Central Registration Office, Aras Brugha, 9/15 Upper O'Connell Street, Dublin 1.	(01) 8746821	(01) 8746078
DUNDALK	Earl House, Earl Street, Dundalk, Co. Louth.	(042) 32251	(042) 34609
GALWAY	Hibernian House, Eyre Square, Galway.	(091) 563041	(091) 563987
KILKENNY	Government Buildings, Hebron Road, Kilkenny.	(056) 52222	(056) 51255 (056) 63498
LETTERKENNY	Government Buildings, High Road, Letterkenny, Co. Donegal.	(074) 21299	(074) 22357
LIMERICK	River House, Charlotte Quay, Limerick.	(061) 318711	(061) 417863
SLIGO	Government Buildings, Cranmore Road, Sligo.	(071) 60322	(071) 43987
THURLES	Stradovoher, Thurles, Co. Tipperary.	(0504) 21544	(0504) 21475
TRALEE	Government Offices, Spa Road, Tralee, Co. Kerry.	(066) 21844	(066) 21895
WATERFORD	Government Buildings, The Glen, Waterford.	(051) 73565	(051) 77483
WEXFORD	Distillery Road, Wexford.	(053) 45555	(053) 47207

12. V.A.T. RETURN FORM

VAT 3

Registration No.

IE

COLLECTOR-GENERAL,
OFFICE OF THE REVENUE COMMISSIONERS,

UNDER NO
CIRCUMSTANCES
SHOULD THIS RETURN
BE USED FOR ANY
OTHER TAXABLE PERIOD.

PLEASE SEE
IMPORTANT NOTES
OVERLEAF.

This return relates to the taxable period (s)
The form duly completed and signed must be returned to me not later than
For payments to the Collector-General, the complete form (including the Giro/Payslip) should be returned.

Collector-General.

REPAYMENT INFORMATION

Any repayment due to you will be repaid direct to your bank or building society account. If you have not previously advised account details to this Office, or if you wish to amend details previously submitted, please tick the box below and complete the information overleaf.

BANK DETAILS INCLUDED OVERLEAF:

Registration No.	Period.	
IE		Q1

VAT
VAT on Goods & Services
Supplied & Intra-EU
Acquisitions.

IR£ POUNDS ONLY

T1

(Instructions overleaf for T1)

VAT on Deductible
Purchases, Intra-EU
Acquisitions & Imports.

T2

(Instructions overleaf for T2)

TAXABLE PERIOD   GCD   UNIT

INTRA-EU TRADE. (INTRASTAT)

IR£ POUNDS OR NIL ONLY

Total Goods to other EU Countries   E1

Net Repayable.

T4

(Excess of T2 over T1)

OR

Net Payable.

T3

(Excess of T1 over T2)

DO NOT LEAVE THESE
BOXES BLANK. SEE OVERLEAF.

Total Goods from other EU Countries   E2

I declare that this is a correct return of value-added tax for the period specified.

Signed _____ Status _____ Date _____

 BANK GIRO
CREDIT TRANSFER

Payslip
(See Instructions overleaf.)

THE
REVENUE
COMMISSIONERS

To		For
BANK OF IRELAND COLLEGE GREEN DUBLIN 2	90 - 71 - 04	COLLECTOR-GENERAL VALUE-ADDED TAX. A/C. NO. 31468191

NAME:

REG. No.   *IE*   PERIOD:

Receiving
Cashier's
Brand &
Initials

I declare that the amount entered below
is a correct statement of Value-added tax payable for the period specified.

£   p

Signed: ....   Date ....

ENTER AMOUNT OF
VAT PAYABLE HERE. ➤   T3 | IR£   00

CASH	
CHEQUES	
TOTAL	

VAT 3 G (A)   *Please do not fold this GIRO or write or mark below this line.*

⑈90⑈7104⑈ 31468191⑈ 80

Notes on the Completion of the Vat 3 Form

VAT Section

(The VAT section must contain a full disclosure of the VAT content of all business transactions for the tax period in question.)

Box T1
should contain the total of the following:- **IR£ pounds only**

- VAT charges by you on supplies of goods and supplies of services

- VAT due on any intra-EU acquisitions

Total T1

(This figure to be transferred to **T1** box on front of form.)

Box T2
should contain the total of the following:- **IR£ pounds only**

- VAT on stocks for resale, (i.e. purchases, intra-EU acquisitions and imports)

- VAT on other deductible goods and services, (i.e. purchases, intra-EU acquisitions and imports)

Total T2

(This figure to be transferred to **T2** box on front of form.)

Box T3 will contain the net VAT payable for the tax period i.e. excess of **T1** over **T2**.
Box T4 will contain the net VAT repayable for the tax period i.e. excess of **T2** over **T1**.

BANK ACCOUNT DETAILS FOR VAT REPAYMENTS

BANK:

BRANCH:

SORT CODE:

ACCOUNT NUMBER:

SIGNATURE:

Intra EU Trade (INTRASTAT)

Box E1 should contain the total value for VAT of Union goods invoiced by you (or sent by you if there is no invoice) to other Member States during the relevant period.

Box E2 should contain the total value for VAT of Union goods invoiced to you (or received by you if there is no invoice) from other Member States during the relevant period.

Both of these boxes must be completed, if you had no such exports or imports of goods, insert NIL as relevant.

In neither case should services or non-Union goods be included. Detailed information on Union goods and INTRASTAT is available in the VIES and INTRASTAT Traders Manual.

Methods of Payment

Payments- Your VAT can be paid by means of the Bank Giro/Payslip overleaf, through any bank. If paying by Bank Giro/Payslip, the VAT return <u>must be</u> posted separately to the Collector-General. A prepaid envelope is enclosed for this purpose.
Alternatively forward the completed Bank Giro/Payslip WITH YOUR PAYMENT to the Collector-General, along with the completed VAT return, using the prepaid envelope provided. N.B. In using the latter payment method <u>DO NOT DETACH</u> the Bank Giro/Payslip.

Cheques - Cheques should be crossed and made payable to the Revenue Commissioners or Collector-General. Please quote your VAT number on the back of <u>all</u> cheques used for tax payments.

Receipts - A receipt will issue from the Collector-General whether you pay by Bank Giro or send your payment to the Collector-General.

Personal Callers - The office of the Collector-General, 2nd floor, Apollo House, Tara Street, Dublin 2 is open to the public from 9.30am to 4.00pm. The Office of the Collector-General, Sarsfield House, Francis Street, Limerick, is open to the public from 9.30am to 5.30pm.

PART I

THE CHANGES IN THE FINANCE ACT 1997

1.   Introduction

In this part of the book, I set out the changes to the law governing VAT on property introduced by the Finance Act 1997. I decided to write a separate chapter on the changes in order to facilitate the reader who wants to study them separately. The changes are also covered in the appropriate parts throughout the book. They were introduced with effect from 26 March 1997 to thwart VAT plans that were being used by exempt persons to avoid irrecoverable VAT on leases.

2.   Derogation

It is required that Irish VAT law is in harmony with the EU Directives on VAT. The main EU Directive on VAT is the 6th Directive (77/388/EEC). On 3 March 1997, Ireland applied for a derogation (See H.9) from Article 21.1(a) of the EU 6th Directive in order to introduce a provision into Irish VAT law which is not in line with the Directive. In the application for derogation, Ireland sought permission to make the recipient of an assignment or surrender responsible for the VAT in certain circumstances. The Revenue Commissions instigating the request from the Irish Government seem not to have considered it necessary to seek a derogation for the new market value rules. That puzzles me in view of the fact that Article 11 of the Directive only allows market value in very limited circumstances. The new unencumbered rent concept seems to go beyond that which is permitted by the Directive.

When the UK introduced market value rules for certain property transactions it sought and obtained a derogation.

The Council granted the derogation on 24 July 1997.

3.   The changes

I will start with the easy changes and move on to the more difficult ones.

The changes deal with six aspects of VAT on property.

1.   An option to extend a lease

2.   Valuing leases

3.   The VAT trap on short lettings

4.   The cancellation of a waiver

5.   Surrenders, assignments and second leases

6.   The reverse charge

4.   The first change - an option to extend a lease

A lease which gives the tenant an option to extend it to 10 years or more is treated for VAT purposes as one which runs to the latest date possible. A 7 year lease, for example with an option to extend it to 35 years is a 35 year lease for VAT purposes. Likewise a 15 year lease with an option to extend it to 25 years is a 25 year lease for VAT purposes.

A lease which contains an option to extend it to less than 10 years is unaffected. For example, a 3 year lease with an option to extend it to nine years is a 3 year lease for VAT purposes.

The legislation is quite clear that the option to extend must be in the lease itself. This means that a 7 year lease which contains an option of extension to 35 years is a 35 year lease for VAT purposes. In contrast if there was a separate option agreement the lease would not be affected. It would remain a 7 year lease for VAT purposes.

The extending affect only arises where the tenant has the option to extend. A 7 year lease which contains a clause whereby the landlord can extend the lease to 35 years remains a 7 year lease for VAT purposes.

5.   The second change - valuing a lease

The new legislation deals with 3 aspects of valuing a lease viz:

1.   It tells how a surrender or assignment is to be valued for VAT purposes.

2.   It introduces a new concept known as "unencumbered rent".

3.   It introduces a new rule for valuing the self-supply of a leasehold interest.

5.1   Valuing a surrender or assignment

Under the new rules a surrender or assignment is valued as if it were a new lease running from the date of surrender or assignment to the leases termination date. For example, a tenant entered into a 35 year lease and after 10 years he surrendered the lease back to the landlord. No money changed hands. The surrendered lease was valued for VAT purposes as if it were a 25 year lease subject to the rent and conditions contained in it.

There are three ways of valuing a lease for VAT purposes viz.

1.   The multiplier: Multiply the rent by the multiplier. The multiplier can be obtained from the local tax office. It is changed from time to time. At present, it is 14.43. This means that an assignment today with a rent of £1m per annum has a valuation, using the multiplier of £14.43m.

2.   The formula: $R \times N \times \frac{3}{4}$. This means an assignment with 25 years to run at a rent of £1m per annum has a valuation using the formula of £18,750,000.

3.   Valuation by a competent valuer.

Strictly under the law one can pick which method of valuation one wishes only if there is no provision for an increase in rent within 5 years. If there is provision for an increase within 5 years valuation by a competent valuer is required. This means that for the majority of assignments or surrenders a valuation by a competent valuer will be required. However, I understand where the VAT is fully deductible Inspectors will cosnider (and more than likely allow) the choice of method of valuation. They are not of course obliged to do provision for a rent increase within five years.

If there is a premium payable on the surrender or assignment it will be included in the amount chargeable to VAT. A reverse premium is ignored.

Where there is less than 10 years left in the lease being surrendered or assigned it is still valued on the capitalised value of the rent using the multiplier, the formula or a valuation by a competent valuer. For example, a tenant who had a 21 year lease at a rent of £100,000 per annum assigned it on 30 June 1997 when it had only 5 years left to run. The lease was valued at £375,000 based on the formula and calculated as follows:

$$£100,000 \times 5 \times {}^{3}/_{4} = £375,000$$

Using the multiplier which is 14.43 at present (July 1997) gives a ridiculous value of £1.443m.

Alternatively, the lease could have been valued by competent valuer.

5.2 Unencumbered rent

Sometimes connected landlords and tenants put restrictive conditions in a lease to support a low rent and thus reduced the leases value for VAT.

To stop this type of VAT planning the new rules require the valuer to ignore restrictive conditions when arriving at a market rent for a property. The valuer must arrive at the market rent that the property would fetch if let without restrictive conditions. Restrictive conditions are not defined in the legislation. I suspect the draftsman purposely avoided defining restrictive conditions on the basis that like the elephant, it is hard to define, but you will know one when you see one! The reality is that most, if not all leases, have conditions that it could be argued are restrictive.

If you have a case where the Inspector is attempting to impose an unencumbered rent as the basis for arriving at a VAT charge you might find it useful to consider whether or not the domestic legislation in this regard is in line with the Directive. Article 11 of the EU 6th Directive sets down the rules for determining the amount on which VAT is charged. Unencumbered rent seems to go beyond Article 11. In addition the derogation sought by Ireland did not include a request for permission to use unencumbered rent. It merely sought permission to use the reverse charge.

In a recent decision, the E.C.J. considered the question of taxable amount of rent under Article 11 (Finanzampt Bergisch Gladbach v Skripalle (Case C-63\96)). In that case, Werner Skripalle charged a market rent on letting a property to a connected company. The German tax authorities attempted to impose a higher charge based on a notional amount in accordance with German VAT legislation. The Court found against the German authorities.

If you are considering the vires of the Irish legislation in the light of the Directive you might also find it useful to read the E.C.J. decision in the case of EC Commission v France (1989) 1 CMLR 505, ECJ 50\87. In that case, French law attempted to deal with below market rents for social housing by restricting the entitlement to inputs. The E.C.J. held that the French domestic legislation contravened the provisions of the EU 6th Directive and that input entitlement could not be restricted in the circumstances.

However, it is unlikely you will have a problem with unencumbered rent in the majority of cases. The Revenue Commissiners have stated in their Guide to the Finance Act 1997 Changes that there will be no change in the methods of valuing a leasehold interest for VAT where a market rent is charged in a commercial arms-length transaction. The Revenue Guide goes on to say

> *"In practice, the unencumbered rent will be substituted for the actual rent charged for the purpose of valuing on interest for*
>
> *(i)   an exempt (or partially exempt) company or a non- taxable entity develops a property through a development company,*
>
> *(ii) the conditions contained in a lease restrict the use of the property to a situation where there is effectively no open market for the interest and the exempt company or non-taxable entity or a related party to it is the only possible tenant and*
>
> *(iii) the cost of the developing significantly exceeds the value of the interest, based on the actual rent charged, effectively confirming that a non-commercial rent is involved.*

5.3   Valuing the self-supply of a leasehold interest

Where a tenant uses a leasehold premises for the purposes of his vatable supplies he is entitled to recover the VAT charged on the lease subject to the normal rules. If he later uses it for exempt supplies he is obliged under the new rules to repay the VAT initially recovered. The legislative mechanics for this are that the taxpayer treats the application of the leasehold interest to exempt use as a notional sale chargeable to VAT. The deemed consideration for this notional sale is the amount on which VAT was charged when he entered into the lease. This is known in VAT parlance as a self-supply.

Before 26 March, VAT on such a self-supply was chargeable on the cost to the tenant. The question arose; what is the cost of a lease to a tenant? Presumably nil!

6. The third change - VAT trap on a short letting

For many years, there was a nasty VAT trap which is best explained by an example. A firm of accountants purchased a property and because it used it for its accountancy business it was entitled to recover VAT on the cost of the building. After some years the firm cut back with the result that it had spare space available. It let half the property on a 4 year nine month lease to a firm of architects. Letting half the property on a 4 year nine month lease was exempt from VAT with the result that half the input credit was clawed back i.e. had to be repaid to the Revenue. Had the accountants waived the exemption within the VAT period in which the letting commenced there would have been no claw back. A waiver of exemption sounds more complicated than it is. A waiver of exemption is simply a letter to the Inspector letting him know that VAT will be charged on the rent.

Under new regulations effective from 26 March 1997 a person who misses sending the waiver of exemption to the Inspector on time may in certain circumstances be allowed a back dated waiver. To get a back dated waiver the landlord must apply in writing to the Inspector stating:

(i)   His name

(ii)   His address

(iii)   His VAT registration number

(iv)   The tenant's name

(v)   The tenant's address

(vi)   The tenant's VAT registration number

(vii)   Details of the letting agreement.

(viii) The date from which the waiver will have effect (no being earlier than 26 March, 1997)

    (i) That he is entitled to full recovery of the VAT on the rents and

    (ii) That he agrees to the back-dating.

The effect of a back dated waiver is as follows:

1. No adjustments are required for the past. The landlord is deemed to have paid the VAT and the tenant is deemed to have deducted it. All obligations such as invoicing are deemed tohave been complied with. Other short term rents are unaffected as regards the past.

2. The application for back-dating is treated from the dateof application (or agreed later time) as a waiver of exemption in respect of all short-term lettings from then on.

A back dating is only allowed where a person is in the first instance entitled to the input credit and subsequently short term lets the property. It is not allowed where the property is let short term from the beginning and the waiver is not sent on time.

7.   The fourth change – cancellation of a waiver

Short term lettings (those of less than 10 years) are exempt from VAT. This means that VAT is not chargeable on the rent nor is it recoverable on costs related to the rent e.g. on the cost of the property, related legal fees etc..

A landlord who has lettings of less than 10 years can waive his entitlement to exemption. As mentioned earlier, this simply means writing to the Inspector telling him that he (the landlord) will charge VAT on the rents. When a landlord waives his entitlement to exemption he is entitled to recover input VAT on the costs and is obliged to charge VAT on the rent at 21%.

There is a facility under the legislation whereby a person who has waived entitlement to exemption may cancel a waiver provided they pay back to the Revenue the benefit gained i.e. the amount of VAT recovered less the VAT charged on the rents.

The regulation which set out how to calculate how much had to be paid back to the Revenue had some gaps in it. The legislation has been amended to plug those gaps with effect from 26 March 1997. For example, if an export company acquired a property VAT free under VATA 1972 Section 13A prior to 26 March 1997 the VAT element on the purchase of the property was not taken into account in calculating the VAT due to Revenue on cancellation. It will be taken into account for cancellations from 26 March on.

Example

Ms. Jane Eyre ran a clothes manufacturing business at Carraroe, Co. Galway. All the product was exported to the U.S. with the result that she had a 13A authorisation permitting her to buy goods and services VAT free. She purchased a premises for £400,000 VAT free. She acquired another clothes manufacturing business VAT free under the transfer of business provision (VATA 1972 3(5)(b)(iii)). A factory premises was acquired VAT free under the transfer for £320,000.

She later fell into bad health and closed down the factories. She let both factories short term at a total rent of £50,000 per annum. She waived her entitlement to exemption. After four years she cancelled her waiver and repaid £44,000 to the Revenue calculated as follows:

VAT on 13A premises	£50,000
VAT on 3(5)(b)(iii) premises	£30,000
Input tax deducted in respect rents say	£6,000
Total £	86,000
VAT on rents £50,000 x 4 x 21%	£42,000
Amount paid on cancellation	£44,000

8.   The fifth change – surrenders, assignments and second leases

To understand the changes to the law governing VAT on a surrender, assignment and second lease you must first all understand some fundamental concepts as regards VAT on property.

8.1   First fundamental – Creating a long lease

A landlord is treated for VAT purposes as disposing of his interest in a vatable property when he creates a lease of 10 years or more. He is treated as having no interest in a vatable property after he has created a lease of 10 years or more. It is as if he had sold the property. This of course is not the case. He still owns the property and is entitled to the rent etc. but VAT law has it that the no longer has the property nor any interest in it.

A landlord transfers the vatable interest in the property to the tenant when he creates a lease of 10 years or more.

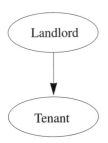

1.   In fact still holds freehold and entitled to rents. For VAT purpose has no interest in the property.

2.   Landlord granted 35 year lease

3.   Tenant has 35 year vatable interest.

8.2   Second fundamental – The ticking clock

The second fundamental concept is simply that the vatable interest is decreasing all the time. It is like all of us at any given time, it only has so long left to live. For example, the tenant who enters into a 35 year lease initially has a vatable interest of 35 years. After 1 year he has a 34 year vatable interest. After 10 years he has a 25 year vatable interest and so on. At the end of the lease the tenant has no vatable interest left.

The new legislation has introduced this new interest in property in addition to all the other interests that are there already. For example, an industrial unit could have the following interests:

Freehold interest held by I.D.A.

999 year leasehold held by an Investor

35 year leasehold held by X Manufacturing Company Limited

25 year vatable interest held by Z Manufacturing Company Limited

What needs to be done is establish and keep track of the vatable interest.

8.3 Assignment of the vatable interest

The tenant who enters into a 35 year lease and who is entitled to recovery of any of the VAT arising initially has, as I said above, a 35 year vatable interest. If after 10 years he sells that vatable interest the person to whom he sells it acquires a 25 year vatable interest.

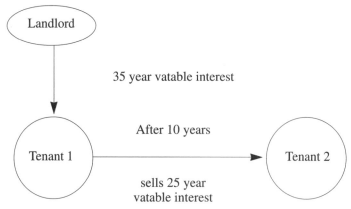

8.3.1 Example

A landlord granted a 35 year lease to a tenant at a rent of £100,000 per annum. The VAT amounted to £180,375 calculated as follows:

$$£100,000 \quad x \quad 14.43 \quad x \quad 12\tfrac{1}{2}\% \quad = \quad £180,375$$

If in ten years time, the tenant assigns the lease the same amount of VAT will arise on the assignment (£180,375) assuming the same multiplier and the same rent.

8.4 Surrendering a lease

Surrendering a lease in property law means giving back the lease to the landlord before it has expired. In VAT law its meaning is extended to take in abandonments, ejectments forfeitures and failure to exercise an option.

The surrender of a lease is similar for VAT purposes, to the assignment of a lease. A tenant, for example who has a 35 year lease and who surrenders it after 10 years is disposing of a 25 year vatable interest. Assuming he was entitled to any input VAT the surrender is chargeable as the disposal of a 25 year vatable interest. VAT arises on the capitalised valued arrived at by using the multiplier, the formula or a valuation by a competent valuer.

Break Clauses

As you know, a break clause in a lease is a clause which allows a landlord or a tenant or both to terminate the lease before it has run its full length. The question has been asked whether the exercise of a break clause is a surrender within the definition in the legislation (VATA 1972 Section 1).

This question was addressed by Michael O'Connor in his article "Changes in the VAT Regime for Property" published in the July 1997 edition of the Irish Tax Review. He states as follows:

"In the writer's view, a lessee does not make a surrender when his lease expires. The lease automatically comes to an end. The same situation applies where a break clause is exercised. Accordingly, because the definition of surrender in the VAT Act does not specifically include the exercise of a break clause, the exercise of such a clause which enables a lessee or a lessor to terminate a lease is not a supply for VAT purposes if the mechanism used is to terminate the lease rather than to effect a surrender. This assertion is likely to be contradicted by the Revenue in a statement of practice which will be issued shortly."

"If the break clause is exercised .... this is the surrender of an interest for VAT purposes" (Revenue Guide para. 8)"

The Revenue's view reminds me of Humpty Dumpty's words to Alice:

When I use a word", Humpty Dumpty said, in a rather scornful tone, "it means just what I choose it to mean - neither more nor less."

In my opinion, the exercise of a break clause is not a surrender for VAT purposes for the reasons set out in the article in the Irish Tax Review.

8.5 A second lease

A second lease is a new lease which is created after the first one has been surrendered back to the landlord provided the property has not been developed or re-developed since the creation of the first lease. The two aspects to be considered when categorising a second lease for VAT purposes are:

1. The length of the lease and

2. The length of the landlords vatable interest.

There are four categories of second leases for VAT purposes as follows:

1. • A second lease for less than 10 years.

2. • A second lease for 10 years or more and

   • the landlord has a vatable interest of less than 10 years.

3. • A second lease for 10 years or more and

   • the landlord has a vatable interest of 10 years or more and

   • the lease is for longer than the vatable interest

4. • A second lease for more than 10 years and

   • the landlord has a vatable interest of 10 years or more and

   • the lease is for a shorter time than the vatable interest.

These categories may be represented by the following diagram.

The shaded areas show the four categories of second leases for VAT purposes.

8.5.1. A second lease for less than 10 years

A second lease for less than 10 years is exempt from VAT. The VAT arising on the surrender of the first lease is not recoverable by the landlord. However, the landlord may waive his entitlement to exemption (i.e. charge VAT on the rents at 21%) and recover the VAT on the surrender. A waiver in the case of a second lease is on a property by property basis. This contrasts with a waiver on a first letting which is on a "one in all in" basis. A waiver in the case of a second lease does not affect other short term lettings.

Example

A landlord granted a 35 year lease to a tenant. The tenant was entitled to full recovery of the VAT charged on the lease. After ten years the tenant surrendered his interest back to the landlord thus giving the landlord a 25 year vatable interest. The landlord let the property on a 4 year 9 month lease. In order to protect his right to recovery of VAT on the surrender the landlord waived his entitlement to exemption on the rents. The waiver only applied to the second letting in question. The rate of VAT on the rents was 21%. (Reference VATA 1972 Section 4(2C)). The waiver must be made within the VAT period in which the second lease is granted.

8.5.2. Second lease 10 years or more: Vatable Interest < 10 years

When a landlord creates a second lease of 10 years or more and his vatable interest is less than 10 years he is treated for VAT purposes as making an exempt supply of goods. This means that VAT on the surrendered interest and any incidental costs is not recoverable. However, he may opt to charge VAT on the vatable interest (at $12\frac{1}{2}\%$) and thus get entitlement to recovery of VAT on the surrender and on the incidental expenses. The landlord exercises the option by deducting VAT on the surrender.

Example

A landlord granted a 21 year lease to a tenant who recovered the VAT charged on the lease. After 13 years the tenant surrendered the lease back to the landlord. The landlord then created a new 21 year lease. The landlord was treated as making an exempt supply of an eight year vatable interest in the property i.e. an exempt supply of his vatable interest. VAT on the surrendered interest was not recoverable.

The landlord had the choice of opting to charge VAT on the supply of the eight year interest and thus gaining entitlement to recovery of the VAT on the surrender.

8.5.3. Second Lease 10 years or more: Vatable interest 10 years or more: Second lease > vatable interest

Where a landlord grants a second lease for 10 years or more and he has a vatable interest of 10 years or more and the second lease is equal to or longer than his vatable interest VAT arises on the second lease. The second lease is valued based on the rent using the multiplier, the formula or a valuation. Where appropriate 4A can be used.

Example

A landlord granted a tenant a 25 year lease which was subject to the 4A procedure. The tenant surrendered the lease back to the landlord after two years and the landlord created a new 25 year lease in favour of tenant 2. VAT was charged on the second lease as if it were the creation of a 23 year lease. The amount of VAT being determined by the multiplier, the formula or a valuation. Section 4A applied to the second lease. As the landlord disposed of more than his vatable interest the question of a reversion did not arise.

8.5.4. Second lease 10 years or more; Vatable Interest 10 years or more: Second lease < Vatable Interest

This category covers a second lease of 10 years or more and a vatable interest 10 years or more and the lease is shorter than the vatable interest. VAT is chargeable on the second lease. In addition, the landlord has to account for a self-supply on the reversion which is based on the difference in years between the vatable interest and the second lease. If the second lease is for more than 20 years the reversion is ignored.

Example

A landlord granted a tenant a 21 year lease who surrendered it back after two years. VAT was chargeable on the surrender. The landlord granted a twelve year lease to a new tenant. VAT was chargeable on the second lease. In addition VAT was payable by the landlord on the reversionary interest of 7 years. This gave rise to an irrecoverable VAT cost to the landlord.

Second Leases from 26 March 1997 – Summary Chart

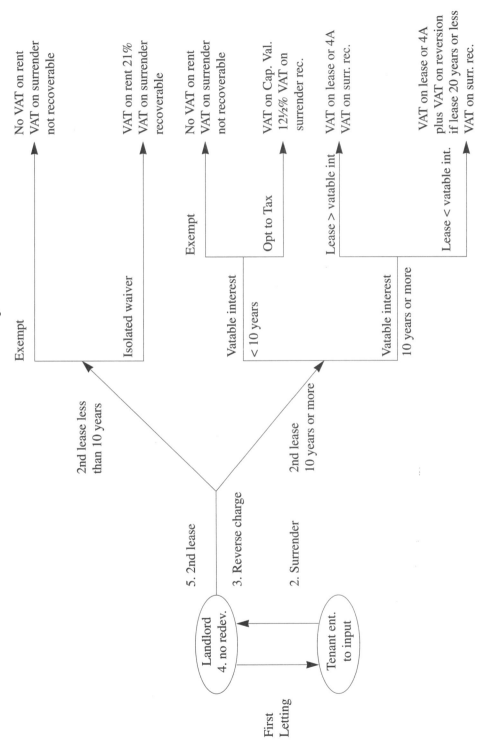

9.   The sixth change – the reverse charge

Normally the person who sells the goods or services is the one who has to collect VAT from the customer and pass on that VAT to the Revenue. Under the reverse charge mechanism the reverse happens. The seller does not charge VAT but rather the purchase is responsible to the Revenue for the VAT arising. This happens everyday when these registered for VAT import goods from other EU countries. The purchaser accounts for VAT to the Revenue by including the amount of VAT in the sales box (T1) of his VAT return. To the extent that he is entitled to recovery he claims back VAT by including the appropriate amount in box T2 of the return.

The reverse charge applies to the majority of assignments and surrenders. That means in the case of assignments or surrenders it is usually the assignee or landlord who accounts for the VAT and the assignor or tenant does not.

The reverse charge applies to the assignments and surrenders if the assignee or landlord is one of the following:

1. A vatable person
2. A Department of State or a local authority.
3. A person supplying exempt property
4. A person supplying financial services
5. A person letting property short term
6. A travel agent
7. An insurance company
8. A insurance broker
9. An Post
10. RTE
11. Transporter of people e.g. a taxi, an airline

I have tried to keep the above list readable and in doing so have lost some of the legal precision. You should refer to the legislation (VATA 1972 Section 4(8)).

The tenant who is disposing of an interest either by surrender or assignment should get confirmation from the landlord or assignee that he (the landlord or assignee) is a person within VATA 1972 Section 4(8) and that he (the landlord or assignee) will account for the VAT.

The landlord or assignee should get confirmation from the tenant that the interest in question is a vatable one.

10.   Key points\conclusion

Where a lease of more than 10 years is created that vatable interest is the reference point for all future transactions in the property until either

1. The lease terminates or
2. The Revenue gets the entire amount of VAT due in respect of the leasehold interest. For example, if the lease is granted to a bank which is not entitled any recovery, or
3. The property is redeveloped.

PART J

INDEX

PART J

INDEX

Subject	Page

PART K

PAGES FOR READER'S NOTES AND PRECEDENTS

Date and Refs.	DETAILS

Date and Refs.	DETAILS